THE
COURAGE
TO BE
RICH

THE COURAGE TO BE RICH

CREATING A LIFE
OF MATERIAL AND
SPIRITUAL ABUNDANCE

SUZE ORMAN

BANTAM BOOKS
SYDNEY • AUCKLAND • TORONTO • NEW YORK • LONDON

*This publication is designed to provide accurate and authoritative
information in regard to the subject matter covered. It is published
with the understanding that the publisher and author are not engaged in
rendering legal accounting or other professional service. If legal advice
or other professional advice, including financial, is required,
the services of a competent professional person should be sought.*

THE COURAGE TO BE RICH
A BANTAM BOOK

First published in Australia and New Zealand in 2000
by Bantam

By arrangement with Riverhead Books, a member of
Penguin Putnam Inc., 375 Hudson Street, New York, NY 10014

National Library of Australia
Cataloguing-in-Publication Entry

Orman, Suze.
    The courage to be rich: creating a life of material and
    spiritual abundance.

    Australian ed.
    Includes bibliographical references and index.
    ISBN 1 86325 224 X (pbk.).

    1. Finance, Personal—Psychological aspects. 2. Finance,
    Personal—Moral and ethical aspects. 3. Wealth—
    Psychological aspects. 4. Wealth—Moral and ethical
    aspects. I. Title.

332.0240019

Transworld Publishers,
a division of Random House Australia Pty Ltd
20 Alfred Street, Milsons Point, NSW 2061

Random House New Zealand Limited
18 Poland Road, Glenfield, Auckland

Transworld Publishers (UK) Limited
61–63 Uxbridge Road, Ealing, London W5 5SA

Random House Inc
1540 Broadway, New York, New York 10036

Australian adaptation by Anne Hartley
Cover photograph © Dana Fineman/Sygma
Text design by Deborah Kerner
Printed and bound by Griffin Press, Netley, South Australia

10 9 8 7 6 5 4 3 2

This book is dedicated to my most precious mama,

who has inspired me with her acts of courage

and richness. All that I am I owe to you.

CONTENTS

◆

ACKNOWLEDGMENTS

◆

After this, my third book, I now know without a shadow of a doubt that no one writes a book in a vacuum, that the process itself is a rich and courageous one, one that involves more people than one can ever count. I would like to thank all those whose names I know, and also all those who, behind the scenes, believed in and participated in the writing of this book.

First, I would like to thank my dear friend and collaborator Cheryl Merser, who brought more to this project than she ever imagined she could and stayed the course from beginning to end. Her family, Michael and Jenna Shnayerson, were, in their way, very much a part of the process, and I thank them as well. May we be friends forever, and collaborators just as long.

Also first—my thanks to my editor, Julie Grau, who has the most extraordinary mind, heart, and stamina of almost anyone I have ever met. This book really is our book, my friend, and I so hope you are proud of it. You are the best, and I feel blessed to work with you.

To my agent and mentor, Binky Urban, who has guided me impeccably on this journey—what an inspiring ride it has been. I love and respect you so very much. I knew for sure God loved me when I was sent to you.

To Sandi Mendelson. Stop the presses for this lady. Sandi, my publicist and buddy, stood behind me from the start, and she is still standing right there, and, boy, do I love it. There are no better than you, my dear, and I hope that you always remember that.

To the people at Riverhead, my total love and thanks for your caring, your attention to detail, and your commitment—all of which has totally overwhelmed me. To Phyllis Grann, Susan Petersen, Marilyn Ducksworth, Cathy Fox, Barbara O'Shea, and all the people from sales and marketing who were involved in getting the word out. To the dedicated and tireless Hanya Yanagihara, Elizabeth Wagner, Kim Seidman, Tricia Martin, Catharine Lynch, Ann Spinelli, Kiley Thompson, Lisa Amoroso, Claire Vaccaro, Bill Peabody, Rachel Krieger, and all the other talented, hardworking people in design and production who were involved in getting the book out.

How can I ever thank the team at Harpo enough for sending my message into millions of homes? To the most creative and courageous production talent in the world, Dianne Atkinson Hudson, Katy Murphy Davis, Kelly Groves-Olson, Ray "Bug" Dotch, Garrett Moehring, and Suzanne Hayward, and most important, to Oprah herself, who has truly changed my life forever.

Incredible thanks and gratitude go right from my heart to the hearts of my QVC family—all the hosts and everyone at QVC and Q Direct who has supported me from the very beginning, especially Karen Fonner, my dear, dear friend who always, always believed, long before anyone else did.

I would also like to thank my PBS team: Alan Foster, Gerry Richman, Larkin McPhee, Tedd Tramaloni, Erika Herrmann, and everyone at KTCA who backed my PBS specials and helped to bring the words of my books to television. Hasn't it been the best?

To Carol Bruckner at ICM Lecture, one of my favourite people in life. We're just starting to cook, my dear. And to Jenna Lamond at ICM, who never misses a trick.

To Anne Heller, my editor and friend at *Self* magazine, who brings my words and thoughts to life every month. Anne, you have such a golden mind; always let it shine, my dear.

A very special thank-you to those who read this book in manuscript and added the wisdom of their hearts and minds: Janet Dobrovolny, Gail Mitchell, Barry Pickers, Frederick Hertz, and John Claghorn; Ann C. Diamond, Esq., of Bronstein, Van Veen & Bronstein, P.C. (NY), for her careful reading of the section "For Love *and* Money"; Kenneth Grau, Esq., and Edward T. Braverman, Esq., of Braverman & Associates, P.C. (NY), and Howard Grossman, Esq., of Goldstick, Weinberger, Feldman & Grossman, P.C. (NY), for lending their expertise to "Buying a Home"; and Ira G. Bogner, Esq., of Proskauer Rose LLP (NY), for his insights into "Thinking Ahead".

My many thanks to the people who shared or inspired the case studies in this book, and with these thanks goes the hope that I was able to help.

My gratitude to the wonderful people at The Literary Guild, Doubleday Book Club, and Bantam Audio for showing their courage in supporting this book.

Thanks again to Esther Margolis of Newmarket Press, who started the ball rolling, and to Chip Gibson and everyone at Crown, who took the ball and ran with it.

To my brothers, who mean so very, very much to me. As I think about both of you, all I can do is say thank you for your love and support. Please know that I can feel it all the time.

To Melissa Howden, who stuck by my side and who over the years has helped me to find my own courage and stay focused on the real goal. What a gift you are to this world. And to Mary Bourn, whose infectious laughter and heart of gold have touched all those lucky enough to know her, especially me. May the three of us always have golden minds and golden lives.

Finally, I would like to thank my friends who have always been there and always will be there—Noni Colhoun, Suhasini, Laurie and Jim Nayder, Woody Simmons, Kai Ekhammer, Karen McNeil, Ruth Carnovsky, Catherine, Bill, and Suzanne Parrish, Pat Holt, Marilyn Golden, Liz Brown, Bobbie Birleffi, Beverly Kopf, Gloria Weiner, Arina Isaacson, Linda Gottlieb and Rob Tessler, Caryn Dickman, Peggy Kiss, Carol Nockold, Connie Palmore, Kimi Beaven, and my dear Laura Duggan.

INTRODUCTION:
THE SOUL OF COURAGE

What would it take for you to change course in your life? For you to feel rich in every way possible, both in the way your bottom-line numbers read and in your heart, your soul, and the way you live each day? What would it take for you to say aloud to yourself in the mirror, "Things are going to be different, starting now"? What would it take for you to believe it? To live it? To make it true?

The single most important quality you need in order to change the course of your life is courage. A great deal of courage.

Can you remember the courage it took to endure a setback or over-come an obstacle in your own life—the unexpected loss of a job, the illness of a loved one, a devastating rejection from someone you cared about? That feeling of waking up in the morning with pain in the pit of your stomach, pain that stayed with you as you went through the day in a fog, wondering how you could possibly cope, how you could go on, let alone rebuild your life. But you did. What enabled you to go on was your courage.

It takes courage to live with financial hardship, and, unbelievable as it may seem, it takes courage to be rich. Why? Because choosing wealth as a goal requires facing everything about your money bravely, honestly, with courage—which is a very, very hard thing for most of us to do. But it can be done.

WHAT WOULD YOU HAVE LEFT IF YOU LOST EVERYTHING?

SUZE'S STORY

After working as a waitress for seven years after college, I applied for—and, amazingly, got—a job as a stockbroker at Merrill Lynch in northern California. To this day I believe they hired me just to fill a women's quota, but who cares? I got the job. My mother was very excited for me, and a little scared, too, I think. To celebrate, she gave me a necklace she treasured, made out of little chips of diamonds from her engagement ring, so I would look as if I belonged. She even went out and got me a proper watch so that people would think I had money and maybe even do business with me.

From my first day, I was in a world very different from anything I'd known before. It felt like a dream to me, working in such a fast-paced office, where the other brokers seemed so self-assured, as if it were a given that they'd make money, lots of it. But I did well, too, and I remember how proud my mom was when, years later, I was able to buy my first luxury car and another watch, this one made of heavy gold. I wore designer clothes and vacationed on private islands. And I kept on doing well, later accepting a position as a vice-president of investments at Prudential-Bache.

Not long after, I decided to start my own business. The doors to the Suze Orman Financial Group opened for the first time on May 1, 1987. I had brought in as a partner a close friend who was a brilliant expert in estate planning, and from the beginning, the office had a wonderful aura around it, one of strength and hope, and was nothing like the tense, pressured offices of the highly structured Wall Street firms I had grown accustomed to. Until the morning of June 22, 1987, that is, when we discovered our office had been robbed, in a very intimate way. A woman working for me had come in after midnight the night before and cleaned out everything—my files, my Rolodex, all my computer programs and records, everything. I'll never know why. I spent the next few days stunned and in shock, trying to find my clients to warn them. I remember thinking at the time that it might take a month or two to sort things out, but I soon learned that reconstructing paper trails and seeking justice are time-consuming matters indeed. In the end, it took me three years and many, many days in court to resume my life and my practice. During those three desperate years, I lost all my courage.

At first, I burned through a range of emotions—rage, self-pity, terror. Sometimes I doubted I would ever re-enter the financial world, thinking instead that I would go back to being a waitress. Maybe that kind of life, which I knew so well, was my destiny. Maybe I had been wrong to ask for more.

I hid my fears and the truth of what had happened from my friends, and was still quick to treat them to dinners, the movies, whatever. Even with no money coming in, I deprived myself of nothing. I used up my savings and retirement money. When I had nothing left, I refinanced my house and began living off that money and my credit cards (debt it subsequently took me several years to clear). I had once been poor, yet had lived with spirit, courageously. Now I was living with the trappings of wealth, but had no money. I was living a lie. I no longer had even the courage to be poor.

But somehow over those years, I found the strength to begin asking myself some hard questions. Why did this really happen to me? Who was I, now that I had lost all my money? Who had I been before, when I thought I had it all? How could I stop the downward spiral, emotionally, spiritually, financially?

I began looking at myself in a new way, too, and didn't much like what I was seeing. I had started to believe that because I made a lot of money I was better than others. I had started looking down on the world, even as my money ebbed away from me. For me, the turning point came when I was sitting in a Denny's restaurant one day, thinking about everything that had happened. Suddenly I looked closely at the woman waiting on me, and it dawned on me that she surely had more money than I did. I might have looked richer, wearing my designer clothes and with my fancy car parked outside. But I knew that the only wealth that I had at this point was a negative, drawn in red ink. Looking again, I could see clearly that this waitress was also happier than I was, and more honest. I was the poor one, inside and out. Where would I find the courage I needed, the courage to change?

I drew strength from a spiritual quest I had begun earlier, which now began to occupy a bigger place in my life and thoughts. I meditated and contemplated the teachings of the masters with a hunger I hadn't felt before. Slowly, I began to consider all that was happening to me in terms of what God might want to teach me. If I could view these years as a gift to be unwrapped, I thought, I might find a way to feel enhanced rather than diminished, grateful rather than bitter. I thought, too, about my parents, the strength—and, yes, courage—they had exhibited through their many hardships, and of a motto I once learned that reminded me of the way my parents lived every day: Be a warrior. Don't turn your back on the battlefield. *I decided I wouldn't.*

At last, after years in the court system, the case was resolved. Finally, I was free to move on. In retrospect, however, the inner battle to restore my courage was the battle harder won. The lesson I learned was that my attitude toward money had made me poor and that with that attitude, no amount of money could have made me rich—the wealth had to come from somewhere else, from inside. Money doesn't bring courage, I learned. It's the other way around. Once I took that lesson to heart, I began to rebuild my life.

In all realms of life it takes courage to stretch your limits, express your power, and fulfil your potential; it's no different in the financial realm. In a buy-now, consume-now culture like ours, it takes courage to make the decisions today that may make us rich tomorrow. It takes courage to face up to the facts of old age and mortality and to prepare for them. It also takes courage to live generously, regardless of your financial state of affairs. I've seen many times in my own life, as well as in my readers' and clients' lives, how easy it is to live within the familiar limits of poverty, however you define it, and within the limits imposed upon you—by yourself or others. It takes courage to ask for what you want. And it takes courage to live honestly, wisely, true to yourself—and true to your desire for more.

DWELLING ON THE HIGHEST, RICHEST PLANE THERE IS

What's keeping you from being rich? In most cases it is simply a lack of belief. In order to become rich, you must believe that you can do it, and you must take the actions necessary to achieve your goal. There is nothing wrong with wanting more. You do not need to feel guilty for wanting more. If, however, you deny the possibility that you can have more, you'll be making yourself a victim of today's circumstances, and the cost will be your tomorrow.

Let me ask you a question: How do you feel about your money? Most of us, when asked, regardless of how much money we actually have, feel afraid. We worry that there isn't enough today and that there won't be enough tomorrow. We worry about what we haven't done with our money, and we worry about what we have done. Try as we might to push the fears away, to deny them, they keep coming back into our thoughts, uninvited, and we must push them away again. If you spend a lifetime pushing your fears away, I can promise you that ultimately you're pushing money away as well. The courage to be rich lies in the opposite stance, when you can give yourself the gift of believing in more.

I wrote my first book, *You've Earned It, Don't Lose It,* to address what I saw as a growing—and legitimate—fear people had about not having enough money to make it through their retirement years. I felt an urgency in alerting people to the dangerous mistakes that could rob them of the financial security they had worked so hard for their whole lives—lessons I'd learned from my ageing clients, many of whom faced real hardship because of poor choices, bad planning, or insufficient or incorrect information.

The publication of that book brought me into contact with hundreds of people whose stories I heard when they would approach me at appearances or speaking engagements, or read in the letters they would write. I listened to their concerns and their problems, and believed that it was important not only to provide them with the practical means to right the financial wrongs in their lives but also to help them truly to understand the relationship between their emotional lives and their financial ones. That was what led me to write *The 9 Steps to Financial Freedom.*

In *The 9 Steps* I hoped to help people come to terms with their past as a way of coping with their present. I firmly believe in the lessons of that book and the path it lays out, but in time I began to feel the need for a new message, a lesson we could take with us into the next millennium. Because it's my belief that the past always holds truths for the future, I looked back a hundred years and thought about the attitude and outlook our grandparents and great-grandparents took with them as they entered the twentieth century. In the strength of their hope and their dreams of a better future, I saw the perfect embodiment of courage and an inspiring example to draw upon as we face the century before us. I wrote *The Courage to Be Rich* not to retread information covered in my earlier books (though a certain amount of overlap in the finite realm of finance is inevitable; in those instances, I cross-reference the earlier books or other reliable sources), but to build upon their foundation a new way for each and every one of us to seize the future. With faith, determination, and courage.

You know, I know, it takes tremendous courage just to keep going, to work hard to pay the bills every month, to meet the next financial or emotional challenge that comes along. The courage to be rich, however, goes beyond the chains and limitations of our minds and present-day circumstances, and it brings tomorrow—when yesterday's defeat will be long past us—into every today. This kind of courage is vision, and it refuses to let today's defeat block our path into the future. This kind of courage is not about just getting by or simply accepting the cards that have been dealt to us. Instead, it is about excelling beyond our own seemingly endless limitations, even in the darkest of financial times—and we all have dark financial times. The courage to be rich gives us the material and spiritual tools to see our way out of the darkness and into the light. For when the light of courage illuminates our way, we always find true richness at the end of the path. Courage is faith. Faith in a higher being, perhaps, or faith in the essential rightness of the world, that correct actions and beliefs are not only their own reward but also qualities that themselves will be rewarded. Is there a grand scheme to the world? I'm not equipped to say. However, if we live each day of our life as if there is, and with courage, we are living on the highest, richest plane of this earth, regardless of the answer.

PART I

ACTS
OF
COURAGE

CHAPTER 1

THE COURAGE TO LOOK WITHIN

Over the many years I've worked with people and their money, I have tried to answer what to me is the most puzzling financial question of all: Why is it that some people have money while others do not? It's almost mystical, really. Day after day I see people who have grown up in similar circumstances, had basically the same opportunities, and earn more or less the same salaries, yet how very differently their bottom-line numbers can read. I'm sure you've seen this yourself. Haven't you known really good, hardworking people who end up with very little? Haven't you met people who should have had less but have more? Or people who, time after time, almost seem to make it and then, boom, something happens and they have to start all over again?

Is it that some higher being looks down on all of us and chooses who among us is going to win life's financial lottery? I doubt it. Is it simply that those who have all the money they could ever need wanted it more than others? Not from what I've seen.

In my nineteen years as a financial planner, never once have I come across a client who didn't have the desire to have more, or the intelligence and the ability to achieve the desire. Not once. So what was stopping them? The same thing that no doubt is stopping you: financial obstacles.

And what are those financial obstacles? Some of the obstacles that are placed in front of us are external and easy to recognise—lack of cash or opportunity, the family we are born into, lack of financial knowledge, or maybe just laziness. Legitimate obstacles, some of these, but after all these years working with people richer and, yes, poorer than you are today, I've seen people overcome each of them countless times. These are the easy obstacles, for what you can pinpoint you can overcome.

Harder to recognise, and much harder to overcome, are the internal obstacles, the emotional obstacles, that keep us from having what we want and enjoying what we have.

I have come to believe that the way each of us thinks and feels about our money is the key factor in determining how much we ultimately have. The main underlying reason that some of us don't have money is that our thoughts and feelings about money have become internal obstacles that prevent us from having or keeping what we want. In the same vein, the reason that others do have money is that, with their thoughts and feelings, they have created the means to achieve and hold on to what they desire. In other words, our thoughts and feelings about money are, to me, fundamental factors in determining how much money each of us will, in this lifetime, be able to create and keep.

LESSONS MY CLIENTS TAUGHT ME

Years into my practice, once I began to understand the powerful hold our thoughts and emotions have on our money, I started to ask my clients different kinds of questions—questions about "how" and "why" rather than simply questions about "how much". I began trying to get to the heart of their financial emotions: "Why have you let all this money just sit in a bank account for ten years earning two percent interest?" I'd ask. Or "How did you begin to get into all this debt?" Or "What are the money issues you and your spouse fight over?" Or "Why, when you have so much more money than most people, do you feel so poor?"

The answers were remarkably similar, regardless of how much money was actually at stake: "I'm afraid to invest. I feel safe leaving my money alone." "Suze, I'm so ashamed of my debt, I can't even tell my husband."

"I'm just so angry at the way he spends our money." "I am afraid. What if I lose it all?"

I listened carefully to the words that my clients were using, over and over, to answer my questions or simply to talk about their financial situations. I noticed that whenever people had financial difficulties, whether they were in debt, had nothing to show for their years of work, had no idea where the next dollar was going to come from, or felt like they never had enough, they seemed to have one thing in common. They all used the same words to answer my questions. Regardless of their particular financial dilemma, their answers all contained at least one of the following words: *Shame. Fear. Anger.*

Let's say a client came in to see me because she found herself in terrible debt and needed help to find her way out. If I asked her, "How do you feel about having so much debt?" her answer would likely reflect one or more of three emotional variations: "I'm so ashamed; I don't want anyone to know about my debt." "I'm so afraid; I have no idea how I will ever get out of debt." "I'm so angry at myself for allowing myself to get into this situation." *Shame. Fear. Anger.* The emotional obstacles to wealth.

Perhaps it's easy to see how staggering debt could incite these emotions, but it's less apparent in situations where there seems to be enough money, or at least no immediate threat to one's security. And yet I can cite countless examples of clients whose deep-seated emotions kept them from achieving greater wealth—be it in the form of emotional or financial security. Fear, loss, shame about the past. Anger at the circumstances over which you have to prevail.

UNLOCKING THE EMOTIONS

You may be thinking, How is this possible? Just because I'm afraid, how does that relate to the fact that I have no money? Isn't it the other way around? Isn't it that I'm afraid because I don't have any money?

That's the way most people think. Especially people who do not have money—or the courage to be rich. It's easy to blame your emotional state of affairs on your financial state. But from what I've learned, the opposite is true. Your emotional state ultimately determines your financial state.

I have found that when negative emotions control the purse strings, money will not flow purely and evenly. When it comes to money, emotions can speak louder than reason or necessity. Your emotions, expressed through your financial actions, got you where you are now and will continue to shape your financial future if you let them. If shame, fear, or anger is at the wheel, then I can promise you, you are not on a course toward richness. By having the courage to face and overcome your inner obstacles, however, you will change the outer trappings of your financial life forever.

YOUR EXERCISE, PART ONE

I want you to take a few minutes to consider how you feel about your financial situation today. Don't think in terms of numbers, the bills, how much you owe, or how much you've saved. Think instead about how you truly feel about your finances. Is money—the money you've spent, the money you have, the money you need—a constant worry for you? Do you feel that you're not good enough to get what you want or that you don't deserve what you have? Are you embarrassed by how much you have? Envious of what others have, angry that you don't have such things? I want you to address your emotions honestly and commit your thoughts and feelings to paper. If you don't have the money to pay your bills, write down how it feels not to have enough money. If you're in debt, write down how that feels. If you have far more money than your friends, write down how that feels as well. On the other hand, if you think you remain emotionally unattached to your money, I still want you to try to complete this exercise, because you might surprise yourself by uncovering emotions that have been long buried. I want you to close your eyes and look deep within yourself until all that exists in your consciousness is a clear sense of yourself and your feelings about your financial life.

After you have spent some time contemplating your situation, please write a few more sentences describing how you feel about it as precisely as you can.

A sample paragraph might read:

"It's terrifying how much debt we've managed to build up in just five years of marriage, with having the children and everything else. I'd be so embarrassed if my parents knew. I'm worried about how we'll make it until the children go to university, let alone university itself."

Now take a good look at the words you have written and see them not as words but as your *current truths*—statements that not only describe your state of mind but also have the power and veracity to determine your outlook and, subsequently, your actions. Underline or highlight any words that have to do with an emotion. In the case above, for example, the writer would highlight *terrifying,* a word describing fear; *embarrassed,* a word describing shame; and *worried,* another word describing fear.

Without having seen what you wrote, I can guarantee that you've used words describing shame, fear, or anger. This is not a financial planner's party trick; rather, it demonstrates the universality of our impoverished feelings about money.

MONEY, POWER, RESPECT

Strange as it may sound to you, money is attracted to people who are strong and powerful, respectful of it, and open to receiving it. I want you to think about this—it is something I firmly believe and have said time and again: Money behaves and responds just like a person—nurture it, treat it well, and it will grow and flourish; treat it carelessly, or with disrespect, and it will dwindle away to nothing. Quite simply, if you respect money and give it the attention it needs, it will respect you back.

Conversely, the emotions of shame, fear, and anger cloud your financial judgment, take away your power over your money. When these emotions determine your spending patterns or force you to deny or defy the truth about your money, they not only wreak havoc on your finances, they actually repel money from you. This is not to say that there aren't people with a lot of money who feel shame, fear, or anger—there are plenty of such people. Although they may have a good amount of money, they're not rich in the sense of living a full, expansive and contented life. And often such people are unable to hold on to their money. How frequently do we read in the tabloids of wealthy people whose fortunes are destroyed by drugs, ugly divorces, unscrupulous business practices, or similar disgraceful causes? Why do you think this happens? I believe it happens because their underlying emotional states are powerful enough, and corrosive enough, to repel even vast fortunes. No matter how much money you have, power and respect—for yourself, for others, for your money—attract riches, and powerlessness and disrespect repel them.

The roots of these emotions take hold in childhood. So strong are they that they grow even if we try to ignore them, gaining the power to control our thoughts, words, actions and fortunes. If we let them. We've all felt shame, fear and anger—the emotions of poverty. And we all have the power to confront them and expel them—from our emotional lives, and from our financial lives as well. I have seen so many people change their financial lives after facing down these treacherous feelings. You can, too. For the sake of your dreams, I urge you to have the courage to do so now.

FINANCIAL SHAME

What does financial shame look like? Its posture is head down, eyes down. It's contained and hidden, but the effects of its presence are apparent even so. It's the most deeply rooted emotion of all, because it cuts to the core of who you are—telling you you're not good enough, not deserving of what you have, less than others, no matter how much you have. Experience the sensation of shame just once, and you're not likely to forget it.

MARK'S STORY

I must have been about nine or ten, and we were having this Sunday school outing. Everyone in my class was going hiking on the nature trail in the morning and then out for lunch afterwards. Our minister was taking us, and we all liked him, so this was a pretty big deal. I can't remember anything about the nature trail, but I will never forget that lunch. There were about ten of us, and we got a big table at a milk bar. Cokes for everybody, in a big glass with a straw. I had a grilled cheese sandwich and french fries, and we all had ice cream for dessert. Then, when the bill came, all the kids put five dollars on the table, and I just froze. I didn't have five dollars. I didn't have any money, my parents hadn't given me money. Not a cent. Ricky, who was sometimes my friend and sometimes

my enemy, noticed and said, "Hey, why aren't you paying up?" I was mor-
tified. Everyone was looking at me, real quiet. I remember getting hot, and
I remember starting to cry in front of everybody, which made it worse.
They all were staring. I felt so ashamed. I'll never forget it.

Powerful memory. And Mark has been paying to make up for it ever since. To this day, he's the one who always treats, the first to pick up the bill, a big tipper and a big spender. His shame that day made such a powerful impact on him that he sees to it that everyone knows he has money to spend. What they don't know, however, is that he spends it all, leaving himself with nothing, ultimately as penniless and ashamed today as he was all those years ago at his Sunday school lunch.

Maybe you were ashamed growing up because your family had less than the other families you knew. Maybe you didn't have the right clothes or car or belong to the country club, or your mother was the only mother who worked, as mine was, which was a source of shame to me. Maybe you didn't have the money to attend or finish university, the way your friends did. In some cases, the shame is "Why me?" shame, because you might have had more than everyone else and didn't feel you deserved it. Your shame might have come from a specific incident, as Mark's did, or from a cluster of incidents you never forgot. In any case, shame has real staying power and can destroy your pride, self-respect, self-worth—and ultimately, net worth.

How does shame come into play in grown-up financial life? If you feel "less than", you'll spend more—possibly even more than you have—in order to feel like more. If you feel you don't deserve what you have, you'll neglect it, it will fail to grow, and eventually it will stagnate. If you feel undeserving, you will never take real pleasure in the money you have and what it can do. If you believe that you truly don't deserve the things you really want, then they'll never be yours. Defeat won't be a problem for you. But success will.

FINANCIAL FEAR

What does financial fear look like? Watch, sometime, when you see a line of people handing over money or a credit card to a salesperson in a store. If there's fear, you'll be able to see it. Watch the way the other customers clutch their money too tightly, take just a second longer than they should to relinquish it, hold out their hand before the salesperson is ready to give them the change, hold their breath until the credit card clears. Perhaps instead you might see them distance themselves from their money, hand it over too quickly, toss it, or push it. When it comes to money, fear is constantly constricting and debilitating, like a companion or a voice in your head, reminding you of all the bills you have to pay, intruding on times that should be pleasurable, keeping you up at night. It can express itself in one of two ways. Fear can prevent you from doing what you should with your money, or it can cause you to do what you shouldn't with your money.

P A M ' S   S T O R Y

My mother wore her money dress my whole childhood. It was a royal blue shirtmaker, and the print was dark golden coins, coins scattered all over it. White collar. The belt was red patent leather, and the belt buckle and the buttons were coins, too. She wore it to church with gloves, and she wore it to take us to the first day of school, to the P&C, every time she wanted to look nice, I guess. We called it the money dress, and we knew that when she was wearing it, it was an occasion. I was always proud of her in the money dress. You could just feel how great she felt in it, and it was as if her pride was contagious. Then one day, when I was about eleven, we were going to my grandmother's house, because my cousins were coming to visit. We all were instructed to wear our best clothes, and after I got dressed, I went into my parents' room. There was my mother, sitting on the bed in her white slip, holding the money dress and crying. I had never seen her cry. It was then that I saw that the patent leather belt was cracked, and the "gold" was peeling off the coin buttons. Then my father came in and screamed at her that he couldn't afford to get her a new dress, just put the dress on and get ready. She cried harder, and he kept screaming. Then I understood. This wasn't about the money dress. It was about money, and we didn't have any. I was so afraid, I ran outside. But I could still hear the crying and the screaming.

The fear is still with Pam today. She and her husband both work, and they make more than enough, but they are anything but rich. Pam overspends, pure and simple, and her credit card debt is keeping pace with her salary. She has a closet overflowing with real money dresses, and her children have the absolute best of everything, at a cost far greater than Pam and her husband can afford. They live in the best neighbourhood, drive showy cars, and live in terror, waiting for the moment when their financial lives are going to come crashing down on them.

If your parents quarrelled about money when you were young, if you grew up feeling there wasn't enough, you almost certainly harbour some fear about money today. Fear has nothing to do, necessarily, with the financial facts of your life; you can certainly have money and still be afraid. Yet you cannot be rich, truly rich, if you're living with fear. Whether or not you have enough today, if you fear you don't, then one way or another you'll make sure that you don't. Or you may go the other way and become a miser, holding on to your money as desperately as you hold on to the fear, unable to take pleasure in spending a penny and unable to be generous, which will render you poor in every way.

FINANCIAL ANGER

What does financial anger look like? It looks clenched. Clenched fists, clenched mouth, creased forehead. It makes you look closed and unyielding. It is anything but welcoming, and it turns away money as readily as it turns away other people. Maybe you feel anger at yourself for what you've done or what you haven't done with your money, for a raise you didn't get, at your parents for the ways in which you still feel they let you down, at friends who have more than you, at a spouse who left you powerless and penniless, or simply at the unfairness of life—and the unfairness of money. If you do, this anger may be extremely well concealed but can still translate into debt and dishonesty with yourself about what you are doing (and aren't doing) with your money.

STEPHEN'S STORY

My family emigrated from Europe to the United States when I was eleven years old, and it was a really traumatic time for us all. For my mother, especially, because she had to leave her mother, who was ill, and her twin brother. There was this sad sense that we might never see them again. I remember we had to sell all our property before we left. For the most part, our furniture wasn't new or nice, so the neighbours just kind of came and paid what they could for everything—the beds, the kitchen table and chairs, the dishes. But about six months before we had known we were leaving, my mother had bought two comfortable cushioned armchairs. I can still see them. She was so proud of these chairs, and she hated to have to part with them, but when she knew she had to sell them, she at least wanted to get a good price. Nearly everything else was gone by then, so there were just these two flowered chairs in the little living room. A man came, some kind of a dealer, I guess, and he paid her only about half of what she expected to get. She tried to negotiate with him—plead with him is more like it—but he was very contemptuous. When he left with the chairs, she cried and cried for hours in the empty house. I was so angry at him—how dare he take such advantage of my mother? I remember thinking that when you have something valuable, people will always try to take it from you.

Stephen is still angry, angry at the unfairness of the world, so angry that to this day he really believes that he has to protect himself and every single penny he has, or else someone will take advantage of him. In effect, he's still buying high and selling low. He's left two jobs, thinking he might be fired. He thinks everyone, from the corner grocer to the people who calculate his phone bill, is probably out to get him. He hoards his money. His anger has so convinced him that the world is a financial minefield that he's virtually retreated from it.

An adult's anger is the same as a child's—anger at not getting what you want. But as adults, we're in control (at least we're supposed to be); we're the ones with the power to say yes or no. If you want something badly, something you can't afford, you're going to be angry if you say yes to yourself and angry, too, if you say no. In this no-win situation, there's nowhere for the anger to go, and it can stay with you, causing a good deal of damage, throughout your life. If you're angry at being deprived, you might keep up the deprivation in order to sustain the anger—or maybe you'll lash out at the anger with reckless spending. Perhaps you will feel suspicious that others are trying to shortchange you, and if you feel it, others will sense it. If anger is a recurring theme in your life, your actions around money will be grudging and pinched, to the point where the flow of your money will become constricted, dwindling, in some cases, to a trickle.

When your outward appearance and way of living suggest to others that you have more money than you do, you're angry. When you've invested more money in today than tomorrow, you're probably angry as well. And no matter where you cast the blame for your anger, in the end the person you'll be the most angry with is yourself.

When emotional reflexes steer our financial actions, we are not acting in our best financial interests—anything but. As you can see from these stories, you are not going to get rich by feeling ashamed, afraid, or angry, but by purging these emotions from your financial life so that they no longer taint your actions, by making different choices, by expanding your financial worldview beyond today and into tomorrow.

If you've made mistakes, so what? We all make mistakes. If you trusted someone you shouldn't have trusted, you can learn to trust yourself. If you are in debt, you can get out of debt—millions of us have. If you face your finances truthfully, just the way they are now, you can begin to change them, a little today, perhaps a little more tomorrow.

But first you have to render those emotions of fear, shame, or anger powerless over you and your money.

YOUR EXERCISE, PART TWO

You can try saying to yourself, Okay, no more anger, but it won't get you very far. Because emotions have lives of their own, it is hard to pin them down, look them directly in the eye, and send them away. First you have to identify their source, then evaluate them with the adult perspective—and compassion—you have now. This begins the process of defusing their power.

I'm asking you to go somewhere quiet, taking with you a pen and the piece of paper on which you described how you feel about your money today. Look closely at the paragraph you wrote at the beginning of this chapter and ask yourself this question about the emotions you identified: Where do you think that feeling came from?

In essence I am asking you to go back in time. Go back to your childhood to find, if you can, the financial memory that planted the shame, the fear, the anger. Use the word that most prominently and accurately describes your present-day feelings toward your finances as a sort of password, a key to unlock painful episodes that still resonate, even subconsciously, in your life today. Was it that your neighbours once offered you hand-me-downs because they thought you were too poor to buy things of your own? Did that make you ashamed? Was it that your mother once took you grocery shopping, filled the whole cart, then discovered that she had forgotten her wallet and had no way to pay? Did that make you afraid? Was it that all your friends went to Europe one summer, while you had to take a part-time job? Did that make you angry? Was there enough, too much, or never enough? Was money a source of happiness or of despair?

For instance, let's say that you're so ashamed of the amount of debt you've incurred that you're keeping it a secret from those closest to you. Shame and secrecy are your passwords. Search your memory and see what those words call to mind. Perhaps they remind you of feelings of shame you had as a teenager, when you felt you weren't good enough and had to pretend to be something other than yourself to gain acceptance with the "in" crowd. But don't stop at the first recollection that suggests itself. If you go deeper, farther back, you might recall where you learned that lesson—maybe your mother told you as a child to keep the family's money problems a secret from your friends, because if they knew you were poor, they might not like you anymore.

Bingo. When you finally get to the heart of the matter, it will be as clear to you as if a flashbulb had gone off. I urge you not to give up, not to turn away until you've reached that moment of clarity. Incidentally, the process I took you through in the previous paragraph was the very one I myself went through to connect to the source of my shameful feelings about my debt. Those memories, those secrets were my own.

When you've reached that moment of understanding, please write your memory down on the same piece of paper you used in the first part of the exercise.

Now let's go deeper. What are you doing today, as an adult, to keep that feeling alive, to allow it to control your financial life? For example, if you don't believe you deserve what you have or can achieve what you want, your feelings of unworthiness likely stem from the shame you've been harbouring since your youth. If you believe that you could lose everything you have or will never feel financially secure, your present-day fear is fuelling that childhood emotion. If it seems to you that everyone else has more and you'll never have enough, your feelings of inadequacy and hostility are nurturing youthful versions of those feelings into adulthood.

Add to the piece of paper what you are doing today in your actions, thoughts, or feelings about money to keep the emotions of shame, anger, or fear alive and in control of you and your money.

In Mark's case, for example, his flamboyant spending today is an attempt to make up for the shame of yesterday, but in fact it is keeping that emotion alive. With the weight of Pam's debt, she is trying, today, to dispel the pain of yesterday's poverty, but her actions leave her even more afraid of not having enough money to pay the bills. Stephen's financial demeanour, suspicious and tightfisted, is keeping his anger alive— and keeping the world at bay. Each is paying an emotional toll today, and a financial one as well.

Now it's time to cut off the power of the emotions holding you back, just as you would apply a tourniquet to an open wound. Think about these memories, the misguided actions you're taking today, and how they might be connected to your past. Think of the child you were when the memory was formed, and why you felt the way you did in the context of who you were then. You were powerless. You were a child and had a right to feel the way you did. Think of who you are now and the power you can summon to change.

You must release yourself from the hold these memories have over you. You can no longer afford to live in the past; make the present your point of reckoning. Today and tomorrow are all that matter. Take responsibility for your life, and for your money, from this moment on.

ALWAYS FORGIVE

The only way to get beyond the emotional obstacles standing between you and more money is to let them go, to forgive. Forgive the people who helped to etch those memories on your young soul. Forgive yourself for the way those emotions have played out in your financial life up until now. Forgive the past and present, in order to make the future a blank slate on which you can engrave different goals and different numbers.

We all know how hard it actually is to forgive—but we all know, too, the healing powers of forgiveness. For me, the shame, fear, and anger I felt from growing up, at least in my own mind, as poor little Suze Orman from the South Side of Chicago, daughter of a chicken plucker, defined me well into adulthood. No matter how well I did or how much money I made, I never felt good enough, smart enough, attractive enough. These feelings were all that my entire being could bear; there wasn't room for any other, more generous emotions. I didn't feel entitled to anything—love, friendship, and especially money. For the longest time, I can honestly say, these thoughts and feelings kept me from being rich.

I didn't realise the extent to which these emotions defined me, even as I grew unhappier, lonelier, and angrier over those years. One day, I was getting ready for work, utterly miserable and about to get into the shower. In the way we all invoke God when we're at rock bottom, I silently screamed out to Him: Why can't I have what everybody else in this world has? Is this all there is for me? I remember it so clearly—my distress and then a feeling of calm as my plea was answered with a prayer that I had learned as a child and which suddenly came back to me. I repeated it over and over as if it were my salvation, as perhaps it was. It went like this: *I ask to be forgiven and released by all those whom I have hurt and harmed, and I ask to forgive and release all those who have hurt and harmed me.*

Forgiveness, for me, was a process, one that took a long time to complete—to forgive my parents who had, after all, done the best they could, and to forgive myself enough to believe that I was fine just as I was, and entitled to whatever I could create and achieve. With my prayer, over time, I released myself from the bondage of those terribly destructive emotions and finally made room for more.

YOUR EXERCISE, PART THREE

Read what you've written from the earlier exercises again. Add to it if you feel the need—if you can recall more vivid details, if there's something you wish to express to another. You may think of this document as a letter to a higher power, a direct line of communication. Purge yourself of all aspects of the memory in the process of capturing it on paper. Read what you've written one last time.

Now I'd like you to take this paper and burn it. Watch it as it is transformed from paper to ashes. Think of the fire as representative of the fire of love that is burning in your heart; see the ashes as all that remains of your past hurts as your writings go up in smoke; release the hurt and pain; let the past go.

It's time to start over. It's time to forgive. To forgive Mother, Dad, the world, and, above all, yourself. Use my prayer or create one of your own. Find the words of forgiveness that bring you release. Articulate your feelings in some form—trust a friend with your story of forgiveness or contemplate forgiveness in a place of worship.

Do it now. Now is the time to forgive the child you were, the child who was ashamed, angry, or afraid. You were just a child. Forgive the shame. You reacted as any child would, and today you can see that whatever you were ashamed of then would pass, and ultimately it wouldn't matter. Forgive the fear. Where did the fear come from? Your parents, who were doing their best to make everything okay? They tried to shield you. They did the best they could. Forgive them. Let your anger go. Today you're no longer angry at whatever made you angry yesterday. Release it with forgiveness. You have what you have. This is your starting point.

Every day things happen that may put more obstacles in your path to wealth, that could create overwhelming hardships, that could leave terrible scars. Forgiveness is a never-ending process. It is not enough simply to forgive what happened in the past. You can learn from the setbacks that happen today, release them, and move on. Over time, with forgiveness, you will stop blaming your past for your present, and you will learn to take responsibility for your actions, financial and otherwise, today and forever. Take your financial destiny into your own hands and your own heart. See it as the act of courage it is.

CHAPTER 2

THE COURAGE TO HAVE MORE AND TO BE MORE

What do you think when you think about your money?

What do you say when you talk about your money?

What actions have you taken with your money?

When it comes to your money, what you think will direct what you say, what you say will direct what you do, and what you do will create your destiny. True richness begins with thoughts of true richness. True greatness begins with thoughts of true greatness, and the potential for greatness resides in all of us.

Over the years, I've heard from many people who think they don't have enough, that they will never have—or be—enough, that they can't: can't get out of debt, can't provide for their children, can't face the future. I have heard tales of sadness, hopelessness, and despair from people facing the facts of the financial lives they have created. There is a vast difference between facing reality, bad as your particular financial reality might be at this moment, and thinking that you can't do anything about that reality. Whether you're wealthy, whether you're poor, the constricting thoughts that tell you *you can't* are immensely powerful and terribly destructive; I have come to refer to them as thoughts of poverty, and thoughts of poverty can dwell in all of us, no matter how much or how little money we have. These thoughts of poverty are insidious; they lead to words of poverty or defeat, and ultimately to actions of poverty and a legacy of poverty that can be passed down for generations. We must learn to still those thoughts.

I learned this lesson from the life of my dad.

MY DAD'S AND MY STORY

At first, children accept the world they're born into, and in my family, our world was my dad's chicken business, a series of small chicken stands, which sometimes did a little better but mostly did a little worse. I felt poor living in a family that calamity struck often—fire nearly killed my dad and left him with emphysema; powerful chain stores threatened our chicken stands; landlords more than once forced out my dad's business.

Growing up, I never once questioned that this was the way it was meant to be for us. It never occurred to me that our lives, my dad's life, might have been different. Then, at a family get-together not long after my father died, my cousin said casually, "I still think it's too bad that your dad never got around to finishing law school." What? It was as if an electric shock went through me. Law school? My dad went to law school? How was it possible that he had gone to law school and ended up plucking chickens? And why didn't he ever tell me?

As the story came out I learned that my father had, indeed, gone to law school, working at a flower shop between classes and selling produce from a cart on weekends to pay his tuition. He lived at home, in a one-bedroom apartment with his parents and brother, and contributed his share toward the family's household expenses. Just as he was about to start his last year of school, however, my grandfather asked him for money to help open a new chicken store. My dad gave up his dreams, gave his tuition money to my grandpa, joined him in the chicken business, and never became a lawyer. Why not? He got sidetracked. He settled. He lost heart. Perhaps he simply chose to think his father's thoughts. No one knows why, and the reason scarcely matters. Regardless of why, ultimately he convinced himself that this was his destiny, not the one he had dared, for a time, to imagine.

It was quite a shock for me to learn how different our lives might have

25

been. My dad had played such a vital role in my life, and I had learned the lesson of my childhood well. This was the plan for us. Who was I to think I could have more, be more? In retrospect, I can see that for a long time I thought his destiny was mine as well, because the message he'd passed on to me was the lesson of less and the thoughts of I can't.

As I look back, and from conversations I've since had with other members of my family, I now realise that my dad's thoughts were always thoughts of poverty, that his internal voice told him you can't. It wasn't as if he didn't try, because he did try. He worked harder than anyone I've ever known, every day of his life. Three times he talked investors into investing in new chicken stands, and three times he started over from scratch. It was not that my father was without courage, for at least in my eyes, he had more than most; he had amazing courage. Despite this, my brothers and I also heard him say, more than once, "This is just the way it was meant to be, and there's nothing I can do about it."

Finally, as an adult thinking back on what I knew of my father's life, I got it. No matter how hard he tried, his schemes never worked out for him because he never thought, deep down inside, that they could, never thought that they would. He thought he was never going to make it, thought it and thought it until he believed it, said it, and made it happen. He stilled the internal voice that said I can't once, by attending law school, but then let it resume its chant and never even got his degree. What a pivotal point in a man's life! He did everything he knew to try to make it, except to think that he could, say that he would, and then, from that position of strength and clarity, take the actions that would have led him to a rich and fulfilling life. With his thoughts he created his destiny, as do we all.

THOUGHTS OF COURAGE

Day in, day out, your thoughts accompany you everywhere: to work, throughout meals, while socialising; you even drift off to sleep with your thoughts. Sometimes they're obsessive—after a fight with your partner, say, or if you've been unfairly reprimanded by your boss. Most other times, they free-float, reminding you that it's time to call your mother, that you're due at the dentist, that you're going to wear your new shoes to the party tonight. Happy thoughts, tedious thoughts, routine thoughts are with you all the time. And so are money thoughts, the thoughts that tell you how much you have, how much you need, and how much you want. Ultimately, these thoughts tell you more about yourself than your cheque book does—they tell you who you are and who you can become. If you can start to change the thoughts that tell you *you can't* into thoughts that tell you *you can,* you can begin to change your financial destiny.

The power of positive thinking is hardly a new idea, and it has helped many people in many ways—in their relationships, in their work, in coping with loss. Now imagine unleashing that power upon your money. Positive thinking is seldom talked about when it comes to our financial lives; it's not a slogan you'd be likely to see hanging in a financial planner's office. But I can tell you that most of the problems we're plagued by in day-to-day life have to do with money, and necessarily, they occupy our thoughts. If you really want to live a rich life, the process must begin in your head, with positive thoughts.

How do you turn your thoughts about money around? The same way you direct any of your other thoughts. Think of thoughts as actors inhabiting your mind, with you as director, in control of where they'll stand—at centre stage, in the background—and when they'll speak. If you're on a diet and determined to do well, you'll be able, with firm stage direction, to still the thought of a hot fudge sundae. If anxious thoughts tell you to call the office and say you're sick, you can overpower those thoughts by reminding yourself that this is the day of your big presentation and you're not going to miss it because of cold feet. In the same way, every negative, harmful, or unproductive money thought can be replaced, redirected, banished from the stage. If your thoughts turn to your debt and how you'll never be able to pay it off, replace the thought: *Yes, I have debt, but there are ways to get out of debt; millions of people have, and I will, too.* If your thoughts turn to your elderly parents who are unwell, turn your thoughts again: *There are agencies that can help with this, and I am going to look into aged care services and see where I can get help for them and for me.* If your thoughts turn to how in the world you'll ever pay for your children's education, redirect your thinking: *I wish I had saved more by now, but I will still do what I can and will look into loans, scholarships, and the best state schools, and find what's best for us.* Replace each thought of powerlessness with a powerful thought, a thought that says *I can,* and then move away from the thought. Think about something else. Replace a thought of powerlessness every time it comes into your mind, over and over again. This is not an invitation to live in denial. You're not pushing the problem away, you're simply meeting it in a new way, head-on, with the strength of your positive new thoughts.

Every day, people confront adversity—destructive acts of nature, tragic illnesses, bills that get out of control, houses that fall apart, lives that are shattered in ways that only money can fix. Why is it that some people triumph over adversity and others succumb to it? You can trace their actions to their thoughts. If they think they'll triumph, they will go on to say they will and to take the actions that lead them out of adversity. Still the thoughts that tell you *you can't,* because *you can.* Beginning today, look toward a brighter future; leave the past behind. The will to change begins with your thoughts, then gathers strength with your words.

THE FORCE OF LANGUAGE

Where there is a flow, any flow, of money, even a trickle, you have the power to increase it. Believe it or not, it almost doesn't matter how much or how little money you have coming in every month. All money has the power to grow or to dwindle, and when you unleash powerful thoughts over even small amounts of money, you are turning toward more. What will begin to make you richer is how you think about yourself, your circumstances, and all the possibilities that lie ahead.

Where do your thoughts take you? They take you to your words, the words you use—or don't use—when you talk about your money.

The connection between our words and our wealth is a subtle one, and one that hasn't been explored very much, but it's a connection that has fascinated me ever since I became a financial planner and began to hear, really hear, the words we use when we talk about money. In my practice, I have seen people who are clearly preoccupied with their debt but whose words try to obscure the damage. I have seen husbands and wives married many years who've never talked honestly about money. I've also seen thoughts and words intermingle in ways that make no financial sense: "But you told me everything was going to be okay." "Well, maybe I did and maybe I was wrong." Do our words always reflect our true thoughts about money? Not always. But if the overriding goal is to create more, then your thoughts and words must be in alignment—toward the truth, toward the goal, toward the means to the goal. When you talk about money, you have to be very careful of what you say, because just as your destiny begins with your thoughts, your words bring you closer to that destiny.

The way we talk about and handle our money is, for each of us, as distinctive as a fingerprint, and as intricate. If you can learn to listen very carefully to the words you use in relation to your money, you will uncover truly important clues as to why you aren't as rich as you would like to be or as rich as you could be.

When clients come into my office and tell me about their finances for the first time, the conversation is nearly always riddled with words of discouragement, limitation, and defeat—words that, in my opinion, drive away any hope of having money. "I'll never get that job, so I'm not even going to try." "I'll never get rich." "I'll be paying off this debt for the rest of my life." "We'll never be able to afford a house." "I'll probably lose everything." I cringe whenever I hear people talk like this, and I find myself spontaneously exclaiming aloud, "Please, God, don't listen to them. They don't mean what they're saying." Then I ask them to take back what they said, to apologise for their words. I've had more than one client look at me as if I'd gone loopy, but when it comes to money, I take words very, very seriously. After years of dealing with people who have it and people who don't, I have learned that words, all our words, hold the power to make us rich or to keep us poor. Your words are as important as your thoughts, because your words are the bridge from thoughts to actions.

Think thoughts of poverty, speak words you don't believe, and you will never take the actions necessary to achieve wealth. You'll never be rich, either, if you think grand thoughts and speak only of poverty. It takes rich thoughts to lead to rich words. It takes rich words to lead to rich actions. All our thoughts, all our words must be compelled in the same direction to inspire the actions that lead to wealth.

WORDS OF POVERTY, WORDS OF WEALTH

Whether you notice it or not, you talk about your money dozens of times a day, even if silence about the subject is your native financial language. *I can't . . . I'll never . . . I don't know how . . . I wish I had . . .* Used in connection with money, these words, regardless of how much or how little money you have, are words of poverty.

To have more, you have to begin by thinking you can have more, but then you have to say it: *I can . . . I always . . . I am learning how . . . I will have . . .* To have more, you must learn to speak in the language of wealth, a language that shows self-respect—and also respect for your money.

You must learn to listen to the language of money around you and the words you choose to express your thoughts. When you begin to do this—and it isn't very hard, it's like listening for a song, or a chord, or a word you just learned—you can read your financial future in the words you speak, hear and exchange every day. Try to listen to yourself to learn what an astute financial planner might know about you after meeting you just once. Speak poor, and you'll be poor. Speak rich, true words, on the other hand, and you start to change your entire outlook.

LETTING YOUR THOUGHTS EXCEED YOUR WORDS

Do you hear yourself in the words and phrases below? If so, you're speaking the language of poverty. Instead, I want you to learn to speak the language of wealth.

- *I'm broke.* The words "I'm broke" suggest, in fact, that you're broken, at rock bottom, unable to function, unable to meet your responsibilities. Is that the message you want to send to the world?
- *I know I should . . .* Anything that you "should" be doing is something you're clearly not doing. "Should" is another way of absolving yourself of responsibility. Any sentence that contains the word is not even close to a statement of intent.
- *It's only money.* There's nothing "only" about money. Money *matters,* plain and simple. If this is your attitude toward money, believe me, your money will take the same apathetic attitude toward you.
- *I need a new . . .* Do you really *need* it? Is "need" the right word? Elevating desires to needs is destructive—to ourselves and to those around us. Let's say you saw a new suit and you thought, I would like to own that—you were able to keep need out of it. Isn't that statement more accurate and therefore truer to the language of wealth?

- *Never.* Never say "never", when it comes to money. "Never" cuts off tomorrow, and tomorrow holds the possibility of always. "I'll never be rich." "I'll always be rich." One word makes a world of difference.
- *I could start investing if . . . When I get a raise, things will be different.* "If" and "when" take us away from the here and now to a place that exists only conditionally.
- *Oh God.* "Oh God, how am I going to pay these bills?" "Oh God, everything is so expensive!" "Oh God, I would love to come with you to the Caribbean if I just had the money." So often when it comes to our money we invoke God, which gives an unnecessary, desperate urgency to what we are trying to say. It's the language of longing, not the language of wealth.
- *Poor Bill,* or whoever. The words evoke someone who is bankrupt, not necessarily financially, perhaps, but certainly emotionally and spiritually. A pitiful case, a person who must be treated with extra sensitivity, a person who's weak. The words evoke poverty. They also enforce poverty. Either Bill, through his thoughts, words and actions, is soliciting pity, or else poverty is being thrust upon him by what other people think and say about him. Either way, the poorer the thoughts, words and actions are, the harder it is to rise above them.

WORDS AND POWER

It is not enough to push away thoughts and words of poverty. You must also use words of wealth, bounty and abundance. Any words, repeated often enough, become true. Begin your process of change with thoughts and words that encompass richness, possibilities, dreams, openness, and hope: "I know there is a great job out there just for me." "I am going to invest and do a great job at it." "I have debt, and I am paying it off." "We will be able to afford a house one day soon." This is the language of more.

Here is an exercise I always practised with my clients and still practise myself. It's a simple, one-step exercise to make sure your thoughts and words are in agreement. Before you say anything with respect to your money—your prospects, your goals, your financial worries—I want you to ask yourself the following question: Are your words stating what you wish to be true? For example, if you are about to say, "I will never get out of debt," I want you first to ask yourself: Is this what I want to be true? Of course it isn't, so don't say it. Rephrase what you're trying to express until it passes this test. In this case, "One day I will be out of debt" is likely what you want to say.

Every time you're about to speak about your money, ask yourself this essential question—*Do I want this to be true?*—and speak only when the answer is yes. For instance:

- "I'll never get around to investing."
  Do you want this to be true?
  Say instead, "I am finally beginning to learn about investing."
- "I just know the market's going to crash."
  Do you want this to be true?
  Say instead, "I believe that the stock market is a good investment over time."
- "My husband will probably leave me with nothing."
  Do you want this to be true?
  Say instead, "If I get divorced, I will take every measure to get what's fair."
- "I'll never get out from under."
  Do you want this to be true?
  Say instead, "Slowly but surely, I am putting my finances in order."
- "I'm an impulse spender. I can't help it."
  Do you want this to be true?
  Say instead, "I spend only what I can afford to spend."
- "I just can't save money."
  Do you want this to be true?
  Say instead, "I am beginning to save a little from every pay cheque."

By asking yourself this one question every time you are about to make a statement about your financial situation, you will learn to speak only in language that's respectful to yourself, your money, your future.

Sometimes—with all of us—words just pop out, or we say something before we've thought it through, but when it comes to money, listen to the words you use. If you slip, simply take it back. Say, "I didn't mean that." Rephrase what you've said to reflect what you want to be true.

Align your words with your goal, remembering the power in each and every word.

THE WORDS CREATE THE VISION

I cannot stress enough the profound impact the words you use today will have on you tomorrow, which is why I want you to speak the language of wealth right now, using the present tense—"I have the courage to be rich"—to create the future you want. Beginning today.

The notion of stating your goals in the present tense rather than as an expression of future intent is neither my own invention nor is it new. It actually dates back to a tenth-century Hindu text called *The Outlook of Shiva,* written by a scholar called Somananda. In it, he instructs us to act as if we already embody our goal, no matter the disparity between what we are and what we wish to become. It is important not to allow doubt to cause us to abandon our intention but to maintain "an unwavering awareness" by affirming our goal with confidence and conviction. In this way, Somananda explains, our being aligns itself with our intention, and the goal becomes manifest.

The wisdom of this teaching is what I draw upon when I urge you to create a new truth by speaking it in the present tense and unifying the sequence of thoughts, words and actions. Become it by being it. Be it by saying it.

PRELUDE TO ACTION

What happens next? After you start to think you can, your thoughts become more powerful; after you start to use only words that say you can, you start to feel more powerful. When you feel more powerful you have the energy to propel you toward the actions that create a life of real wealth. There's the cycle: from your thoughts and your words to your actions. Every time you go through the cycle without wavering from the goal of oneness, your assurance and determination build, paving the way toward more.

If you learn to compose the thoughts and words of more, you're partway there. What once seemed impossible now seems inevitable. Richness, remember, begins with your thoughts, because your thoughts create your destiny.

CHAPTER 3

THE COURAGE TO MAKE ROOM FOR MORE MONEY

There are so many things we imagine when we dream about having more money, when we think about what it would be like to be rich. The things we could buy, the places we could go, the problems money would solve. We think about how much better we would feel, less anxious and afraid, how much happier. We could be more generous, perhaps, donate money to charity, surprise our parents with some great present, and certainly not worry about sending the kids to university, or our own retirement. If only we had more money, we think, everything would just fall into place. If only . . .

It's true that money can buy things and solve problems, but in the fantasy, we're also imagining other things that money might provide—extra time and the capacity to use it well, a once-and-for-all cure for fear and anxiety, peace of mind, generosity, even happiness. That's a lot to ask from some paper and shiny pieces of metal. In the dream we give such powers to money because the dream is of more than money itself. Dreams like these suggest that we believe that with more money, we'd not only have more, we'd also *be* more. Richer not only in dollars and cents, but richer in soul and spirit, too. Is it possible that dreams like these can become a reality in which we are richer on all planes? I not only think it, I know it; with faith, integrity and courage, anything is possible.

We have seen how emotional obstacles—shame, fear, anger—stand between us and more. We have seen how our thoughts and words must be in alignment in order for us to achieve more. We have seen how important it is to clear away the internal clutter that keeps us from having more, being more. But we still have to overcome one last obstacle before we can start taking truly strong financial actions that will permanently create what we want and so deserve when it comes to our financial lives. The last obstacle that must be cleared away is material clutter: the sheer volume of items in your life that you no longer value and no longer need; the confusion in your finances that allows you to obscure what you actually have and what you don't have; the chaos of all the financial tasks you intend to get to but until now have left undone.

If you are not making the money in your life that you think you should be making, if you have debt, if you cannot save a penny, I am willing to bet that clutter is standing smack in the middle of what you have today and what you could have tomorrow.

CLUTTER'S COMPOUND INTEREST

Clutter in our lives leads to more clutter—the clutter of stuff in closets, cupboards, basements and attics. Think of your bedroom, your bathroom, your kitchen and kitchen drawers, the garage, your shelves; just think of the clutter. A huge industry has arisen to help us manage and contain our clutter. Think of the irony. We spend good money to buy stuff, to hold stuff; we pile it up in corners, under beds, in closets, where we surely forget about it, where it almost never gets used. Overflow clutter ends up in rented storage bins, at a cost, say, of seventy dollars a month or more, which can mean a loss of thousands of dollars over time. What are the items filling these storage bins and our basements and attics? Items we think we might need some day, items we are not yet ready to part with. Items that, in all likelihood, we'll never use again—yet we still won't let them go.

Why won't we let these items go, the useless items we keep around us? It is the profound fear of loss, which prevents us from gain. We keep so much stuff around us because we fear that if all our material possessions were taken away, we'd be left with nothing—and who would we be if we had nothing? It's this same fear of loss, however, that cuts off the possibility for more. You've heard the phrase *Less is more*? In this context it means that clutter blocks the way for more. Surrounded by clutter, you can't find what you need, see what you have, notice what you value, or pinpoint what's missing. In a rich and radiantly abundant life, on the other hand, one in which there is clarity, there is always room for more to come.

In the purely financial realm, when our papers are cluttered and our affairs unattended to, we create a swirl of financial chaos around us. We bounce cheques, we pay late charges on our mortgage, we forget to renew our driver's licence or pay our rates. Why? We do this to obscure where we really stand, because we can't face our true financial selves, so we choose instead to ignore it, forget it, lose it, not face it—all actions that lead us away from money, not toward it, and keep us from creating.

Money can't see its way through clutter and chaos and confusion. It hates being spent on items stuffed into a cupboard and never used. It dislikes being shoved into a drawer, in the form of unopened or unpaid bills, or crammed into a wallet any which way. If you hold on to what you have for longer than you should, you're using yesterday's space to hold tomorrow's offerings. If you allow the clutter in your mind to push out the true facts of your finances, you're not leaving room for thoughts of more. But if instead you clear its path of obstacles like these, you will be able to find your money, and money will be able to find you.

UNLEASHING THE POWER OF MONEY

As the bearer of your money, you are the one who determines—with your thoughts, your words, and the financial actions you take—whether your money will be fat, skinny, full of vigour, or listless: how well, in other words, it will treat you in return. Give it the full power of its life force, and it can provide you with every material thing you wish for, increase its value many times over, help charities, buy education, and keep you and your family safe forever. Does money have a life force, an energy force, of its own? I truly believe it does, for I have seen its force at work, in small amounts of money that, invested wisely over time, thrive and prosper into fortunes—that's the life force of money given its full rein. I've also seen it allowed to languish. A twenty-dollar note stuffed into the back pocket of your jeans and sent through the washer and dryer is money languishing. I believe that the life force of money is vital, given all that it has the power to achieve. The conditions under which you and your money live will in the end determine whether your life will be a rich one or not.

Conditions have to be optimal for any force to be unleashed; a hurricane, for example, will lose its strength before it gets very far inland. In the same way, certain conditions must prevail in order for you to attract money, make it feel welcome, and make it want to stay with you forever and grow. Only you can create these conditions. In order for money to find you, it has to work its way through your emotions, your thoughts, words and actions. In order for you to become a beacon that illuminates the way for money, you have to clear the way for money, clear its path of the emotions, thoughts, words, actions and external objects—the clutter, the chaos—that are blocking the way for more money to come in. This in turn will bring you closer to your true self and light the way for more.

J O H N   P A U L ' S   S T O R Y

I wanted to be an accountant mostly because I love numbers, always have. I live in a small town, and I know my clients really trust me, but I've always known, too, that other accountants in town have made a lot more than I have, which has frustrated me because I know I'm a better accountant than many of them.

Not long ago I started going out with Sherri, a woman I fell for the very first time we met. I began to think about marriage, children, a life beyond numbers, and how we could have a great future together. But Sherri came to my office one night after work, and suddenly that future began to fade. She sounded almost sad when she said she would never hire an accountant with an office like mine. I looked around and saw what she meant—dust and chaos everywhere, files falling down. The place was a mess, but I hadn't noticed; all I do is look at numbers. That night I felt that I had lost her respect, and we didn't have a great evening together. At the end of the night—it was a Thursday, I remember—I told her that I would have a surprise for her on Sunday.

Friday I couldn't concentrate on work at all, but was full of energy. I had a plan. I put the work aside and began cleaning my office, top to bottom. I did the files, and dusted, vacuumed, cleaned the windows and the blinds, everything. As I was cleaning, I found many things—papers I'd misplaced, several old cheques I had forgotten to cash, bills I wasn't sure I'd paid, correspondence I hadn't answered. It really dawned on me then that it wasn't enough just to be good with numbers. Here I was, supposed to be on top of things, and my own affairs were one big mess. By midnight on Saturday I was finished, and I felt so much better. But then I looked around at the walls, all scuffed and dingy, and I thought, More mess. This is actually what clients saw when they came to my office! Sherri was right. I wouldn't hire me, either. I went to the hardware store the next morning and bought some paint and brushes. When Sherri came at noon, I had two walls painted, and the place already looked a thousand times better. She was really pleased, I could tell, but I was even more pleased. She later said that was the moment when she fell in love. That was about ten months ago, and the funny thing is that since I've cleaned up my act, my business is really picking up, too. I still have to make a conscious effort not to be disorganised, but I'm also doing so well that I'm thinking it might be time to hire a secretary. It was looking beyond my numbers that made the difference.

Being good with numbers is not necessarily the same thing as being good with money. John Paul was burying his money and potential under piles of clutter and chaos, leaving money with no ready way to find him, which in fact was turning money away. When he cleared the way for more, more came in: more business, more money, a richer life in more ways than one.

P E N N Y ' S   S T O R Y

I'm your basic stay-at-home mother, I guess you'd call it, and I always left the finances to Charlie, my husband. With two kids, we've never had that much extra, but we always tried to put a little away into the savings account with every pay cheque. We used to talk about what we would live on when we retired, but those conversations never went very far; there was too much to pay for every day.

When my father died, my mother was hit all at once with trying to figure out what she had. There was enough money there, which was a relief to everyone, but what surprised us was that Mother really got interested in her money. She said she couldn't believe how conservative Dad had been all those years, and she was seeing for the first time how much more there could have been. She joined an investment club and put some money into it which she said she wanted to go toward education for my kids, who are now seven and nine. This got me excited, and I began to watch my mother's stock portfolio on television periodically throughout the day. The market would go up, then down, all day long, and I got really hooked on what was happening.

Then I started bugging Charlie about our money. I was thinking that we could do better. He has this drawer where he keeps our papers, and I kept saying, Let's go through it together. For the longest time he wouldn't, but finally we did. It was a hodgepodge of little bits of money. Six hundred dollars in a savings account from when I was working, before I had the kids. Three personal superannuation funds. Two savings accounts we'd started when the children were born but had forgotten to add money to. Papers from Charlie's superannuation at his old job. Plus our savings account. But it added up to fourteen thousand dollars. We were amazed. We actually had fourteen thousand dollars that we didn't know about stuffed into this drawer.

We cleared everything out and then looked into what would be best to do with it. We kept two thousand dollars in the savings account for emergencies and invested the rest in these great managed funds we read about and we amalgamated all of the small superannuation funds into one good one. I figured out how to do the paperwork, which wasn't that complicated once I actually sat down and did it. It was a great feeling, thinking that we could actually begin to make some money.

Then one day, I was watching a financial show on TV, and I thought, What am I doing sitting here, watching money? The kids are at school, and I should be making money instead. Charlie and I had already agreed that I wouldn't go back to work full-time for a few more years, but I figured I could do something. So I've been casual teaching a couple of days a week ever since the beginning of the school year. And all that money goes into our investments. I really feel like a grown-up for the first time, and it feels good.

By clearing the way through their financial clutter, Penny and Charlie found they had more than they imagined: enough to begin to see a clear path to a promising future. Stuffed in a drawer, their money was neglected and suffocating. When they let it out and treated it with respect, they were empowering it to grow on their behalf in the years ahead. Penny then took that power to heart and, with her actions, turned toward more.

JEFF'S STORY

You can imagine what it's like having five kids—sheer mayhem. It's fun for the most part, this high-energy household. But it's also hard to keep track of everything. Meg, my wife, is basically a saint. She runs the house, gets the kids off to school and camp and lessons, buys them what they need, and keeps track of the money. I'm a lawyer. I make good money, and we live in a nice neighbourhood, but with five kids, it never seems like enough. Meg doesn't complain, but she's always sort of hinted that the money isn't exactly under control and let it go at that.

Then one day it all started to fall apart. It was a weekend, and I went to send a fax to a client, and the machine didn't work. No dial tone, either. So I called the phone company to complain, and they said that the line had been turned off for non-payment. We get a separate bill for the fax line, because it was installed at a different time from the phone line. How long had it been off, I asked, and they said two weeks. Two weeks! Think of the work I might have missed, plus who wants their clients to hear that their lawyer's line has been disconnected when they try to fax you? Meg wasn't home, so I went to her desk to look for the bill and found a lot more than I bargained for.

Bills everywhere, especially for credit cards I didn't even know we had. Some bills weren't opened yet, but were already overdue. I looked in her cheque book and saw that she was paying a little here, a little there, trying to keep us afloat. Then I came across a sweet note she had written to her sister but never sent, promising to send the money she'd borrowed next month. It broke my heart, but clearly something was really wrong with the way we were living. Here I was making a perfectly good salary by any standard, and my whole family was sinking.

The timing was unusual because the house was absolutely empty— soccer games, play dates, who knows where they all were. Shopping, maybe. Anyway, I started looking around, going from room to room, and there was so much stuff. Rollerblades still in the box, toys and cosmetics still in bags, clothes everywhere, and, believe me, I wasn't exactly innocent, there was plenty of my stuff, too. I looked in some drawers and what did I find? Five rolls of Scotch tape, partly used. Five rolls! Who needs five rolls of tape? There was this pasta-making machine in the kitchen that we'd used maybe once. Books all over the place, three children's tape players, jumpers for the dog, and about a dozen lunch boxes. I just can't begin to name all the stuff.

When everybody came home, they ran laughing and screaming into the house, and then they got quiet when they saw me. I called a family meeting right then and said, "This has got to stop." When I get serious, they really pay attention, even the little ones, and there was silence in the room. I walked them through every bedroom, even mine and Meg's, because this wasn't the children's fault. Then I said we were having a garage sale next weekend, and everyone should round up stuff to contribute to it.

We made over a thousand dollars on our garage sale, which left us with twenty-three thousand dollars in debt, five kids, and a big mess. It was Meg's idea that we go to a consumer credit counselling service, which was a big help. It got us organised and focused, and the counsellor showed us how to deal with the debt first, and how we could begin to save later, once the credit cards were paid off. We sent all the garage sale money to the credit card companies, which felt pretty great, I have to say.

I look around at my neighbours, and they have the same stuff that we had and still have. And I wonder, Do they have the same kind of debt? Or could they really have so much more money? I had a hint at the garage sale, when more than one of my neighbours said they should do the same thing. Maybe we all have too much, or maybe we all just owe too much.

The weird thing is that since we started paying attention, which is basically what we're doing now, paying attention, everything seems more possible. Last week, we got an offer for a credit card with a really low interest rate for six months, and Meg said, Let's do it, roll over some debt, and that will make a difference. Then for the first time, our town announced a summer program for kids, with swimming and tennis—free. So the kids can go to that. Strangest of all, though, is that just the other day I got a letter from my father, with a cheque for five thousand dollars. He'd done well in the market, he said, and wanted us to put the money toward an education fund, a thousand dollars for each of the kids. He's never in my life done anything like that before. Weighed against our debt, it's hope. The debt feels lighter. We can deal with it.

With the best intentions in the world, Jeff and Meg filled up their house with children—and filled up their lives with clutter. When they finally faced their clutter, they also came face-to-face with their finances. And made some changes. They got rid of some of yesterday's spending, yesterday's clutter, and what's happened? Already, more is coming in. Reduce the clutter, they learned, and you can make way for more.

Drawing upon the courage to be rich does not mean denying yourself the important things in life, but changing your thoughts about money, your words about money, and the actions you take with the money you have and the items your money has bought. In essence, I am asking you to change your current money reflexes, so that you start thinking, talking, and behaving with money, your money, in a new way—with clarity. If you have very little right now, I know that it takes immense faith to believe you could have more. But you can. How can you start a fortune with, say, twenty dollars? With faith, with that twenty dollars, the next twenty dollars, and the clarity to see all the way to tomorrow, when the first twenty dollars has disappeared into a sea of plenty.

But you must start to clear away the clutter now, as John Paul, Penny, and Jeff did. Money needs time and space to grow, and the "seed money" you plant today must be treated the way you would a garden: planted and nurtured and given time to grow. Tiny seeds can grow into huge plants, and tiny sums of money can grow into great wealth. Perhaps at this point in your life it sounds hopeless, but with faith—and, yes, courage—you can turn your life around and find the clarity in today, along with the clarity to look forward to tomorrow. Clear a path through the clutter and chaos in all aspects of your life, and you can see the way ahead and find the capacity for abundance in the clarity.

YOUR EXERCISE: FOUR STEPS TOWARD CLARITY

You make room for more by knowing what you have, by not owning anything you don't want or need or love, and by valuing every item you own. You make room for more, literally and metaphorically, by creating a place for more to enter.

Your possessions are the earthly, material objects that represent who you are, what you care about, how you define yourself: your taste and your value system. You spend hours of your life working to pay for these possessions. Over time, your possessions change, from the makeshift objects that furnished your first apartment, when you were starting out, to the items you bought later with such care, perhaps with the idea of permanence. The following actions toward clarity will take you on a tour of your house and its contents, four times. I want you to think about the value of each object—what it cost you when you bought it, what it is worth in dollars today, and what it is worth as an earthly, material representation of who you are now.

1. The first time, wander through your house, your garage, look through your drawers and cupboards with the goal of finding at least twenty-five items that you are willing to throw away—yes, throw away. Anything from worn-out shoes, grimy duplicate can openers, broken toys, and lipsticks that were definitely a mistake, to spent toothbrushes, unused cleaning products, and earrings with one half of the pair missing. Broken umbrellas, dried-up cans of paint, candle stubs. Bits of things where there's not even enough left to use. Twenty-five items. Keep looking until you find them. These items are gone, and I want you to throw them away.

2. Now go through your house again, this time in search of loose change and the occasional bill squirrelled away. Look in your handbags and your briefcase. Look in the pockets of your cardigans, pants, jackets, skirts, shirts, dresses, and coats; look under the cushions of your chairs and couches, and in between the seats of your car. Do you have a jar of coins somewhere? Go and get it. Look through your jewellery box or where you keep your cufflinks. Rummage through the kitchen drawers, any other secret places where you might have left or put some money. If you are like most of us, you will find, altogether, thirty dollars or more. Then put the money you've found into a jar—call it a jar of abundance—or a bowl—a bowl of bounty—to remind you of what you didn't even know you had, and put it near where you keep your bills.

3. Go through your house a third time. This time, find at least twenty-five items that are still in good shape but are truthfully of no further use to you. Clothes you or your family no longer wear, winter coats, scarves, hats, old belts, handbags, dishes, a working appliance you have replaced, videos, a stack of books you no longer need, still-good toys. Twenty-five items that someone else could use and would be grateful to have. After you have gathered everything, reflect for a minute on the money you spent, how much of it was wasted, and how little you have to show for it now.

Now clear away the clutter. Take these items to a collection bin, a charity thrift shop, a nursing home or day-care centre, the Salvation Army or St Vincent de Paul. Take them, in other words, to a place where people who need them will have the readiest access to them.

Could you have a garage sale instead? You could. But I want you to begin thinking expansively. By having a garage sale, you see, you'd get only a fraction of what these items are really worth, which diminishes both your purchase and your purchase price. They are better given to someone who will appreciate them and use them gratefully, rather than sold to someone who will gloat over getting a bargain. This can actually raise their worth to full value. Rather than trying to make up for your mistakes, you will have made a generous offering to the world. Make your donations within one week.

4. Now go through your house a fourth time, pausing to touch and look at the items that mean everything in the world to you, the items you would never part with, ever—photographs of your children, a ring your mother gave you, the desk that was your grandmother's, scrapbooks, perhaps the painting in your living room that was the first big thing you and your partner ever bought together. Now think of these items so precious to you, and how little in fact they cost you. Define for yourself the true meaning of worth.

Just a rough estimate—what do you suppose your clutter cost you at the time you bought it, and how much money does that mean you no longer have today? Ten fifteen-dollar T-shirts, an ill-fitting forty-dollar skirt or seventy-dollar shirt, the toaster oven that never worked properly, the bread maker that made oddly shaped and funny-tasting bread. What did these things that you had to buy because you thought you couldn't live without them—and then didn't use them—really cost you in the end? Note, too, the items that served you well; these are items from which you "got your money's worth"—a fair and equal trade.

What I want you to do is to begin to think about money, what it can buy and when it can serve you better kept, simply, as money. Remember that most items, the minute they're removed from the store in which you bought them, lose their financial value or are certainly worth far less than what you paid for them—you can bring value to them only by using them.

By removing the first of your clutter, you have already begun to create more—more space, more awareness, more honesty, more possibility, more hope for tomorrow, and, ultimately, more money. What you don't want is gone, and therefore meaningless clutter is out of the way. The chances are good that you've also filled a jar of "found money", to remind you that you had even more than you realised. By treasuring anew the items you could never part with, you've been reminded of the things that money cannot buy. These are lessons in more, lessons in clarity. Facing up to your money, probably for the first time in your life, will leave you with a sense of power, with the feeling that yes, you can figure this out. When clutter is in control, you leave that clutter with the last word, and clutter has only the power to destroy. When you take control of the clutter, you are left instead with the power to act and the power to create.

FINANCIAL CLUTTER

Unpaid bills create financial clutter, as does debt, and they both work against clarity. Unopened monthly bank statements clutter up your clear thoughts about money, for when you don't know how much or how little you really have, you do not know what you can (or cannot) afford to spend.

More clutter arises from the things you know you must do—set up your will or trust, arrange guardianship for your children in case something happens to you, get your debt under control, begin investing for your future—but haven't yet done. Bank or credit card statements you don't read or understand are costing you, blocking you, and getting in your way financially. Changes you mean to make but haven't made to your superannuation plan preoccupy your mind and keep your finances in a frozen state of chaos. Financial papers kept for years, unsorted, in a filing cabinet; a messy wallet, with the bills stuffed in or folded or out of order— these things mean you aren't paying attention to your money, which is tantamount to pushing it away. Items as seemingly insignificant as over-due library books or videos cost money by the day, clutter your thoughts, and give you the feeling that your life is in disarray. Even in the neatest and tidiest house, financial clutter can stand in the way of more.

Remember your jar of money, the money you didn't even know you had? I asked you to put it near where you keep your bills. Just leave it there for now. By stating your desire to be rich, in drawing on your courage, in taking the actions that will lead you toward more, you will also leave your financial clutter behind you. In the chapters that follow, we'll get to what you must do to create a new future. We'll get to what you must do with your found money. And it will be so much easier to move forward once you have left this clutter behind. Having come this far, you have cleared the way toward wealth, toward richness of all kinds. Now it is time to make your dreams come true.

PART II

THE VALUE OF MONEY

CHAPTER 4

THE COURAGE TO VALUE MONEY

Not long ago, I was talking to my next-door neighbour Elysia, who was outside selling lemonade with her sister, Naomi. We were having a conversation about raising her prices from ten cents to twenty-five cents per cup. I asked her, "Elysia, what are the five most important things to you in life?"

She contemplated the history of her seven years, then looked at me and said, "First my family, then my house, television, candy, and then money." Impressed that she had come up with exactly five items, I probed a little deeper.

"Elysia, what do you need to get the candy that you love?"

"Money," she said.

"And how about the TV, what do you need to get that?"

"Money."

"And how about your house?"

"Money," she replied once again.

And then I asked, "How about your family, what do you need to get them?"

Just as quickly, she replied, "Love."

"That's right," I said, "but don't you think that maybe you have to re-order your list? You see, if you need money to buy the candy, the house, and the TV, then don't you think money should be more important than what it can buy?"

She thought about this, and then she looked at me and said, "I think you are right."

Elysia, in that short period of time, was introduced to the first law of money, a law that serves as the foundation for wise spending:

THE FIRST LAW OF MONEY

People first. Then money. Then things.

You see, most of us are just like Elysia, in that we value things more than we value money. We care more about having what money can buy than we care about having money itself. If we valued money more than we valued things, we would not part with it so freely, nor would we think of parting with money we didn't have in order to buy something on credit. This is a vital law, a law that is respectful of money, a law that, if you follow it, will keep what you have and what you spend (or don't spend) in full harmony. It is a law that, if you follow it, will make you truly rich.

People first. Those things that are created by and kept with love must always come before anything else. Family, friends, your partner, your children, yourself. The adage that money can't buy love is true, and a life without love—regardless of how much money one has—is a poor life indeed.

Then money. Can you imagine going to someone's house and having them proudly show you a room filled with thousands of dollar bills and telling you the history of how all that money came to be? You would be appalled at the vulgarity. At the same time, you would think nothing of it if you were to go to someone's house and be given a tour of a room they had just redecorated. What did it take to redecorate that room? Money. Money exchanged for furniture, paintings, carpeting, lamps, and so on. In either case, you're being shown a room full of money. The difference in your perception was the value system that you applied—a room full of things is okay, whereas a room full of money is not. That is because you value things more than you value money.

Then things. When your financial priorities are in order, things come last.

GETTING AND SPENDING

We work hard for our money, forty hours or more a week, and once we're set loose from the workplace, we go shopping. We buy food and clothes and stuff, and then we say we just don't know where the money went. But if we valued money over things, over the items it can buy, then we would know exactly where our money went. We would change our money/thing ratio so that we'd have more money than things. We would take great pleasure in seeing our money and watching it grow. Barring unexpected illness, we would have no debt—and, for that matter, no doubt. We would always know when we could afford something we wanted to buy, and we would also be more likely to be able to buy the things we truly wanted.

YOUR EXERCISE: FIND THE COURAGE, FIND THE MONEY

Our consumer culture makes us want things, and easy credit enables us to have them, long before we've paid for them. Bigger and better, or smaller and better. New. Improved. Entire new arenas of consumer goods keep opening up, enticing and seducing us. No one can say no all the time, so I'm not going to ask you to do that. I learned long ago that restricting my clients to a budget works no better than forcing someone overweight to diet—sooner or later there'll be a financial tantrum. Instead, I am asking you to start making some choices about today and tomorrow.

Not long ago I was in a gourmet and gift shop where there were give-away samples on all the display tables, making the shopping experience feel like a party. On one table they were offering slivers of very pretty fragrant soap. You bought this brightly coloured soap not in standard bars but by weight; they'd cut what you wanted from a bar the size of a loaf of bread: $20 a kilo. I did a quick calculation, and figured that if I were to switch from my ordinary soap to this fancy soap, I would be spending $100 more a year on *soap*.

At another table, they were offering teeny cups and spoons with various kinds of gourmet vinegars for customers to taste—blueberry tarragon, cabernet sauvignon, cognac, and fig. They were exotic-tasting, it's true, but each bottle of vinegar cost $14—$10 more than I usually pay for my perfectly fine vinegar. Another quick calculation, and I realised that if I switched to these fancy vinegars, I would be spending maybe $50 more a year on vinegar than I do now.

At the next table I tasted some raspberry-mint jam: delicious. But worth $6 more per jar than I usually spend for jam? I don't think so.

But it is in just this way—premium this and designer that—that our spending inches up, our scale of living inches up, we upgrade a little here and a little there, to the point where those things we once thought of as luxuries have become necessities. With three relatively small indulgences at that store, assuming I never went back to my usual brands, I would have raised my cost of living by almost $200 a year.

Now, it could just so happen that soap, vinegar, and jams are items that really matter to me and that the thought of having these exquisite varieties makes me feel so great and pampered that the extra $200 a year would be worth it to me. If that were the case, well then, I might have decided that I was going to buy them anyway, extravagant or not. But if I valued money over things, I would find that $200 from somewhere else in my life, not simply tack on to my spending an extra $200 a year in order to feel good. Because it's not just $200 today that's at stake. It's also $200 next year and every year thereafter. Beyond that, it's $200 that's being used for today's small pleasures at a far greater cost tomorrow.

If you're not on a course of getting rich but want to be, you have to change course; it's that simple. To choose rich is to make every penny count, every dollar count, every financial choice count. To erase the bad habits that make money vaporise into nothingness. To distinguish between necessity and luxury, and to choose your luxuries very, very carefully. Case in point: the fancy "designer" lemonade I also sampled that day at the gourmet shop.

Let's say I drink six large bottles of lemonade a week, all three months of summer, and let's say I switch to premium lemonade. One summer's cost? $180. Let's say I don't switch but stick to the 65-cent version. One summer's cost? $23.40, which I've been paying all along anyway. I put the $156.60 I didn't spend into a good low-fee managed fund for 20 years at 10 percent interest, and it grows to $8992.

Now I want you to examine the necessities in your own life, and also the luxuries. Next, choose a few luxuries which you wouldn't mind "downgrading" to the necessity category—$500, $1000, $2000 worth each year; you pick the number that feels right. Regardless of how much or how little you think you have, you can find money by examining your expenses, trimming your spending here and there, and learning to choose and value money over things.

What I want you to do is to think about everything you own, everything you owe on, everything you want, everything you actually need. Examine your spending carefully and honestly, taking note of items you don't use, items where maybe, just maybe, you don't need the top-of-the-line version next time, areas where you're apt to waste money flagrantly. In Chapter 3, we removed some of the clutter from our past, and with this exercise, we will turn future clutter into money instead. This exercise will help you find $500, $1000, $2000, or more, every year—money that you will think about and treat differently after you read the chapters that follow.

What will the money be used for? First, to speed up the process to eradicate any debt you have, for once and for all. After that, the money will be used to invest in your future.

Here are some thoughts to get you started:

♦ Your morning coffee. Do you make it at home (cheaper) or grab a cup on the way into the office (more costly)? One medium-size coffee and a small snack a day costs at least $2.75, which means you're spending $1004 a year on morning coffee. Invested at 10 percent, that's $57,504 over 20 years, $98,740 over 25 years, and $165,152 over 30 years.

- Somewhere along the line, did you switch from an old-fashioned blanket and bedspread to a luxurious doona? That's a step up from necessity to luxury. What about extra-fluffy towels, lovely scented soaps, rich shampoos, and accessories for the bath? Have you turned your daily bath into a luxury at-home spa? At what cost? If you can cut back just $10 a month on these luxuries, you will have $120 more a year to invest.

- Have you added to your phone line extra features like call waiting, call forwarding, or caller ID? At what cost per year?

- Mobile phone. Do you really need it? What is it costing you per year?

- Designer sunglasses. How much did you spend on your most recent pair of sunglasses? Have you looked into cheaper brands? How often do you lose a pair? Are expensive sunglasses a downgradable luxury for you?

- Have you made the switch from two-litre containers of ordinary ice cream to small tubs of premium? What about biscuits—do you buy "designer" brands rather than big bags of no names?

- Do you and your partner go to the movies once a week? Luxury or necessity? If you skipped one week a month, you'd save $200 or more a year (not to mention considerable additional savings from not eating out afterward).

- How many things are there in your kitchen that you rarely or never use? Appliances—pasta maker, bread maker, ice cream maker, popcorn popper, waffle iron? Rarely used pots and pans? How about serving bowls and platters? Do you need all the ones you have? Is all your equipment top-of-the-line? Do you use it enough to justify having the best? Might you think twice before buying something else for the kitchen?

- Do you buy books that you know you're going to read just once, rather than take them out from the library? Four fewer hardcover mysteries a year, at $25 each, puts you $100 closer to your goal.

- How extravagantly does your garden grow? Gardening is suddenly a big new "necessity" and can be a costly one. Could your garden budget take some pruning?

- Daily bread—have you decided that the best thing since sliced bread is French baguettes, bread that goes stale after one day? Have you switched from ordinary loaves of bread to gourmet bread? Luxury or necessity?
- Designer underwear—luxury or necessity?
- How many power tools are in your garage, and how often do you use them?
- How much unused exercise equipment do you have around the house? Have you discarded your old tracksuit in favour of slick new exercise wear?
- Must you have an expensive camera? A video camera?
- How often do you feel you need a new car? Could it be less often?
- Remember the days when every family had one TV? How many colour televisions do you have now? How many VCRs? How many videotapes? Do you tape over things you've taped before or use fresh tapes every time? How many videotapes do your children actually own? Would you consider replacing an old TV with a newer model (bigger screen, sleeker console) before the old one actually stops working? If so, could you reconsider?
- Have you signed up for more than one cable TV plan or just one basic plan? The difference can be $25 a month, or $300 a year.
- As a kid, did you drive to holiday spots or visit your grandparents on holidays? These days, do all your holiday destinations require planes and hotels? At what cost?
- Does someone else do your cleaning? Luxury or necessity?
- Do you routinely take your clothing to the dry cleaner when all it needs is a pressing you could do yourself? If your dry-cleaning bill were just $10 less each week, you would have $520 a year to invest.
- Do you use disposable razors? Buy expensive juice poppers for the kids? Small cost, maybe, but the cost of disposables adds up.
- Have you switched from old-fashioned vegetable oil to the much more expensive extra-virgin olive oil?
- Do you drink premium beer instead of regular beer? How much, over the course of a year, is this costing you?

- Do you have a really great "designer" bike? How often do you use it?
- Do you buy a lot of costume jewellery, wear it a few times, then forget about it and go on to other, newer costume jewellery?
- Do you need a separate phone line for your fax? For your computer? Is this a genuine need?
- Luxury or necessity—that bouquet of fresh flowers you routinely pick up on the way home from work every single Friday, even if you're not going to be home much that weekend? At, say, $8 a week, you're spending $416 per year of the money that could be making your future more beautiful.
- Do you buy lottery tickets twice a week? This can cost $104 a year, and the odds of creating your own fortune with $104 a year are far greater than the odds of your winning your fortune in the lottery.
- Do you use more expensive whitening toothpaste rather than standard varieties? How much extra does it cost per tube and per year?
- Do you love the luxury of manicures, pedicures, and waxing so much that you wouldn't think of going without them? A $20 manicure every two weeks costs $468 over the course of one year.
- Are your cosmetics department-store varieties or chemist brands? Does every single cosmetic item you "need" have to be premium? How many cosmetics currently in your bathroom have turned out to be mistakes? At what cost? Could you trim $200 a year from the cost of cosmetics?
- How much do you truly spend on convenience foods, gourmet takeaway, restaurants, and entertaining? Might there be a way to trim a few hundred dollars a year here and there?
- Do you have an electronic personal organiser? Are you more organised? Do you even use it?
- Did you raise your children with disposable nappies and pre-moistened baby wipes? Are there a lot of seldom-used toys around the house? Could you pare down by $200 or more the mountain of stuff you buy your kids each year?

+ How new is your computer? Are you constantly trading up for faster, more powerful models? Could you wait a little longer next time?
+ Do you really need all the clothes you have? Do you buy clothes simply because they're on sale? Can you trim $300 a year from your annual clothing budget?
+ How often are you assessed a late charge on videos, library books and bills?
+ Do your kids have a separate phone line? Luxury or necessity?
+ Have you switched to more expensive disposable contact lenses?
+ Do you pay for "designer" bottled water and fancy fruit juices?
+ Do you belong to a gym? Do you use it?
+ Did you leave the barber behind years ago for an expensive hairstylist? Do you pay for colouring as well? Some hairdressers charge $100 for a haircut; investing this money once a month for 25 years, at 10 percent, you'd have $132,683.
+ Have you ever "needed" cosmetic surgery? Cosmetic dentistry? A massage? A personal trainer?
+ How many compact discs do you have that you never listen to? Or tapes?
+ How often do you go into stores or look through mail-order catalogues without any particular "need" in mind? How often do you buy?
+ Might you be able to say no to the next high tech/high fashion/ high concept item that appeals to you, at least until you see how much other people "need" it after they've had it for six months?

Did you find $500, $1000, $2000? Here's how it will make you feel to become rich, over time. You made the money materialise, and maybe you can come up with even more. After you rid yourself of the burden of debt, you will begin to invest it. Soon, the interest begins to add up. Then the interest compounds, month after month, year after year. Then there comes a point where the money you have put away begins to matter. It begins to make you feel good. And then it begins to matter more. You begin to make decisions differently—an extra $50 toward tomorrow begins to seem much more valuable than another jumper or another dinner out or another CD to play once or twice in the car on your way to work. There will come a time when the money you have created matters more than the choices you will make in order to create it. At that point, you will choose—without regrets, in a kind of excited state—to keep pouring money into your tomorrow ($50 extra a month, $100 extra a month, or more). You will choose to value money over things. After a while, you begin to grow with your money. You stop cringing every time the bills come, the unexpected happens, the fear begins anew. When getting rich becomes your true goal, you're on your way.

That's how we get rich, financially speaking. Little by little. Every fortune in this world began with a balance of zero. Oddly enough, that's also how we get rich, emotionally speaking—by the way we make our choices and the choices we make.

CHAPTER 5

DEFINING VALUE
AND WORTH

YOUR MONEY REFLEXES

In a financial planner's version of a party game, I often ask people this question: If I were to offer you (a) $1000 a day for 30 days, or (b) a cent on day 1, two cents on day 2, four cents on day 3, and so on, doubling the amount every day for 30 days, which would you take? Invariably, people will start mentally adding up numbers, maybe getting as far as day 10, when the amount I'd give them would be a whopping $5.12. At that point, most people go for the sure thing and as a reflex action take the first offer, the automatic $30,000. A few people, even without doing all the maths, will always opt for the unknown, figuring there's a trick in here somewhere; even without knowing the outcome they will just as reflexively choose b. Only very occasionally will someone actually sit down and start doubling cents on paper and realise that by day 22 the amount I'd give them is up to $20,971.52, and know which option to pick. Pick b and you'd have amassed $5,737,418.23 by day 30.

Aside from the fact that there's no actual money at stake, why don't people want to play this game through to see where it might go? I am convinced that no one wants to play for the same reasons that most of us don't want to deal with our real money in our real lives. We prefer instant gratification (you can add up the $30,000 in a second) to what money can do over time (five or ten minutes to double up the cents). Because we don't respect small amounts of money enough to believe that they can grow to a fortune, many people won't pick up a coin off the street. Unbelievable as it sounds, for many of us our gut reflex is to turn away from money, which essentially is turning away from what we can truly become.

Do you compete with your money? Try to prove love with your money? Try to please others with your money? Does charging something give you a kind of high from which you later crash? Do you tend always to say yes when asked to spend money or, conversely, tend always to say no? Do you hate to part with your money? Like the automatic a or b response most people offer to my game, before even playing out the possibilities, all these are reflex responses to money, not responses of reason, and when you let your gut reflexes govern your behaviour with money, or when you want money to say something to others about you that isn't true, you're in effect answering before permitting your courage its voice. You're silencing your courage, and with that action, you're not acting in your best interests.

EMILY: *"It makes me so mad. Every other weekend, the twins come home with some expensive present from their father, even though I have asked him not to buy them so much stuff. So the next weekend, my weekend, I always go out and buy them some nice present, too—nicer, I might add, than I can afford."*

Emily's reflex is to compete, not with love but with spending, with the result that she's angry at her ex-husband for overspending, angry at herself for competitive spending—and also angry at herself for conveying to her children values of which she does not approve. The courageous reflex is to look within, not without, when deciding what to spend. No child is born to expect or demand a big treat every weekend, but every child will thrive with a full weekend's worth of love and attention.

BRIAN: *"We have a superannuation plan at work, but my employer doesn't match what the employees put in. I'm going to sign up for it anyway, as soon as I have the money."*

Each of the five years that Brian has worked for this firm, he has been given a raise, even though he was managing just fine before the raise. The greatest pity here is that Brian, who is in the early stages of his career (and his spending/saving habits), is at a point in which time could benefit him so much more with every contribution he makes today. But his reflex is to put today's desires before tomorrow's needs. The courageous reflex is always to keep tomorrow in mind today.

LIZ: *"I am so excited about my new unit. Usually I'm not quite this bad with credit cards, but this time I kind of went overboard. I wanted it to be perfect."*

Liz's reflex is to spend money before she has it, to get to the goal without taking pleasure and gratification in the process. Do you really think that after this surge in spending and debt, Liz is going to want to listen to her voice of reason, pay off her debt, and stop making her home her dream home? With courage, you choose to put money in before you take it out.

As their words suggest, these people know that they are acting impulsively, without letting reason—and courage—have their say in the decisions they're making and the money they're spending or not spending.

When you live with the courage to be rich as a financial and emotional constant, your life will open up in a number of new ways. You will be able to temper your reflexive spending or your refusal to spend, without feeling anxious or deprived either way, because you will be making your choices from a rich place, not a place of poverty or uncertainty. When you value money over things, you will shop with a sense of calm that you don't have now, because your debt will be gone, your spending will be in harmony with your investing, and you will choose to buy only things that you value more than the money it costs to buy them. When you choose to live a rich life, you feel rich in every way, you act expansively and generously with your money, and your money responds to you in the same way.

RICH THOUGHTS ABOUT SPENDING AND VALUE

When it comes to most things that matter to us—a relationship, our job, office politics, how well our children are doing in school—we tend to obsess about them. We talk about them constantly with our friends, and we look at them from every possible angle, trying to understand every nuance, trying to make things work out in the best possible way. We'd all agree that money is important, right up there with our relationships, our jobs, the things that define us. But when we obsess about money, what do we obsess about? Maybe we're buying something important, and we obsess about getting a good deal. Often we obsess about whether or not we can afford a certain item, which almost always means that we're trying to talk ourselves into buying something we cannot afford. We may obsess about the things that other people have and how much they cost. Certainly we obsess about those things we don't have. For all this, how-ever, we seldom pull close to the heart of money, or its true value, when we talk about money. We rarely talk about what it can do rather than what it can buy, which means that we value things, not money.

Here are some questions I want you to think about now:

+ What is it in life that you truly value?
+ Do you value the possessions you have around you?
+ Do you value your money?
+ What do you value most?

SUZE'S STORY

For years, I played a little game with my clients to try to make them think about what was really important. I would ask them to pretend that there was a huge fire coming their way, and to pretend that they had just thirty minutes to get everything out of their house. What would they take?

It never failed. Without hesitation, the answers always came flowing back in a stream of sentiment—my wedding pictures, my mother's wed-ding dress, family scrapbooks, a bracelet my grandmother gave me, an oil portrait of my child.

After years of pretend fires, such a fire became a tragic reality for me and many of my clients. A number of years ago, the Oakland Hills experienced one of the worst fires in history. I was visiting a friend and will never forget looking out the window and thinking, What is all that smoke? The skies were quickly turning from a gorgeous blue to the most ominous black I have ever seen. The hills were on fire. Just then we heard from a neighbour that the fire was spreading, and if you wanted to get anything out of your house, you had very little time. I jumped into my car and headed up to my house, which was in the direct path of the fire. When I got home, some of my neighbours were already loading their cars to evacuate the area. As I began doing the same thing, in a state of sheer panic, I remember thinking, Oh my God, I am doing in real life what I have been asking my clients to pretend to do all these years. I then took a good look at everything I had packed, and sure enough, I was bringing with me the things that money could never replace. Items of the highest personal value to me, but worthless to any other soul on earth.

I drove down the hills and joined the other evacuees watching the smoke from a safe distance. I began asking others what they had chosen to bring with them, and, like me, most had chosen those items that had deep meaning only to themselves, items that money could never replace.

By the time the fire died down, at 4.15 that afternoon, stopping about a mile from my house, some three thousand homes were lost. As I drove through what used to be some of the most beautiful areas in Oakland, there were charred ruins wherever you looked. The only things left standing were some chimneys. I thought then of the solace their priceless mementos would give to those who had otherwise lost everything.

When we are faced with a situation like this, we know beyond a doubt what has value for us and what does not. We know what to take and what to leave behind. We act in an instinctive way—and yet perhaps this is when we behave most purely with our money. But it's rare that we're asked to make these kinds of choices. Day to day, we lose touch with these, our purest values; we obscure them in the way we spend, neglect to save, fail to take the financial actions we know we should.

The courage to be rich comes alive when you have the courage to know what you really do value in this life, when you live—and spend—with the clarity with which my neighbours and I expressed our values that desperate day of the fire. In order to be truly rich, you have to not only value what you have, but also have only things in your life that you value.

You have to value doing what is right over doing what is easy. You have to value tomorrow along with today. Finally, once you internalise these qualities, you have to think them, say them, and express them in your actions. At that point, you will want for nothing, and you will have what you want. Your financial reflexes will be pure and true to your goal of becoming rich.

ASKING FOR MORE

In order to become rich, your self-worth has to rise along with your net worth—you must feel you deserve to be rich, you must never cast yourself as the victim, you must stop settling or feeling as if you're just getting by, and you must make the most of what you have. This is a hard concept for many of us to grasp, for most of us feel as if we're already doing the best we can—but are we, really?

TRACY'S STORY

My marriage was basically a disaster. We had been married for only a year when I found out that Mark was sleeping around, but by then I was pregnant, so I stayed with him for two more years before I took the baby and moved out. I'm a personal trainer, and one of my clients had a garage that had been converted into a little cottage that he rented to me for eight hundred dollars a month. I figured it was probably the best I could do, so we moved in, Maisie and I. I teach at a gym, and I also have private clients, so I figured I could get by.

The heating in the cottage didn't work too well, so I first had to buy a space heater to keep us warm, then some blankets—all the things I needed to set up house—and everything went on my credit cards. There's day care at the gym, so when I'm there I'm fine, but whenever I was training clients at their houses, I couldn't exactly bring Maisie along, so my day-care costs kept going up. Then half the time my clients had excuses for why they couldn't pay on time, and sometimes they'd call and cancel, and never pay what they owed me. So I was getting pretty desperate. It didn't help that my car needed a new transmission, which was another thirteen hundred dollars on my credit card. I was up to my credit limit, so what did I do? I got another card.

I was talking to Ron, one of the other instructors at the gym, one day, a really nice guy, and he mentioned that he had just upped his rates for private clients to sixty-five dollars an hour. What! Then he said that he had all the clients he could handle; did I want a couple of referrals? I couldn't believe it: How was it that he was charging twenty-five dollars an hour more and he had more clients than he could handle? I asked him if he ever had trouble getting paid, and he kind of looked at me as if I were crazy and said no, he always got paid up front, plus he had a policy that if a client cancelled less than twenty-four hours in advance, the client had to pay a thirty-dollar cancellation fee. I felt like such a jerk. This guy does exactly what I do, and he's probably making three times the money. Not to mention having more work than he can handle.

Embarrassed, I told him what I charged and how half the time I never got paid anyway. He thought I was nuts. He told me that he wouldn't give me a single referral unless I charged sixty-five dollars an hour, and he said it hurt every one of us if we didn't all charge the going rate. Then he made me promise only to take money up front. He really got me thinking: Why not be a grown-up about this?

With my favourite clients, I couldn't suddenly raise my rates by twenty-five dollars an hour, so I told them that I was raising them by ten dollars, up to fifty dollars an hour. I was pretty scared to do it—I hate talking about money—but I did. I told my undependable clients the same thing and also told them that I had to be paid up front. Well, that was pretty much it for some of them, and I got a little panicky that I wouldn't have enough clients. But then I got three extra clients from Ron and charged them all sixty-five dollars an hour. It felt great. One of my new clients has a friend who wants a trainer, too, so that will be one more client at the top rate. I've lost a few clients, the ones who were kind of deadbeats anyway, but I am actually making more money than I was before. And I can't tell you how much better I feel about myself.

Inspired, even encouraged, by her competition, Tracy began asking for more, stopped settling and getting by, and ceased to allow herself to be a victim of clients who had no intention of paying her. Hard as it was for her to ask for more, she did it—which was asking more of herself, as well as asking more of her clients. The result? Her self-worth rose, as did her net worth.

Tracy, in other words, began living up to an important law of money:

LAW OF MONEY

When you undervalue what you do, the world will undervalue who you are.

Do you see the connection? You cannot feel poor and undeserving and expect to become rich. Instead, you must be certain of your claim on the world, and stand up for your rights in this world even as you stand up to your responsibilities. If you don't have as much as you truly feel you should have, you must ask for more—more of yourself and more of others—as Tracy did. The act of asking is itself a rich act, a powerful act, an expansive act. By asking, you are opening yourself up to receive more, and you will—perhaps not today, but you will. People who expect more get more, it's that simple.

MONEY AND GUILT

What if you were to have all the money you needed and your financial ducks were in a row? What then? Would you be happy? Or would you feel guilty about what you had?

If you don't have as much as you'd like to have or you spend more than you should, do you feel guilty?

Do you have enough money right now? Do you take great pleasure in it, or does it make you feel guilty?

If the relationship between you and your money is harmonious, regardless of how much you have, your financial transactions will be harmonious as well. By this I mean that you will take such pleasure in what your money brings to your life, what your money—whether large amounts of it or small—can do to help the lives of others, and what spending it on life's simple or sophisticated pleasures can do to enhance your quality of life and well-being. Let's face it, money is great. Then why does it—or the lack of it—make so many of us feel racked with guilt and miserable?

I have never met a person who feels guilty about how much they love their children, how much they love their parents, their family, their partner. I have never seen anyone hide the fact that they have a loving family. If there is lots of love in your life, if your family is close or your marriage is happy, you will tell me with pride and respect and gratitude how rich you feel, rich with love. No guilt there, not a bit. We never feel guilty when we have more than we could ever want of the things that money can't buy; it's only when money comes into the equation that guilt makes its way in, too.

LINDA'S STORY

I think I knew what my life was going to be like from the time I was fifteen. Jake and I were high school sweethearts, and that was that. Every summer, he worked in his father's boatyard, and I worked in my parents' shop, and we just knew that he'd take over the boatyard one day, and we'd also run the shop. Which was what happened. We got married after high school and now have two children, who aren't really children anymore. Our son's finishing university, and our daughter is already out on her own. But all the time they were growing up, it was a small-town story, and we were pretty happy. The boatyard did fine, and the shop pretty much stayed as it always was. Then, about five years ago, our little town began to wake up; suddenly it wasn't just the fishing boats in the boatyard, pleasure boats began coming, too. More and more people were building weekend and summer houses here, and now the house we inherited from my parents is suddenly worth a lot. About a month ago, we got this amazing offer to sell the shop. It's on the corner of Main Street, and it's a pretty big space. The rates have been going up, and we were wondering anyway if we should keep it going. But now that the town is getting spiffed up, we're just this poky old shop, and people keep coming in and asking for cosmetics I have never even heard of. So in comes this offer, out of nowhere. Jake's ecstatic and keeps talking about how we should take it and all the things we could buy. The kids, too. And my friends, I don't know, I think they're a little bit jealous. They're saying things like maybe we'd start hanging out with the summer people instead of them. Me, I feel really torn about it. We didn't do anything to deserve this. What would we do with so much money? I almost wish this had never come up.

When it comes to money, if you have it, you may feel that you don't deserve it—guilt. If you don't have it, you may feel that you should have it—guilt. If you are working toward having it, you may feel that all you're doing is working for money and you are not enjoying the process. And if it just happens to come your way, as with the offer that Linda and Jake are considering, then guilt can keep you from taking what could be yours. Money guilt can take the joy out of what you have created as well as entice you to do things that are not necessarily in your best interest— Linda's temptation to turn down the offer on the shop, for example.

If you do not have the courage to face this guilt straight-on and bankrupt its power over your money, then you really will never be able to experience true richness. The mere fact that we judge ourselves by how much we have shows what an important touchstone money is in telling us who we are. Inwardly we say we go for it, aim as high as we can, but outwardly we question why we deserve what we can attain.

At this very moment in time, each one of us holds before us an offer much like Linda's, the offer of a bigger cup to fill with riches. If you are not achieving all that you can in this world, you can change course and claim your potential. If you are in debt, you can turn away from your guilt and self-pity, methodically get out of debt starting today, and put that money you have used month after month into your future. If you have everything that you could need yet remain plagued by guilt, you owe it to yourself and your money to make yourself worthy of what you have, embrace it, and send it flowing back out into the world— through investments, through contributions to charity, through careful spending on yourself and on your loved ones' pleasure. If you have not saved a cent for retirement and feel guilty about it, you can begin saving today. I am a financial planner, not a psychiatrist, but I do know that your net worth will rise to meet your self-worth only if your self-worth rises to accept what can be yours. Feeling guilty about money does no good whatsoever, is disrespectful to you and your money, and will keep more from coming to you. If you have accepted love into your life, then you must accept money as well, for if you don't, you are implying that you are not yet worthy of money and are placing a higher value on money than you are on love—a violation of the first law of money: *People first, then money.* Make yourself worthy of money, and money will make itself worthy of you.

CHAPTER 6

THE COURAGE TO FACE THE UNKNOWN

LOOKING AT YOUR MONEY

Your overall financial picture encompasses all that you have available to you now, all that you have put away for later, all that you owe, perhaps the equity in your home, and all that you will be able to create from now on, starting now. There's a sequence to getting rich that first involves making settlement with the past, which is to say clearing out your finances so that you know exactly where you stand and, if you are bearing the burden of debt, getting rid of it, to clear the way for what you can create tomorrow. First step: knowing where you stand right now.

YOUR EXERCISE: FACING THE UNKNOWN

Please go to where you keep your bills, and where, if you did the "found money" exercise in Chapter 3, you've placed your jar of "found" money. What's there? I want you to find out.

First, look at your cheque book. Have you recorded all the cheques you've written? Have you balanced the cheque book on a regular basis? Have you made certain that the bank has credited you with every deposit you made? (Banks are not infallible, you know.) Now open all your bills, bank statements, and insurance and rates payments—anything that has to do with your money, what you have and what you owe. Look at every statement and any bill that you do not pay in full monthly. Write down the balance of what you owe on every bill. Maybe you still owe your gardener three hundred dollars for clearing out a hedge, even if you've already paid him the one hundred dollars you owe him this month for mowing the lawn. Possibly you owe the gym two hundred dollars for this year's membership. Or you owe the dance studio for your child's ballet lessons, after you've paid only the deposit. Record every credit card bill, every balance that remains on your statements and invoices.

After you have written these amounts down, take a deep breath and total them. What do you owe? Is it more or less than you thought? Regardless of how you feel about it, at least you now know where you stand, and some financial clutter—the clutter of guessing, the clutter of estimating, the clutter of worrying—is gone, replaced by the truth, for better or for worse. You have faced your finances.

Now I want you to open up a brand-new cheque account and start over, start facing your money honestly every month and with each cheque you write. If you don't care about your bank one way or another, go to a different bank. If you're happy with your bank, then open up a new cheque account there—with a different account number, a new promise to yourself, a new approach to your money. Take with you your jar of money. Deposit a sum of money, including the money from your jar, and start fresh with this new cheque account.

As your old account is laid to rest, your outstanding cheques will eventually clear, and soon you will be able to close that account and work only with your new account, fully balanced every month. It will feel great, starting over. I can't ask that you go back and balance the past, but I do know that with a new resolve, you can face your finances in a fresh new way—and a new cheque account will enable you to do this. You will know what you own, you will know what you owe, and much clutter and chaos will be removed, which is the way to make room for more money. In this moment of reckoning, I want you to face the truth. Do not be afraid.

From this day on, as soon as a bill comes in, I want you to open it, look at it, write a cheque for it immediately, and record it in your cheque book. Put the cheque in an envelope, put a stamp on the envelope, and get it ready to mail. Write on the inside flap of the envelope the amount of the cheque and the due date. If you are customarily late in making your payments or if you dread having to sit down and pay a daunting stack of bills all at once, this technique will help you begin to deal with your money and keep your affairs in order. If you can send off the cheques with the bills as soon as they come in, great. Then the bills will not clutter your physical or mental space even for a day. If you do not have the money to send off the cheques right away, no problem. As soon as you do have the money and deposit it into your cheque account, you are to mail off as many cheques as your deposit will cover, according to their due dates. If with that deposit there is enough money to cover them all, then send them all off at once. Remember, they have already been written and recorded, so the only thing you have to do now is mail them.

And the money from your money jar or bowl? That extra twenty or thirty dollars or more? That money is to be applied to the credit card that carries the highest interest rate.

The hardest part of paying the bills is actually sitting down and facing them all at one time. It really can be overwhelming, we don't like to do it, and so we don't. We also don't like to let go of money that we have just received. We like to hold on to it, because we do not like to see money flowing away from us. The fact that this is money that isn't really ours but money we owe to others—to the mortgage company, for insurance, for cable TV, to the department store—doesn't make it any easier to relinquish. Simply having it makes us feel richer for the time being, and we like that feeling. Yet this is where financial clutter starts to build—and it's also the point at which we begin to create more clutter: As soon as we feel a little richer, our natural tendency is to spend a little more, and then when the bills come due, we don't have enough money left to pay them. Don't hoard the money you owe—free yourself up instead by paying your bills as soon as you possibly can. If you want to turn financial chaos into financial calm, I am telling you that paying your bills in this way will make you feel clearer about where you stand and ultimately will make you feel more powerful. And it's when you feel powerful that more will come your way. What you know about your money can never hurt you as much as what you do not know about your money.

CREDIT CARD DEBT: THE WEIGHT AND THE BURDEN

Having been in credit card debt myself and having seen many of my clients struggle to fight their way out of it, I know what credit card debt can do, to both your net worth and your self-worth. When you're in credit card debt, you and your self-worth are in a kind of free fall, because you're literally worth less than you have, which makes you feel less than you are—a negative balance on both accounts. Deep in credit card debt, you can't see your way out—the minimum payments get you nowhere, you're constantly juggling payment due dates, and simply by looking at the monthly finance charges (if you can bear to look at them at all), you know, even if you can't run the numbers, that the situation is hopeless. In terms of self-worth, you feel that you're living a lie. Surrounded by things you don't own, you have the odd sense that nothing is yours but the debt—to the extent that you become the debt itself. And what is a debt? It is less than zero. And that's what you feel you are. That's the inward manifestation, and it's with you all the time, like a Greek chorus, reminding you that, financially and emotionally, you're trapped.

There's often an external manifestation of debt, too, which one of my clients and I discovered together.

A M A N D A ' S   S T O R Y

Amanda, a long-time client of mine whom I had not seen for quite a while, came to see me one day a few years ago, and when she arrived, I noticed that she had put on a lot of weight. Obviously, I said nothing about it—she had come to see me about her money, not her weight. We were going over her current finances, and because I had consulted my notes from our last meeting just before she came in, I noticed that this time Amanda had $20,000 more in credit card debt than she had had a few years before. When I asked her what had happened, she said that her business had got into trouble and that she was taking cash advances from her credit cards to keep it going.

As I went through her papers, I noticed, too, that Amanda had more than $20,000 in a savings account, so I asked her why she was incurring debt on her credit cards and not drawing on her available cash. She replied that if she did that, then her husband would know that her business wasn't doing so well. "You mean your husband doesn't know you have twenty thousand dollars in credit card debt?" I asked.

"That's right," Amanda said. "I pay the bills, so he has no idea." I then asked her how she felt about that, and she said, "I feel as if I am carrying the weight of the world on my shoulders."

I asked Amanda how long she had been hiding the debt from her husband, and she said for a year. Summoning up my courage, I also asked her when she'd started gaining the weight. She began gaining weight, she answered, about a year ago as well. With that, flashbulbs went off for both of us, and our conversation very quickly turned into a financial Weight Watchers meeting. We couldn't be sure, of course, whether her weight gain was the result of anxiety over her business, over deceiving her husband, over the debt itself, or whether it was the result of something else entirely. But we could both see that she had to do something to relieve her stress.

After talking it over, we agreed that she must tell her husband the truth about their finances. Amanda promised that when she went home that night, she would tell him everything. She called the next morning and said that even though the discussion was a little rough at first, they decided in the end that they should take the money out of their available cash and pay off the credit cards, which, as far as I knew, they did.

About six months later, Amanda called to say that her business was doing even worse than it had been, and wanted my reassurance on their decision to close it down and stop throwing good money after bad. After reviewing the numbers, I said with confidence that I thought that was a good idea. Before she hung up, she said, "By the way, I've lost fifteen pounds and am feeling much better about myself." I thought about this when I went to her folder to update her records and read my notes from our last meeting: Has gained weight, does not know why. Business failing, hiding $20,000 debt from husband, is to tell him tonight. Called to say she told him, they will pay off the debt with their available cash. *As I was about to write this update—*Is closing business, lost fifteen pounds, sounds great—*I began to think again about Amanda's weight gain and loss. It clearly hadn't been caused by her business. Her business continued to fail after she came to see me. Still, she had lost weight. What was different was that: (a) she had gotten rid of the debt, even if it left her and her husband with no savings; and (b) she was no longer holding on to the secret of hidden debt. And with that I began to follow my hunch that perhaps the weight of debt is not simply an emotional burden but a physical burden as well.*

From then on, when clients came into my office burdened with debt and weight, I would try to find out, as politely as I could, whether their weight had risen commensurate with their debt. I am not claiming to be a sociologist here, but surprisingly often the answer was yes. I would then try to find out whether they were hiding the fact of their debt from someone they loved; again, more often than not they would say yes. My clients, I found, were carrying the weight of their debt in more ways than one.

One of the most disrespectful and powerless ways to live a life is to live a lie, and when you are mired in credit card debt, I am sorry to say that you're living a lie. You're presenting to the world as your own possessions things that do not belong to you, things that you cannot afford. If your debt is carefully hidden, particularly from those closest to you, you are not only living a lie but also putting your loved ones' financial lives at risk. You are being dishonest about yourself and your future, because juggling credit card debt today jeopardises all of tomorrow's dollars. You are also being disrespectful of money itself, because the way to treat money is to value it and enable it to grow, not to send it off to credit card companies in interest payments higher than the cost of an item in the first place. True richness is attained when our net worth and self-worth have met the challenges of life and risen above them.

GOOD DEBT, BAD DEBT

There is a place at times for debt in all our lives, but the debt, if it is to be worthy debt, must be in alignment with the other goals in your life.

Student loan debt, for example, is in alignment with your goals for the future, for this kind of debt enables you to pursue your dreams in a way you couldn't without incurring the debt. Student loan debt is debt to feel proud of.

A mortgage, assuming you can truly afford the house, is worthy debt, for it enables you to pursue the dream of home ownership and to create a safe haven from the world for yourself and your family. You can be proud when you get to the point where you can qualify for, and afford, a mortgage payment.

If you have stretched beyond what you can afford today in order to help your parents, then you have achieved worthy debt. *People first, then money.*

If you borrow to buy an investment property where the rental return and tax savings will pay off the loan for you, you've incurred a good debt—but only if you have enough savings to cover the mortgage payments for several months if ever the property is untenanted.

If you have gone into debt to cover medical expenses for yourself or a loved one, then your debt is honourable for the same reason as above.

If you have taken out a car loan, assuming you need a car and can afford the payments, then your debt is worthwhile, because a car is a necessity for most of us, and to pay for it all at once is beyond the means of most of us.

A loan from a friend or family member to cover a cash-flow crunch, when you know for certain that the money will be coming by a specific date, is a loan of convenience and needn't be a burden.

Extending your limits for extenuating circumstances, such as getting through a pregnancy or an adoption, is a finite loan, and, assuming you have figured out when and how you will dispense with it, will not cost you your future but will help you create it.

Overspending on credit cards merely to accumulate things to wear or display or to satisfy the desire for travelling, eating out, or entertainment is paying tomorrow for today's pleasures. This is the most dishonourable kind of debt there is.

Credit Card Debt

Whenever I ask people whether they have credit card debt, those who don't have debt invariably answer with a triple negative: "No, uh-uh, not me. I pay my bills in full every month." In their vehemence is discipline and pride. If they do have credit card debt, on the other hand, without fail their reply is always in the form of a question: "Do I have credit card debt?" or, more often, "Who, me?" even if we are the only two people in the room. I puzzled over this for years, until one day I had my answer. I was watching a group of kids play that round-robin children's game "Who stole the cookies from the cookie jar?" Each child, when accused of stealing the cookies ("Suze stole the cookies from the cookie jar"), replies with a question: "Who me?" ("Yes, you"; "Couldn't be"; "Then who?"). Each child is accused of stealing the cookies, denies it, and then accuses another child as the game comes full circle.

The people who answer my question about credit card debt with another question are those who have stolen the cookies from the cookie jar. They are trying to buy some time to think about how to answer the question. In fact, they don't want to have to answer it at all. Not only do they not want to face the truth by answering the question aloud, they also don't want me to know.

If you have credit card debt, do you think, do you really think, you're the only one who has messed up in this way? Do you really think you're alone with this dark secret? And is it really such a source of shame that you can't even admit it aloud to someone else?

Do you see the damage your debt is causing, not only to your finances today and tomorrow but also to your sense of self-worth? I have said this before, but it bears repeating: *You are not a bad person because you have credit card debt, you are simply a person who has managed your money badly.* There is a huge difference between those two. What others think of you is far less important than what you think of yourself. If you think less of yourself because you have debt, most likely your thoughts, words, and actions will render you unable to get out of debt.

If you proceed with your financial life the way it is now, you are settling. You are doing absolutely nothing to change your situation. In order to live a life of richness, a life free of the bondage, weight, and burden of debt, you have to summon from the deepest recesses of your soul every ounce of courage you have and put the process of getting out of debt in motion. You must turn your fear into action, your self-pity into resolve. You can no longer grant yourself permission barely to get by, to float the debt from month to month and year to year, or to ignore your situation. Getting out of debt is without a doubt the single most important action you can take on behalf of your future financial and emotional security.

DENIED CREDIT?

Over the years, I've received many letters from people who've been denied lower-interest-rate credit cards and want to know what they can do about it. Credit card companies, banks, mortgage lenders, and credit unions buy information about you through the Credit Reference Association. They use a formula to decide whether to approve or deny credit. Here is what you need to know about what your credit report contains and how to fix incorrect information.

You are entitled to a free copy of your credit file if you have been denied credit. I recommend that you check your credit status from time to time anyway, in order to make sure that it is accurate.

The information that is contained in a credit file is your full name (and any previous names), telephone number, current address, employment history, marriages, divorces, loan defaults, bankruptcy information, and, most important, your credit history. It will list the names of anyone who has done a credit check on you. This could be an existing credit provider or any company that you have applied to for a loan or credit card. This information remains on your file whether you took up the loan or not and includes the amount of the loan applied for. Defaults are also recorded, and a default is usually registered once you are two months in arrears with payments. This information remains on your file for five years, or in the case of bankruptcy, for seven years.

There are strict privacy laws to ensure that personal information does not fall into the wrong hands. An employer or real estate agent cannot access your file and even when you apply for credit you must sign an authority authorising a credit check before anyone is allowed access to your file.

Upon receiving your file, review all the information to see if everything is accurate. Make a list of everything that is incorrect, out-of-date, or mis-leading. In particular, look for mistakes in your name, address or phone number, and for missing or outdated employment information. You'll also want to look for: bankruptcies that are more than seven years old, any negative information about you that is more than five years old, credit accounts that are not yours, incorrect account histories (especially late payments when you've paid on time), and a missing notation when you've disputed a charge on a credit card bill.

Once you've made the list you can use the update form which is on the back of your credit report. If you received a fax copy of your report and do not have this update form you can write a letter, listing each incorrect item and exactly what is wrong. Be sure to make a copy of the form before sending it back. This service is free.

Once the credit bureau receives your update request, it must get back to you within a reasonable time. This is an easy process for them, since they are all linked by computers.

Here's how to contact the credit bureau in Australia:

Credit Reference Association of Australia
PO Box 964
North Sydney 2059
Ph: 02 9464 6000

In New Zealand, here's where to contact the credit bureau:

The Baynet
15 Hopetoun Street
Ponsonby
Auckland
Ph: 09 356 5855

If something in your credit report is incorrect, or if the creditor who provided the information can no longer verify it, the credit bureau must remove the information from your file.

Finally, if you feel the bureau is not abiding by the law or has treated you unfairly, you can send your complaint to the the Privacy Commissioners in your state. Be sure to send a copy of your correspondence with the bureau about which you are complaining. If a credit bureau insists on reporting out-of-date or inaccurate information, writing to the Privacy Commissioner can put an end to it.

Your Debt Set Point

How much debt are you carrying right now? Does it make you nervous and uneasy? If it does but you haven't taken any action to eradicate it, then you haven't yet reached the "set point" of your debt. I believe that each of us has within us a point at which anxiety over our debt turns to panic, and it is at this point that we are finally moved to take action. One person's set point may be $2000; another's may be $20,000; still another's may be in six figures. You know your set point instinctively—without a doubt you'll know it when you reach it.

What I have noticed is that often there is a correlation—an inverse relationship—between this set point and a person's self-esteem. The lower the self-esteem, the higher the set point. If you are spending money you don't have, and continue to do so even as the possibility of paying it off becomes more and more remote, then you are probably spending money not to *have* more but to *be* more. The less self-esteem you have, the more debt you create.

The first step, then, is to work on your self-esteem. Easy to say, but how do you do it? Start by knowing that you are more than the negative balance on your credit card statement. Begin to tell those close to you about the debt you are carrying, relieving yourself of the burden of secrecy. Know that you are not a bad person because you have credit card debt, simply a person who has managed your money badly. Once you free your notion of self-worth from the bonds of material things, you will "need" less and you will spend less. As your self-esteem rises, your debt will diminish. Call it a law of financial physics.

Paying Off Credit Card Debt

With credit card debt—among the rich and the poor—at epidemic proportions in this country, there have been many television programs and dozens of articles about how to get out of debt. The subject is well covered in books, too; in my last book, *The 9 Steps to Financial Freedom,* I offer a step-by-step plan. In short, there is plenty of help available to show you how to get out of debt. You already know why you should do it; now I want you to take the actions that will enable you to reach that goal.

Millions of people have done it, and so can you—but only if you raise it to a top priority and keep your vow to become debt-free.

Having covered the topic at length elsewhere, I am not going to summarise it here, because if you have debt, you should learn everything you can about paying it off. However, here are some important points to keep in mind:

1. Face your debt by telling others about it.

2. If you are in credit card trouble, you must cut up all of your credit cards now, with the possible exception of one card for emergencies; do not carry this card in your wallet, however.

3. Call the credit card company of the one card you've kept and ask them to lower your credit limit to a level that will provide you with security in the event of an emergency.

4. You must pay more than the minimum payment every month, as much more as you possibly can. Here's an example to illustrate why: If you owe a credit card company $1000 at an 18.5 percent interest rate and you just pay the minimum of $17 every month, it will take you about 12.5 years to pay it off and cost you $1550 in interest. Pay just $10 extra a month and you will cut down the payback time to 4.6 years and pay $512 in interest. That's a saving of over $1000. Higher balances take exponentially longer to pay off; a balance of $3000 can take up to 30 years to pay off if you just pay the minimum due every month. You can calculate the amount of time it will take you to pay off your debt on the FinanCenter, Inc., website (http:// www.calcbuilder.com).

5. You must pay off the credit card with the highest interest rate first, and the rest in descending order.

6. You must negotiate for yourself the best interest rates, even if it means switching credit cards every 6 months.

7. You must understand everything about how your credit card works—all fees, how the company charges you, all about the so-called grace period—everything.

8. You must honour all your debts equally—whether it's the money you owe Visa or the money you owe your brother.

9. After you pay off one credit card, you must apply the money you have been paying that particular company to paying off another credit card.

10. If you doubt that you can do this by yourself, you must get in touch with a counselling service such as Credit Helpline. The Financial Counsellors Association can let you know who to contact in your area, and can be reached on 02 4229 4711. They will help you organise and consolidate your debt.

11. You must never let this happen again.

12. After all your debts have been paid off, you are to apply the money you were paying all those months toward creating your future.

BANKRUPTCY

I can't tell you how many letters I have received from people who have got into financial trouble and are now wondering if bankruptcy is a viable way out for them. After all, more and more people are claiming bankruptcy—the number in 1999 was 26,376, an increase of 8 percent.

So far as I know, there has always been a provision for declaring bankruptcy and a way to start over. Sometimes, for no apparent reason, anyone among us can be struck by illness, death, a natural disaster, a financial blow that sends us farther back than zero, to a place where there is no reasonable way out, hard as we may work. Yes, yes, then, of course, we should be permitted to start over.

If your financial troubles arise instead from credit card debt, if you're overextended because of irresponsible actions, should you then be permitted the legal means to start over? That's another question entirely, and one you have to answer yourself. Why? Because even though your financial record may be cleared after seven years by declaring bankruptcy, there is also the record of your soul to consider, and that record has no stated time frame. If you declare bankruptcy, someone will have to pay for what you are not paying for. It might be the merchant you cheated, or your debt might be passed along to the rest of us to absorb. Declaring bankruptcy is not simply a way to cop out on overspending. And should you choose to do it, you must understand that fact for your own sake, not just for the sake of the rest of us, who will surely, one way or another, be required to pick up the pieces.

If you are in a position where bankruptcy seems the surest way out, then there are several information pamphlets available from the Insolvency and Trustee Service, Australia (ITSA) in Canberra, or you can visit their website at: http://law.gov.au/itsa. If you decide to take this course of action, you must understand the magnitude of what you are doing, you must understand what you are asking of others, you must understand the sacrifice you are making as well as what you will gain. There is a time and a place for declaring bankruptcy; otherwise we wouldn't have a provision for it in our system. And if you do decide that it is the right solution for you, I hope that you will take your actions to heart, know that it is your only way out, then start over from a place of pride, not shame—pride that will never allow you to find yourself in this situation again. If bankruptcy is truly your only way out, then face it with courage.

RICH THOUGHTS

RICH THOUGHTS ABOUT CHILDREN

Every parent dreams of the world for his or her child; trouble is, the dream gets a little fuzzy when it's not reinforced by action. Presenting the world to a child—teaching a child what to expect, how to conduct daily life, what responsibility means, and how to handle money—is perhaps the most awesome prospect any parent faces in a lifetime. Yet, for all the care and concern with which we teach our children, we rarely stop to reflect carefully about what we want to teach them about money or what kinds of lessons our own actions convey.

If you want your child to have good table manners, you will constantly remind her to hold a fork properly, to keep her elbows off the table, and never to slurp the soup. It becomes a reflex, a refrain, and you keep repeating the lessons until her table manners are excellent—and automatic. At the same time, you know that if you want her table manners to be good, your own table manners must be impeccable, because she'll watch you, study you, learn from you—and catch you when you slip up.

Your child will learn about money from you in the same way: by intuiting what you think, hearing what you say, and mimicking what you do.

With the twentieth century behind us, what will your child need to know in order to prosper in the twenty-first? No one can say for certain, but he or she will need financial skills much more sophisticated than those that many of us learned. Your child likely will not work all her life for some benevolent corporation that looks after her and sees that she gets a pension to keep her safe in the long years of her retirement. With many kids mastering computer skills even as toddlers, your child will have to be adept with the tools of the future. With technology continuing to advance at such a staggering pace, your child will need to know how to think and adapt.

So often I'm at an ATM and observe a parent letting a young child pull the money from the machine. Kids know what money is and does, they love it, and they adore this transaction, pulling out a hefty stack of notes and holding the cash. "Let's get some money from the cash machine," the parent will say—and in that there is a big lesson, for I have yet to hear a parent explain to a child that in order to get the money out of the machine, you first have to put it into the machine. Yesterday's children learned that money doesn't grow on trees. Today's child learns that it comes from machines.

Do you see? Allowing your child to hand over the plastic credit card to a clerk in a store or pull the money from the cash machine is not teaching your child about money. Only you can decide the money values you wish to impart to your child, but I am asking you to stop and give some real thought to the lessons your child learns about money and values. In the swirl of everyday life—school lunches, daily bathtime, play dates—it is easy to turn the lessons of wealth (the lessons of more, of less, of possibility) into afterthoughts. For the sake of your child's future, I ask you to turn often to the subject of money, to teach your children confidence and competence.

Nowhere is this truer than when it comes to planning for your child's education. Providing a top-notch education is a part of every parent's dream, yet only a small percentage of today's parents are actually saving for the education they dream about providing.

Too often, then, the scenario works something like this: As the time to pay for tertiary education grows closer and closer, your anxiety grows greater and greater. In this case, less money really does translate into more—more anxiety and more guilt, that is. But here's the catch: Your children are inevitably going to intuit the anxiety, which passes a troubling message down to them. How do you think it makes them feel to know that their mere existence and desire to better themselves through a university education is causing a financial hardship to those they love most? Always, when this happens, the size of the child's internal bank account diminishes.

Then what happens? Let's say that, one way or another, the child gets to university. If you do manage to send him to university, he goes knowing that he is taking from you more than you can afford. Feeling poor and "less than", he obtains a credit card. Having received unclear or ambiguous money messages from you, he somehow thinks that using this credit card, which he doesn't quite understand, will help ease the burden. Before even starting out in the world, he gets himself in debt, a position of powerlessness. When that child enters the job market, he or she will enter it from a place of fear, guilt, or abject gratitude—not, in any case, from a powerful place. In essence, at this point your child's self-worth will come to be determined by your net worth and your feelings about your net worth. And this is the stance with which he enters the adult world.

It does not have to be this way. Attend to matters now. If you do not think you will have money to send your children to school, tell them as soon as you can. It is not a statement about how worthy a person or parent you are if you cannot pay for a university education, nor does it make your child a victim. There are many ways to finance an education if you can't pay for it outright; I have discussed these in *The 9 Steps to Financial Freedom*. But don't spring it on a child at the last minute. The time to start communicating the truth about your financial situation to your children is when they are young. Do not be ashamed to talk about money, about what you think you will be able to contribute, for being honest and forthright about this important subject is one of the most valuable lessons you can ever impart.

If, on the other hand, you have the means—or plan to have or create the means—to save for an education, the sooner you take action the sooner you will assuage your (and your child's) anxiety, thus beginning to pass on a positive money message. With a savings or investment vehicle in place, you are far likelier to save or invest. Taking action also makes any far-off prospect seem suddenly real. Think about it, take action toward it, and talk about it—with your children.

RICH THOUGHTS ABOUT CARS

If it's not a component of the Australian dream, it's certainly a component of our collective consumer machismo: You are what you drive, for as long as you drive it. Cars are our ultimate symbol of success, and they display the level of success we've achieved—or the level of success we want others to think we've achieved: This is who I am, because this is the make and model I drive.

Now it's true that most of us need a car, but even a modest car is a big-ticket item, one of the biggest purchases we will make, not just in terms of today's dollars but also—especially—in terms of tomorrow's. I am asking you here not to let what you drive today drive your destiny tomorrow. I am asking you to value money over things. I am asking you to value your money over your car.

In the first place, think of the language we use when we talk about cars. "I bought a Toyota Camry." Done deal, even if the bank played a part in the purchase, and the car is somehow a past-tense item, over and done with. What if instead you were to say, "I invested in a Toyota Camry"? An investment is something you nurture, care for, and expect to grow in value on your behalf in the years to come. Shouldn't something as important and expensive as a car, any car, be accorded that respect? Instead, we tend to treat our cars like junk, forget to change the oil, neglect to keep them clean so they don't rust, skip the engine tune-ups. We say things like, "Well, they don't make cars like they used to; this car simply won't last that long." Not true. What kind of a way is this to treat such a big investment? Is this showing respect for your money? You are not what you drive.

In the second place, think what you might well be spending over your lifetime in order to drive. What if you were to buy a car, take out a five-year car loan, pay off your car in five years, and then drive it for another five years. What if you continued to "make" your car payments once the car was paid off—investing that money rather than letting it drift back into your pool of available cash? You could make yourself a lot of money.

Let's say you were to buy 5 cars over the course of 50 years' driving, and drive each car for 10 years. You spend 25 years making car payments and the other 25 years investing the money you'd been using to make your car payments. And let's say, for argument's sake, that those car payments remained a steady $350 a month. Investing $350 a month at

9 percent for 25 years will yield you $392,392.67. If you've invested the money for long-term growth and earn 11 percent on it, you will have, at the end, $551,646.65.

Or let's look at it another way. Let's say the car you decide to buy in round one costs $25,000. You make a deposit, take out a loan, and pay it off, at $350 a month, in 5 years. You will end up having spent $26,172 for your car. Now for the next 5 years that you keep the car, you invest the $350 each month at, say, 8 percent. At the end of 10 years, when you decide it's time to buy a new car, you will have nearly enough invested with which to buy a new car outright—over $25,000. From then on, taking this approach throughout your lifetime, you can have a new car every 10 years in effect for "free".

What about leasing—no money down, basically. Isn't that the wisest way to own a car? No—because to begin with, leasing means you will never own your car.

No deposit, low monthly payments, then start all over with a new car in three years—sounds great, doesn't it? That's probably why so many of the people driving new cars last year leased instead of buying. But I want you to keep the big picture in mind—tomorrow's dollars and not just today's. Would you rather lease your life or own it?

When it comes to a car, buying a reliable model, paying it off in four or five years, and planning to own it for at least eight or ten years may not sound like the sexiest decision you could make, but it will ultimately free up more money for you, now and in the future. There's a reason most dealers are encouraging you to lease, and it's because it's in their best interest—which means, too, that it's probably not in your best interest.

Let's say in this case that the car you want costs $25,000. A typical ad will offer a lease with no deposit. At the end of the lease, you still have to pay a residual if you wish to keep the car; this lump sum usually amounts to 25 to 30 percent of the purchase price. If you hand the car back to the finance company, you have nothing and have to start all over with leasing fees and monthly payments. If, however, you bought the car and kept it for a number of years after it was paid off, you would have a car still worth something in a trade-in, as well as the money you'd invested after you paid off the loan.

Bottom line: Are you the make and model of the car you drive? Yes, you are.

RICH THOUGHTS ABOUT TAXES

Whenever I ask people what's the one thing, when it comes to their money, that they have the hardest time with, a surprising number say to me: taxes. As inevitable as death, as inevitable as springtime, taxes are inevitable for all of us; we postpone facing them, we brood about doing them, we worry about what they will cost each year (even if we already know, give or take), and we let them take up a great deal of our psychic financial energy for at least several months of the year—every year.

Why do we do this? Over the years, all the tax write-offs we used to hear about or take advantage of have been disappearing, one by one. Rich or poor, there is very little you can do this year to manipulate your tax bill into being less than it is destined to be unless you have planned ahead. It's true that you can invest your money with the tax ramifications in mind, but that's rarely the main concern among sophisticated investors; making money is. In fact, people who have power over their money, people who are in control of their money, people who are certain of their goals for their money are the least likely to worry about taxes. Rich or poor, you will worry about your taxes if you feel powerless over money, and you won't worry about your taxes if you feel in control of your finances.

The taxation department, faceless and mysterious, is a powerful organisation indeed. They have the power to collect vast amounts of your money. They have the right to audit you, whether you made a mistake, didn't mean to make a mistake, or didn't make a mistake—just because they think you might have made a mistake. Now, that's power. They have the power to make you organise all the paperwork they ask for, and they have the power to make you feel faint every time they send you a letter. Most people can't find one good thing to say about the taxation department.

Despite all this, fear and loathing of tax season is a waste of your time, a waste of your energy, and most likely will not make one bit of difference when it comes to your finances, for you will owe what you will owe, and there is nothing you can do about it. Spending many anxious weeks over taxes causes emotional clutter and it won't save you any money or paperwork, or even undo anything you did in the past year.

And you know what else? If you pay more in taxes than the next person, it means—bottom line—that you made more, and that you'll get to keep more. In fact, the most rich and expansive way to think about taxes

89

is this: I hope I pay a lot more in taxes every year, because it will mean that I am making a lot more money. I'm not going to ask you to go as far as to do that (it's a hard one for me, too, believe me), but at least think about it.

Is there an up side to taxes?

If you can think of tax time as your annual clearing out and cleaning up of your finances, then it still may not be your favourite time of year, but it can certainly be a productive one in which you get your financial life in order. Some things to think about:

- If your returns are in any way complicated (for example, by possible deductions, investments to figure into the overall picture, or earnings from self-employment), then do seek a good accountant to help you file your returns.
- One of my financial planning refrains is that getting a tax refund is a waste of money. If you are due a refund, this means that you have been paying too much tax throughout the year. The money is returned to you, but without any interest. So in essence you are giving a tax-free loan to the government. However, if you are a real spender, this might be a great opportunity to save. Losing interest is better than losing the money altogether. Rather than blowing your tax refund in one lump sum, it would be such an expansive act—to yourself and your tomorrow—if you were to take that tax refund and invest in a superannuation fund, or other long-term investment such as a managed fund.
- Use this time of year to eliminate financial clutter.

DOING AWAY WITH FINANCIAL CLUTTER

Almost always, whenever new clients would come into my office, I would encounter a whole new variety of clutter. Some would arrive with their papers jammed any which way into large manila envelopes; some would arrive bearing shopping bags of statements. Others would bring orderly clutter, papers rubber-banded into neat stacks but in no particular order. Others still would choose folders to enclose the clutter. Occasionally, clients would dispense with the clutter altogether, arriving with just a few sheets from a notepad with some random numbers on them. As my clients presented their papers, I knew that they were presenting their lives to me; the event always took on the air of a ceremony. I saw my job ultimately as sending my clients home with the power and courage to create abundance. But first, my job was working to help to organise the chaos.

Many times clients arrived literally with years of stuff—bank statements going back a decade, stacks of pay slips, so much of their financial past that it made it hard to see their financial present, let alone tomorrow. In order to see where you stand, I want you to use tax time to bring your finances totally up to date.

- First, get rid of taxes from the past. If your taxes are relatively simple, keep the documentation for five years, which is the length of time required by the taxation department. Keep a copy of your tax return, group certificates, bank and investment statements and any other income (rental income, for example), and tax deductions, including all receipts.

  If your returns are more complicated (by capital gains or losses, if you have your own business or are self-employed, if you bought and sold a lot of property), keep all records for seven years, and preferably longer, just to be on the safe side.

  If the taxation department suspects you of big-time cheating or fraud, they can audit you for whatever year they want. If, God forbid, you have committed fraud, your papers won't do you much good, but you probably ought to hang on to them anyway.

- For stocks and investments outside retirement funds, in most cases you will receive statements either quarterly, every six months, or each time you deposit more money into the vehicle. Hang on to these interim statements until the end of every year, then keep only the year-end record.

- If you suspect you may be headed for divorce or if you are thinking of selling your home, hang on to all household bills for at least the past six months. In the case of divorce, you will need to demonstrate what it costs you to live month to month. If you decide to sell your house, a potential buyer might ask to see what you spend on utilities, heating, and so on, and the more cooperative you can be, the better.

- If you are self-employed, keep all bills until you do your taxes, then discard anything that is not remotely an itemised deduction.

- It is not necessary to keep every ATM printout. When you balance your (new) cheque book every month, throw out all ATM receipts.

- If you are disputing any bill, keep the bill until the dispute is resolved.

- If you are withdrawing money from retirement accounts, if you have sold real estate, or have cashed in investments, keep records of those transactions for at least five years.

- Keep all your medical records for the entire year, and hold them until you file your taxes and can see whether they add up to enough for a deduction.

- Try to be organised in keeping permanent records, such as the deed to your house and records of capital improvements, your marriage certificate, birth or adoption certificates, insurance policies, the title to your car, pertinent death certificates, veteran's records, contracts or warranties involved with big-ticket items—both for the sake of insurance and in case you need to use the warranty.

RICH THOUGHTS ABOUT
TOMORROW, TODAY

As an old adage has it, the rich get richer; and rich and poor people alike believe it, as if it were some fundamental principle about money, like compound interest, say, or investing for growth. But is it true?

Well, it's true in the sense that the more money you have in place to earn money, the more money you'll earn over time. That's indeed a fundamental principle of wealth. Nevertheless, remember that most rich people didn't start out that way. How did they get there? By taking rich actions. And you can begin to think rich, too, no matter how little money you have right now.

As we've seen, scaling back your luxuries here and there can create a lot of money to invest today for tomorrow. You can find much more money in addition to that, but you have to look for it. Another old adage states the importance of making every cent count—and, I might add, counting every cent. How many of us do that? The rich do, I can promise you that.

How can you create more money? By looking at every cent you spend. With the baffling array of long-distance telephone choices, for example, have you ever really figured out which one would actually save you money, even a little bit of money, every month? Why not? Ten, twenty dollars a month—it's a lot of money to create, and it could be worth so very much more, over time. Do you buy in bulk when it makes real financial sense to? Why not? Do you neglect to pay attention to weekly supermarket specials? Why? Have you tried, where available, a generic version of every item you use? Why not? One more adage: A penny saved is a penny earned.

Another way of creating money is by redirecting your money. You see, most of us think of our money as existing in a pool: Here is the pool of what I have to spend this month. And, no matter what, the pool gets drained every month, replenished, then drained again. But think about this. So many of our expenses are finite—we pay for a one-time item or some expense goes away. Then what happens? The money we have been paying for an expense that is now behind us simply goes back into the pool and gets drained away, one way or another, with the rest of our money today, when it could instead be redirected into money for tomorrow. For example:

- Let's say your child has been in day care or a preschool program, or has had a baby-sitter or nanny in her preschool years, then "graduates" and moves on to public school. You now have $100 a week or more that you no longer have to pay for your child's care. What do you do? If you put that money back into the pool, you will spend it and never see it again. If instead, with discipline and respect, you redirect that money toward tomorrow, you will be investing at least $5200 a year toward your future.

- You bought a dining room set for $2400 and paid $100 a month over two years to acquire it. If you put the money that went toward making those payments back into the pool, it's gone. Redirect it toward tomorrow, and you will have an extra $1200 a year to invest.

- You needed a TV and sound system when you moved into your house, and borrowed from the bank, repaying $65 a month for five years. Finally it's paid off, but it was never that big a deal— just $65 a month. Put that money into the pool, and where will it go? Redirect it instead, and that's $780 a year toward tomorrow.

- You are a family of four with a food bill of $300 a month, give or take. Your older child leaves home and your food bill is cut by roughly one-quarter. That's $75 a month, or $900 a year. Unless you isolate that money, you will never see it again. If you redirect it toward tomorrow, you will.

- You finally decide you are going to get out of credit card debt, and though it takes you five years at $400 a month, you do. Drop that $400 a month into the pool, and it will cause ripples but eventually be absorbed. Keep it out of the pool, redirect it, and you will have an extra $4800 a year toward your future.

- You are managing perfectly well, and you get a raise. What do you do with the money? Redirect it.

Redirecting money is taking money that you have been paying every month anyway, or have had added to your income, and reclaiming it to work for your future.

PART III

FOR
LOVE
AND
MONEY

CHAPTER 8

THE COURAGE TO OPEN YOUR HEART,

THE COURAGE TO OPEN YOUR HANDS

Think of all the money that will flow through and around you every single day of your life. Your parents' money and possibly money that filters down from their parents. Money to be apportioned among you and your siblings. Money that arises as an issue between friends and colleagues. If as an adult you marry your future to another's, then you are also combining your fortunes. Your money will flow to your children, if you have them, and perhaps on to theirs. And yet, despite its constant presence in our lives, money is a subject we draw away from, even in our most intimate relationships. It's hard to face money directly, to ask for what you want, to claim what's yours, to learn what you have every right to know. If it is your intention to be rich, then you have to introduce the vocabulary of richness into your relationships. It takes courage to open yourself up to money, to ask others to do the same, to make true wealth one of the goals of true love.

LOVE AND MONEY

It never fails. When everything is working out between two people, they think love is so simple. Yet when the disagreements start, love becomes a complicated venture indeed. Often, the central complication is—surprise, surprise—money. Couples are always saying things like "Oh, money is killing our relationship" or "We were doing fine until money came between us." When I hear this, all I can think is that money has never done a thing to anyone, never hurt a fly. Money is just money. But it is the power you give your money, or your attitudes toward and your fears about your money, that can wreak havoc on the most important relationships in your life.

Not surprisingly, by now you may realise that you are in a relationship with money, whether you think of it in these terms or not. And like the other relationships in your life, this one needs work to make it successful. You must take actions that will create possibilities rather than destroy them, actions that will help you feel secure rather than afraid, and above all else, actions that will establish, in your private world, the sense that you are unconditionally loved for who you are and not for what you have. The first law of money states: *People first, then money.* It is also an essential law of relationships: *People first, then money.*

Which doesn't mean that money doesn't matter when it comes to love, because it matters a great deal. Of all the kinds of intimacy there are—physical, emotional, domestic—financial intimacy is perhaps the hardest to achieve, and, it could easily be argued, the most important in the long run. You can turn over your body, heart, and soul to someone, but the union will never be complete unless you link your fortunes (and misfortunes) together, too, for better or worse, and forever.

THE FINANCIAL COURTSHIP

You have met the person of your dreams. You have never loved anyone so much in your entire life. Finally you decide to get married or join lives and live happily ever after, till death do you part. The vows truly are holy, and you mean them with every ounce of your being. Could money get in the way of this love of yours? Not possible, you say. Until it does.

If you haven't walked carefully and honestly through all the money issues ahead of time, I can promise you that money will one day become an obstacle in your relationship. Even if you think you have the subject well covered, you'll probably find that money becomes a problem later on: you change, your partner changes, the money grows or fails to—all potential reasons for disagreement. Arguments over money trigger divorce in more cases than you can imagine—arguments that are not necessarily based on deceit or lies but on how we deal with money. Because most of us deal with it very, very differently.

This is so hard to understand ahead of time and so painful to discover after the fact. On your own, you handle your money your own way. You worry, sure, and sometimes perhaps you spend money you shouldn't— you go overboard on gifts for yourself and others, occasionally you're late in paying your bills. Yet when someone else has a stake in your money and you have a stake in theirs, sloppy habits or reckless spending or even wildly divergent views on how to manage money can strike at the core of how safe and secure you feel and can make you feel violated in a very intimate way. When the first argument over money erupts, most of us are taken by surprise. And the only—the only—way to protect yourself and ensure that your relationship will thrive is to look at money issues in the most naked and honest way you can. Before you utter a single vow, and many times thereafter.

You must open the dialogue. Not just "Oh gosh, who's going to pay for what?"—which we'll get to. But you must attempt to talk together in a rational, candid way about the serious side of money, matters that over time go from being background issues in a relationship to those of the highest priority—how you spend, how you save, how well you share.

- How do both of you feel about saving money for the future? How committed are you both to investing for tomorrow? Do you both agree that money you've saved shouldn't be touched, or would one of you be willing to tap into your savings for such luxuries as holidays or a spa or a new sound system?
- Are your investment styles—be they aggressive or conservative—in sync?
- Can you talk together, no matter how young you are, about retirement?

- Are you in agreement over who does the bookkeeping and pays the bills?
- Do your notions of generosity match?
- Do you agree about your responsibilities toward your respective families?
- Do you have a prenuptial agreement? Do you want one? How does that make each of you feel?
- In the case of a job transfer, whose job takes precedence?
- If your incomes vary greatly, who is expected to pay for what, and how do you come to that decision?
- If you have children, what will happen if one of you wants to stay at home with them? How will the money work then?
- Do you feel the same about the financial aspects of child rearing—public vs. private schools, etc.?
- Are relations with any ex-spouses clearly defined?
- Do you know how much your partner earns? How much he or she spends every month? How much his or her bills are every month?
- Do you both pay your bills on time, or is one of you consistently late?
- Is any past credit card debt, HECS debt, or bankruptcy being brought into the relationship?
- Do both of you have a good credit record, or does one of you have the credit rating from hell?
- Are you both prepared to share your assets or your income, or does one of you feel the need to keep some aspects of your financial life separate? If so, why? Can you both live with that?

Do you still think love holds all the answers?

AMY'S STORY

After three years of dating, you'd think I would know enough about my husband when it came to money. Boy, was I wrong.

I thought I was falling into heaven. I met Bob and thought right away that maybe things could be different. We had always been so poor, my mother, my sister, and I. My father had split when I was nine, and Mother always had to work two jobs to make ends meet. Not that she didn't do a good job. She did, and we always felt very loved, but my sister and I grew up with the knowledge that life is very difficult. That's what I believed. My mother even managed to find the money to put each of us through university, and so what did I do? I had a baby in my second year, my wonderful daughter, Caitlin. And then my life cycle became like my mother's—working around the clock to make everything work out. Caitlin's seven now, and I have held down two jobs ever since she was born. But I found a decent flat for us, and we were managing just fine when I met Bob. I was knocked out by him, he was so self-assured and seemed to have everything under control. And he was amazed by me. He loved Caitlin, plus he always seemed so impressed by the way I handled everything that I felt impressed by myself, too, maybe for the first time.

I felt like I was managing the world. Then it got more amazing. It turned out that Bob was from a wealthy family, and they took us in, Caitlin and me, as if we were their own. We'd go to their house for barbecues, and it wasn't hot dogs and hamburgers, it was grilled salmon—really elegant. For the first two years everything was wonderful. And it kept getting more wonderful. When we decided to get married, Bob's parents paid the deposit on our house as a wedding present. I was so excited—our own house! We settled before the wedding, and I couldn't believe how lucky I felt. I painted Caitlin's room myself and was so proud I could give her her own room; I never had my own room growing up. The deed to the house was put in Bob's name alone, which his parents felt was fair, since they gave the money for the deposit, and I thought, Fine. Everything was perfect. I gave up my flat when we got married, and we moved into our house, like in a storybook.

We hadn't really talked about money much, other than to agree that we would split everything, and I thought, Fine, it's all our money now anyway. I made $36,000 between my two jobs, and Bob made $60,000, working in the marketing department of a big corporation. At first, it seemed like so much money, but then I began to feel poorer than I had before, when I had my own little flat. My half of the mortgage was more expensive than my rent had been, and on top of that there were insurance and rates. Since the house was bigger than my flat, my half of the bills was as much as or sometimes more than what I had been paying before. Then there was the cost of the extra food. I spent most of my savings on new furniture for the house. The expenses kept adding up, but it all seemed okay, because we were building this great new life.

I guess the scales began to fall from my eyes when Bob bought his new Jeep, which he paid for in cash, with money I assumed he'd been given by his parents. And here I was, driving around in a fifteen-year-old Ford. All my money went into our life and the house, all of it, but then Bob had enough to go buy this new Jeep. What really hurt is that he didn't seem to care that I was still working two jobs, which sometimes meant eighteen-hour days, and I got so tired while he worked an easy nine-to-five and had lots of extra money. When I tried to talk to him about it, he said, "Hey, I'm not asking you to do anything you weren't doing before we were married." He got really angry. Then I thought about how I was paying half of the mortgage, so I asked him when my name would be added to the deed. Never, he said; that was the deal, his parents were protecting their invest-ment. I didn't think it was fair because, after all, I was paying half, but he said if I were paying rent on a flat I wouldn't have an owner's stake in it, so why should I care?

Caitlin loved Bob, and she was happy, so I stayed in the marriage, even with all the anger—and I couldn't believe the anger. But finally, I had to go, and after only three years of marriage we separated. Was the divorce fair? No way. I had lost my affordable flat and had spent too much on the house—and I got nothing. No child support, because Caitlin isn't his child. No alimony, because I had been pulling my weight all along. Nothing except the furniture to show for all that I'd put into the house and the mar-riage. Caitlin and I are poorer than ever, living in a studio apartment. My savings are gone. I married this rich man, hoping for a better life, and lost everything.

Amy started out with such high hopes and had quite realistic dreams of the life she and her husband would lead. So where did it go astray? Remember, in order to follow a course toward wealth, what you think, say, and do must be one. Let's track Amy's thoughts, words and actions.

What Amy thought was that when she and Bob got married, her life would get easier, not harder—fair enough. She thought that she would no longer have to carry the financial burden all by herself, and that she and Bob would join forces to make a better life for all of them. She was no gold digger—in fact, proportionately she contributed more to the marriage than her husband did—but had thought that, with the two of them work-ing, she might be able to give up one of her jobs so that she wouldn't have to work so hard. She thought that she could have an easier life than her mother had had, that she could give a better life to her daughter. She thought that Bob would want this for her as well. What did she say about it to Bob—before the marriage? She said nothing and kept on doing all the things she'd done before, working two jobs and so on. Then what happened? When her marriage didn't fulfil her desires, she got angry. Angry at Bob, angry at herself. From that point on, everything she did—whether it confused him, hurt herself, or destroyed any chance at compromise—resulted from her anger.

How could it have been different? Amy could have communicated with Bob, at least enough to make him aware of her fierce need to provide for her child. She could have shared her hope—ahead of time—that life might become easier for her after their marriage. If he had baulked at that, everything might have been different. If Amy had known how Bob felt about splitting bills, whose name the deed to "their" house would be in, as well as all their other financial differences, Amy might have decided right then and there, even though it would have broken her heart, that Bob was not what she wanted—not what she could afford. It wasn't as if Amy was waiting for a knight in shining armour to save her. Amy had tremendous courage and was doing fine on her own. When she fell in love with Bob, however, she thought that life could be even better. Had she and Bob each understood the other's position, it could have been. In the end, though, Bob felt used, felt as if Amy was trying to change the ground rules of their relationship. She, too, felt used, because she thought the ground rules would, and should, change with their marriage. Whatever love they had was lost to money. And, in this case, Amy and her daughter ended up poorer, financially and emotionally.

FINANCIAL PREVIEW

Even if Amy wasn't comfortable initiating intimate financial conversations, when she thought about it, she saw—with the inevitable clarity of hindsight—that Bob had many financial habits that should have clued her in to what he was really like and what she was getting herself into by marrying him. Whenever they went out to eat, for instance, they always split the bill fifty-fifty. Same with the movies and any holidays they took. On shopping trips, Bob would routinely go to David Jones, while Amy shopped for herself and her daughter at Kmart. If he borrowed her car, he never filled it back up with petrol. Once he even put a little dent in the car and showed it to Amy, but never offered to pay for the repair. She was definitely not marrying a man with an "our" sensibility, and much as she hoped for more, he never gave her a glimmer of a reason for that hope.

Every day you see how the person you love acts with, and reacts to, money. The big things, like whether debt is a part of the picture. And the little things—the man who has to have every high-tech gadget there is, the woman who loves to buy shoes—which, if they irk you now, will irk you much more over time. At first you ignore what you don't like, in a much more forgiving way than you would other bad habits—personal hygiene, for example, or bad manners, or constant broken promises. Money is at once too small a subject for confrontation ("I don't want it to seem like I don't trust him!") and too great a subject, for you have given it the ultimate power, the power of silence. But listen closely. Money is one of the most important parts of life—my life, your life, the life of the person you love. If you sense your partner will put his or her money above the needs of your relationship, then I ask you to have the courage to admit to yourself what you already know in your heart.

What you see now is what you'll get later, although you may feel differently about today's financial qualities as they play out farther down the road, when there's perhaps more at stake. The little things get bigger over time, whereas qualities of prudence, which may seem a little stuffy now, become far more important in the long term. There is no way to see clearly into the future, but you can certainly face what you see today. This quiz offers a sampling of financial habits, good and bad, all of which suggest character traits. Please circle the letter of the habits which apply to your partner. Somewhere in this quiz, too, you might find yourself.

A. Fails to tip waiters and other service people as a matter of course

B. Seems unusually taken with luxury items, like wildly expensive cars, clothes, or gadgets

C. Has a weekly date with friends at the racetrack

D. Never balances the cheque book, or regularly bounces cheques

E. Keeps the cheque book balanced at all times

A. Invites you to dinner, chooses the restaurant, then complains about the prices on the menu
B. Expresses material longings for things—holidays, jewellery—way beyond his or her budget
C. Buys and sells stocks constantly for the thrill of it rather than as wise economic moves
D. Seems to regard his or her parents or others as a source of income
E. Is saving the maximum allowed by law into superannuation and monitors these investments to make sure they are performing to the best of their ability

A. Complains about child-support obligations
B. Tries to impress your friends by bragging about money
C. Prefers to take holidays in places with gambling casinos
D. Has a messy wallet, or a wallet full of maxed-out credit cards but absolutely no cash
E. Never buys an item to impress others or brags about money

A. Talks about using his or her work expense account for personal items
B. Cannot pay off credit card bills at the end of every month
C. Cannot get up and walk away from a gambling table, even if losing badly
D. Spends money on a new pair of shoes even though other bills are overdue
E. Loves to talk about finances and is open to teaching you

A. Seems uncomfortable using the pronoun "we"
B. Can never go into a store without buying an item, whether he or she needs it or not
C. Is constantly baffled as to where the pay cheque went
D. Receives calls from bill collectors
E. Is charitable and generous and does not define him- or herself by how much is in the bank account

A. Would never put loose change into a donation box after making a purchase

B. Gives you unusually expensive gifts that you know he or she can't afford

C. Is constantly placing bets, be it on the races or buying lottery tickets

D. Avoids talking about money and acts like everything is just fine when you suspect it isn't

E. Pays all the bills on time and rarely carries a balance on credit cards

Scoring: Count how many of each letter you have circled and record the number below.

A_____   B_____   C_____   D_____   E_____

The letter with the largest number reveals your partner's primary money traits.

Key

A = PENNY-PINCHER

B = SPENDTHRIFT

C = GAMBLER

D = FINANCIAL WRECK

E = FINANCIAL CATCH

While it's true that we all have our financial quirks, any of these undesirable financial qualities taken to their worst extreme could signal trouble ahead—and you don't want to end up with a penny-pincher, spendthrift, gambler, or financial wreck, or someone with qualities of each. Hard as it is to do so, you must open a dialogue about money with your partner now, because it is impossible to join hearts without your purse strings interlocking as well.

If you're close to commitment or in a long-term arrangement but still not comfortable with the way you communicate about money, begin the dialogue now. Can people change their money habits just by talking about the subject? Yes, they can. Once you open the dialogue honestly, you will be better able to see each other's perspective and to act out of compassion for your partner's fears and concerns. Maybe the changes won't come all at once, but I've seen many people open up about money, change their habits, and work together toward a harmonious financial relationship. If you can state clearly what you find problematic or troubling, then at least there's a new perspective out in the open. Expect changes to come not at once but over time, as you initiate a chain of compromises. The most important catalyst for improvement is opening the dialogue in the first place. And being open to change yourself.

When talking in an intimate way about money, it is essential that you do it from an understanding and compassionate place, not spurred by anger or defensiveness. It is not necessarily true, for example, that penny-pinchers are stingy—most are simply afraid of losing what they have; they think that there isn't enough money to go around. In the same way, a spendthrift often uses money to try to make up for low self-esteem or self-worth. A financial wreck also needs to be addressed with great care. It has taken him or her a long time to get in such terrible financial trouble—and there's a reason someone actively goes about making his or her own affairs chaotic. In the case of a gambler, the damage may call for professional help. Regardless of the tendency that signals trouble to you, silence on your part will only prolong and worsen the damage.

YOUR EXERCISE

I want you to sit down together and figure out a sum of money that feels like a generous discretionary amount, an amount that would enable each of you to buy something to show for it, something you cared about. Use as your starting point the amount of money you each spend each month on things you want, things for yourself. Maybe the sum will be the same for you both.

More likely, one of you has more money and should therefore choose a discretionary amount that's proportionately higher. Maybe the figure is two hundred dollars, three hundred dollars, less than that, or much more. You decide, but it has to be a sum of money that matters.

Now go to the bank and withdraw, each of you, your amount of money, in cash. Put it into an envelope and give it to your partner. The rules are that you must neither talk about what you plan to buy nor report on your purchases until the end of the month. Keep the money in the envelope, apart from your own money, and keep all receipts. What should you buy? Anything you want, things that you'd probably buy anyway, somewhere down the road. Anything that you'd buy with your own money—because if you're thinking of merging money, this will, one day, be your money.

At the end of the month, open the dialogue, with honesty and compassion. Here are some questions for discussion: How did it feel to be spending the other person's money? How did you feel, knowing that the other person was spending your money? How do you feel about what your partner bought with your money—pleased, angry, resentful, surprised? Did one of you buy things with both of you in mind, while the other bought things with just him- or herself in mind? Did one of you have money left over at the end of the month? Did you both do a good job of keeping track of where the money went?

Keep your discussion limited to this money as you answer these questions. You have been playing house, but it will give you some idea about what it will feel like to be keeping house.

Financial Intimacy

What if your particular lovebug spent the three hundred dollars you apportioned on car parts, while you spent it (in your view) judiciously, buying the ingredients for a romantic dinner, a few cosmetics you had run out of, a birthday present for a mutual friend whose party you were both attending, and two tickets to a play? Add years' worth of car parts that only your partner enjoys against spending with both of you in mind, and the result is not going to total an equal partnership or a happy one. True, the money was to be spent as discretionary income, but if your ideas about spending in general are worlds apart, you must bring them closer, through dialogue.

Perhaps the formula is pretty simple now. Let's say you're playing house in a one bedroom unit, each earning about the same amount, splitting things pretty much fifty-fifty, with enough left over to buy what you want. So what's the problem?

Any little twinge about money you feel now is going to be amplified later. Our ideas and compulsions about money change as we age—none of us is the same financial being at twenty-five or thirty-five as we are at fifty, when we begin to internalise the fact of retirement and the eventuality of mortality. We may change our money habits, too, as we make more money. Buy a house together, a house that needs a new roof, and then see how you feel if that money goes to car parts. The addition of children to our lives changes, sometimes drastically, our ideas about the money we have and the money we need. It's a process, learning about someone else and money, and it can last a lifetime.

A relationship deepens as the stakes get higher. At the beginning, it's easy to say what's yours and what's mine, when very little is "ours". As time goes on, though, those easy boundaries blur, and what's "ours" begins to take precedence. The house, the furnishings, the car, the children, the family and friends you share, and the rituals you establish can make the marriage a rich place to inhabit. A relationship counsellor will tell you to keep close track of the emotional pulse of your relationship. As a financial counsellor, I can tell you that the financial pulse is equally important, because the financial stakes in a marriage start out high and only get higher.

LEGAL INTIMACY

It is essential to disclose to each other your personal financial histories, money habits, and financial likes and dislikes, and it is also essential that, whether you decide to live together or get married, you know your legal obligations to each other. In particular, marriage, where the financial issues are considerable, must not be entered into lightly. Nor should you agree to purchase a large asset together without thinking things through completely, considering every possible eventuality. A marriage that goes sour and ends up in divorce can leave scars that even the best financial plastic surgeon in the world cannot cover up. Scars that could have been avoided. Few things are as difficult for me as a financial planner as meeting someone forced to start over by a marriage gone bad, especially at an age when he or she should be about to enjoy retirement. Such people are riddled with anger and fear, but they also feel hurt and humiliated.

It's beyond the scope of this book to set forth all the contractual obligations of marriage or those that can arise from a long-term nonmarital relationship. I do know, however, from the many financial questions that have arisen in my office, how few of us, whether we're entering into a lifetime partnership or a marriage, think through—or talk through—

ahead of time all the responsibilities we may one day have to face up to. Here are some of the questions I have had to answer for my clients:

Am I liable for the debts my spouse incurred before our marriage?

No. You don't marry debt. But as soon as you commingle assets, any joint account you set up is fair game for prior creditors. You can get around this by keeping or opening a bank account in your own name, which creditors theoretically can't touch.

Am I liable for debts incurred after our marriage that are only in my spouse's name?

No, but creditors can make a claim on your partner's share of joint assets; this could mean that you could be forced to sell your car or home in order to repay your partner's debt.

If my spouse has children he or she is required to support, will my income be considered by the court when deciding how much the payments will be?

Child support is based on a fixed formula. This formula looks at the income of both parents and takes into account the number of nights a child spends with each parent, who is paying the mortgage on the custodial home, and the number of children for whom a parent is liable. Your income is not included in this formula.

What happens if my spouse files for bankruptcy?

The creditors are unable to touch assets in your name, but again this does not stop them making a claim on your partner's share of joint assets. If the debt is in joint names, one spouse's discharge of the debt in bankruptcy will not relieve the other spouse of the debt. Don't transfer assets from one spouse to another in order to avoid repayment of the debt because in the case of bankruptcy this transfer can be reversed and the asset or money would still be included in the bankrupt's assets.

What are the presumptions with respect to custody of children?

Even if you do nothing you retain joint custody. It is preferable for the parents to agree on who the children will live with and how often they will visit the non-custodial parent. This is called a parenting agreement, and should be made in writing. If you cannot agree, the court will make parenting orders after conferences with family and child counsellors.

If my ex-spouse doesn't pay child support, can the court still enforce visitation rights?

Yes. Financial and custodial arrangements are viewed by courts as distinct and separate issues.

Who is responsible for an incapacitated child?

The father and mother share equal responsibility for an incapacitated or disabled child. If you have a child (or, for that matter, a parent) who will need long-term assistance, please see a good trust lawyer who deals with asset protection.

Are there common-law marriage rights that accrue to a person who lives with you as a spouse for a long period of time?

De facto relationships are covered by state laws and because of the complexity of these laws, legal advice is essential. The division of property in this instance is governed by general law unless there are children from the relationship, in which case it could be assessed under family law.

Can I throw my spouse out of my house, especially if I owned the house before our marriage?

The Family Court can change the legal title of a property, and the Court can order a party to give up an interest in a property. Each case is assessed individually.

Can your spouse leave you, move to another state, and sue for divorce there to get a better deal for himself or herself?

The Family Law Act (Commonwealth) 1975 was passed to eliminate the differences that once existed between state laws. The law is now uniform for all of Australia. However, because amendments have been made by the states since that time, there are slight discrepancies in some areas such as spouse maintenance.

In a divorce, can a spouse take back a gift given specifically to you—or at least claim his or her "half" of such a gift?

Maybe. It's very hard to prove intention, especially if you don't have any written instrument to show it was a gift to you alone. In the case of an inheritance, that's generally considered separate property—unless you commingle it.

Can I disinherit my spouse?

You can state your wishes in your will, but your spouse can apply to the court to have those wishes overturned.

Do I have a legal duty to support my spouse during marriage?

Yes. Husband and wife contract toward each other obligations of mutual respect, fidelity, and support. This applies if a spouse becomes ill or loses—or quits—a job.

If you are in a same-sex relationship or you have chosen to live together but remain unmarried, you still have some serious questions to consider, such as the following:

If we're unmarried but own property together, what happens if we break up?

The property will be divided according to who holds title or whose name is on the account, unless the unnamed party can claim that he or she had an agreement with the partner to share the asset. The dispute will be resolved under general law, rather than in the Family Court, unless children of the relationship are involved.

If we're unmarried and haven't bought any property together, can either of us still face financial obligations toward the other?

Only if you signed contracts together. Contracts between unmarried couples are legally binding. It's better for the contracts to be in writing, since proving a contract is pretty hard to do if it isn't written down, and oral contracts are rarely enforced. But if you strongly believe that you and your partner had a firm contract and you can afford to fight for your rights in court, you may be able to prove your case.

Do unmarried partners ever owe each other alimony after a breakup?

Not unless there is proof of a contract to provide such post-separation support, which is rare and not necessarily legally binding.

Are unmarried couples liable for each other's debts?

Not unless they co-sign on a loan or have a clear contract with each other to accept such liability.

These questions are not meant to scare you or dissuade you from making a commitment. Rather, they point up just how solemn lifetime commitments, especially the legal institution of marriage, really are. You must be emotionally ready to marry, it's true, but you also must understand the financial and legal ramifications of the institution, because there's more at stake here than your heart. If you are in a troubled relationship and any of these questions struck too close to home, please think carefully before you put at risk all you have today and all you might have tomorrow.

THE BUSINESS OF LOVE

When two or more people enter into a business relationship, legal documents are usually drawn up to explain how the business is going to run, who is paid what, and who owns what. These documents may also contain a clause stating that if something was to go wrong—let's say the business partners wanted to break up—how the partnership would be dissolved. Details might include a predetermined formula as to how the business would be valued, as well as a calculation of what each partner would have to pay to buy out the others and how that process would be carried out. It is also not uncommon for the principals of the business to purchase an insurance policy known as *key man insurance,* which protects the surviving partners in the event of an untimely death of one of them. None of this suggests that any of the partners expects the business to fail—quite the opposite; otherwise they wouldn't be going into business together in the first place. Rather, it means that the partners are wise enough to lay all their cards on the table ahead of time, that they want to protect one another and themselves, and that they want to get on with the business.

When it comes to the business of marriage or a long-term commitment, however, most of us would never think of enacting such a plan or muster up the courage to talk about it—but make no mistake about it, marriage is a business, and one with a one-in-three failure rate at that. The time to talk about the what-ifs in marriage or a committed unmarried relationship is the same time we'd talk about it in starting a business, when we are most optimistic—at the outset. When we love and trust each other with all our hearts, before we know what the future might bring.

S U S A N ' S   S T O R Y

I can't believe the way it turned out and what I might have lost. Mark was not that eager to get married, especially since he felt he had lost too much in the divorce after his first marriage. We'd been together for about five years, though, and then I got pregnant. He said he would marry me, but he wanted a prenup. I hated that; I would never take more than my share from anyone. I said yes, but I felt hurt about it for a long time. He went to a lawyer to have the prenup drawn up, and then I showed it to a girlfriend of mine who's a lawyer. The prenup was all about Mark's future earnings, that he should get to keep his superannuation funds and everything if we got divorced. My friend said fine, that was okay, but she added to it that I could keep all my future money, too. What did I know? I was thirty years old, working as an administrative assistant in a start-up computer company. Mark had much more money, and he was already a financial officer at a big company. Fine, I said, and we both signed the papers.

For a long time everything was great. When Max was born, Mark fell in love with him; he was a great father. I kept working and began to really enjoy it, because the company was growing by leaps and bounds. The more I got into programming, the more I loved it. There was a program at work where the company would pay tuition for relevant classes. I decided I didn't want to be an assistant forever, so I signed up for some courses and did really well. It was as if all of a sudden everything clicked, and there I was, getting promoted, installing software for lots of companies. I'd never thought about having a real career; I always thought I would just have a job, but this was great. I bought a BMW, plus some stock options in the company, and began to feel really good about what I was doing. I had a superannuation plan at work, too, and little by little, that money was really adding up. And I could work from home a lot, which meant I was there for Max.

Mark was doing great, too. He got a promotion about the same time as I did, so we were both happy. It didn't seem competitive or anything. We bought this great house and put Max into private school. And for twelve years everything was so good—until three years ago.

Mark was basically downsized because of office politics. Everyone at the top was moved around, and two of his good friends were also fired at the same time. It was awful. Here he was, forty-six years old and out of a job. The severance package seemed good at the time, and he got to take his superannuation money, but he was shell-shocked. His company sent him to a headhunter, but nothing came of it. I knew it would take him some time to get back on his feet, but months went by and he didn't even try to find work; he just sat at home watching television. I thought maybe he was depressed and tried to get him to go to a doctor, but he wouldn't. Now we're in the gym phase—he goes to the gym every day for a couple of hours. It's been three years. Both his friends have jobs—not great jobs, but they're working. Mark is resentful toward me all the time, and God forbid I should buy new clothes for work or do anything nice for myself. His severance money is long gone. He says he's trying to find a job, but I'm home enough to know that's not true. After this year, Max will have to go to public school, and I don't know what's going to happen to the house. I'm doing everything, and I am miserable. Mark won't even write the cheques to pay the bills. Not long ago, I blew up and asked for a separation. We haven't mentioned it again, but I'm walking on eggshells in this marriage. I really am thinking of getting out. I was so supportive for so long, but one person can't do the whole thing. Three years is enough.

I don't see another way out. And you know what? I'm so happy he made me sign that prenup. If we get a divorce, I won't have to pay for him to sit around feeling sorry for himself. I have my job, my stock, and my superannuation. I can take care of me and Max. And maybe then, finally, Mark will take care of himself.

Premarital and Cohabitation Agreements

What I would ask you to do is unconventional: I am asking you to plan for the what-ifs while you are still totally in love. In the name of love, plan for anything and everything that could happen. Decide now how things will be split up should your feelings for each other change, and put it in writing. Have a legal contract known as a *premarital agreement* (or *prenuptial agreement,* or *prenup*) drawn up before you are married, or, if you intend to stay unmarried, draw up what's known as a *cohabitation* or *property agreement* before you solidify your relationship. If you have the courage to take this bold step out of love, not greed, out of wanting the best for each other, not only now but forever, regardless of what happens, then you have nothing to lose. If you stay together happily, so much the better; the agreement will never come up again. If, however, the marriage ends, and you do end up getting divorced, you will have planned for this eventuality ahead of time. If I ran the world, I would definitely pass a new law: Before anyone could get married, there would have to be a prenup.

Time and time again, when I raise the subject, people say to me, "But Suze, why do I need a prenup? I don't have any assets to my name." Those are words of poverty. Prenups are for tomorrow, not today, and no matter how deep your love is today, nobody—not you, not your partner—can see what tomorrow might look like, to see ahead to what you might have in the years to come, and what you might stand to lose.

The myth is that the very subject of prenups will cause contention. In reality, it's a way of bringing to the surface your deepest concerns about money and security and the unknowns of the future. It's not a sign of greed, weakness, or fear to want the reassurance that you both will be safe, whatever happens, and, in my experience, opening up these issues can bring partners closer together in ways they rarely comprehend until they do it.

PRENUPTIAL AGREEMENTS

A prenuptial agreement is an agreement in writing which clearly states who owns what assets before entering a relationship. This document has often been considered by the Family Court when it comes to division of property but at the time of writing it is not legally binding. All of that, however, is about to change and consideration is being given to making prenuptial agreements compulsory.

Here are some scenarios in which prenups come into play:

- You have been through a nasty divorce and you know very well what can happen and how costly it can be to decide who is going to get what, and you want to make sure that you never have to go through that again.

- You built up or inherited an extensive portfolio, or maybe a successful business or considerable real estate holdings before you were married. These holdings may take considerable time to maintain, possibly by both you and your spouse, and you will both reap the rewards during your marriage. Even so, you want to make sure that this property and its growth remain in your name alone should the marriage dissolve.

- You are in a fast-track career, stand a good chance of becoming extremely wealthy one day, and want to protect what you hope to earn.

- One day you'll inherit your parents' holiday home—they've already laid the legal groundwork for this. As your parents no longer use the house very much, you and your fiancé have begun using it every weekend and are full of plans to fix it up. Even so, this house has been in your family forever—and you want to make sure it remains in your family.

- You are not rich, but you are about to marry a rich man. By the end of the marriage, he could claim (possibly correctly) that everything he has derives from his separate property and that everything earned during the marriage was spent—thus claiming that there is nothing to split. Even if he's wrong, he has the money to fight you in court. You need a prenup so that you will know where you'll come out in the event of a divorce.

- You are a widow (or widower) with children, and you want to protect their father's (or mother's) money for them before you remarry.

- You are remarrying and don't want your grown children to be suspicious or resentful of a new step-parent. A prenup will demonstrate to them that assets due to go to them one day will in fact do so.

- Your future spouse came to work in your business and was so devoted to the business before you fell in love that you want to put some of the business into his or her name.

- You have managed to save about sixty thousand dollars, which you are willing to use as a down payment for the house you and your fiancé, who has no savings to speak of, plan to buy. Should something happen, you want to make sure that your life savings are protected.

♦ You've been working for twelve years at a great corporation and to your surprise have accumulated a substantial amount of money in your superannuation fund. The man you are marrying is younger and just starting out at another corporation. While you agree that you will share retirement plans from this point on, you'd like to keep your present benefits protected in the event of a divorce.

♦ You know that your future spouse has debt or is prone to spending unwisely, and that you do not want to be responsible for debts he or she incurs in his or her own name while you are married.

♦ You are in a committed long-term unmarried relationship. You want to live together and share some assets, perhaps even buy property together, but you aren't ready to commingle all your assets.

HOW PRENUPS WORK

Below are questions and answers detailing the main points that you need to consider with respect to prenups.

What exactly is a prenuptial agreement?

A *premarital* or *prenuptial agreement* is a legal contract you enter into before marriage which states how a couple's assets as well as debts are to be divided in a way that is fair and reasonable to both spouses in case of a divorce. A *cohabitation agreement* works in the same way. You can also enter into such an agreement while you are married (a *marital agreement*) or, in the case of a cohabitation agreement, while you are living together.

Do judges really pay attention to prenups? If not, is it worth making my fiancé sign one?

Until recently, judges weren't favourably inclined toward prenups. Perhaps they did not want to honour prenups because the belief was that they encouraged divorce. Now, generally, the courts will take these agreements into consideration. The contract won't be enforced if it's viewed as a contract to evade creditors illegally, or if the court believes that one party was intimidated during the process.

What is the best way to go about getting a prenup?

Prenups must be put in writing and signed by both parties. My best advice is for each of you to retain an individual solicitor to represent your interests or at least to review the contract and advise you about its implications before you sign it. These contracts can be complicated, and you want to make sure that each of you knows exactly what you are signing. Not only should both partners sign the agreement, so should both solicitors.

Do prenups have to be witnessed to be valid?

It is a good idea to have any type of contract witnessed.

Do I need to disclose everything I have?

If anything, err on the side of more rather than less. Disclose it all— your assets, debts, income, expenses, and anything else that will affect the value of your estate, now or in the future. If you are not completely honest and open with each other, a court could re-examine your agreement and refuse to honour it.

Does a prenup only have to do with property ownership?

No. Other items such as debt, say, or future stock options or superannuation benefits can be designated in the agreement. There have been prenups that covered everything from who will get the season football tickets to who has to feed the dog. Almost anything can be covered as long as it does not violate public policy—such areas, for example, as insufficient child support, because you cannot contract away a child's right to support.

What, exactly, is the definition of property?

In most courts of law, property includes everything from your sewing kit to your retirement funds. It also includes debts, patents, intellectual property (such as novels and screenplays), artwork— you name it. When it comes to the definition of property, expand your thoughts to go way beyond things like your car, boat, furniture, jewellery, or house. Property essentially includes everything.

How is property that I acquired before the marriage regarded by the courts?

The court assesses each case individually. Your partner can make a claim against it if your partner contributes time or money to the maintenance of a premarital property, thus increasing its value.

What if I'm left an inheritance or will be given a gift by my parents after I am married? Is that property considered joint property?

No. If those funds were given specifically to you, and you keep those funds in an account in your name only, or you buy something with those funds in your name only, they'll remain your separate property. However, the longer a marriage goes on, the more boundaries between separate monies can blur. Let's say you buy some managed funds, for example, and it's most convenient for the moment to name your spouse as joint owner. You may have just converted your separate property to *joint,* or *community, property.* Where you want such assets to end up should be spelled out in the prenup.

What if I owned rental property before I was married and continue to earn from it during the marriage—is the rent still my separate property?

This can be tricky. If you both invest your labour in the management of the property, the current income is considered a joint asset, since it's the product of both partners' labour, rather than a passive investment. If you use a management company, on the other hand, the rent is more often considered a separate asset. Again, however, it doesn't hurt to clarify ownership in the prenup.

What if, after the contract is drawn up, we want to make some changes?

No problem. You basically follow the procedure that you followed when you had the contract drawn up in the first place. Have the agreement witnessed if necessary, and state expressly whether you're replacing the earlier document with this one or simply amending certain terms listed in the previous agreement.

When should the agreement be signed?

Do not sign it on the way to the church. The court will throw out your prenup if it feels that in any way either party was under duress when signing, or that the parties did not have ample time to think about it and to seek professional help. Make sure that you draw up your agreement under normal circumstances. Normal circumstances means that the person signed of his or her own free will and without any kind of gun-to-the-head coercion.

YOURS, MINE AND OURS

All your adult life you've been managing your own money your own way, and now you're supposed to share everything? Not just the rent or the mortgage, but everything? This has been the traditional idea behind marriage: total financial togetherness. From football tickets to facials, everything that the two of you need and want is supposed to come out of your suddenly "joint" funds. This presumes that you will both want the same things at the same time, that your money habits (balancing the cheque book, for instance) will blend harmoniously, and that you both come from families where money is handled and treated in approximately the same way. It presumes, too, that if one or both of you become more successful, you'll be able to grow together financially as well as emotionally, and that you'll be able to survive the financial down times together. And it presumes that if children enter the picture or ageing parents get sick and need your help, you'll be able to accommodate these new responsibilities peaceably. All this, in other words, presumes a lot, and presumes a transition that most of us, when we get married or start living together, can't make all at once.

Merging finances means compromise, it means sometimes putting someone else's interests and needs ahead of your own, and it requires negotiation and careful thought. No two couples are alike, and no two couples manage their finances in quite the same way—whether they manage them well or poorly.

KATHERINE'S STORY

We got married almost nine years ago, and I guess we didn't really talk too much ahead of time about money. It was pretty clear-cut at the time. I moved into Richard's unit before the wedding, actually, and we didn't make many adjustments. He owned it, and he kept paying the mortgage and maintenance, plus the electricity and so on, and I began paying for food and everything else I could. I bought some houseplants and window shades and a nice halogen lamp and fresh flowers every week. Still, it continued to feel like his place—I think he wasn't quite used to my being there all the time—and I never made an issue of how to divide up the expenses. I just tried to pay for every single thing I could. Plus the unit felt temporary. We were already talking about buying a house together, so I figured we'd just let the money stuff evolve.

Eventually we did find a house to buy. We also sold the unit really fast, and the profits were enough for a deposit. Even then it was okay. We decided that he'd pay the mortgage, rates, and insurance, plus a few other bills, and I would pay pretty much all the rest—food, cable, the gardener, dry cleaning, phone, electricity, whatever. At the time, Richard was making more money, and splitting things, about two-thirds to one-third, seemed fair to us both, I think. Or at least I don't remember very many fights about money this early on.

But then the bills started to escalate. The "everything else" part, the part that I was paying, just kept going up. There was suddenly the pool cleaner, then firewood for the fireplace, and the windows were filthy, so we called a window washer. The house ended up needing a lot of work. Richard paid for some things, and I paid for some. There was work to fix the leaky basement, which he paid for, then I paid for the new hot-water heater, and it just kept going on. I was trying to think of it as "our" money—who cared who paid, anyway, so long as we had the money?—but there was no way to do that. Richard had his cheque account, and I had mine, no joint account, and he'd always talk about "my" money and "your" money. Soon there was no way to keep track of the one-third, two-thirds split anymore. I'd go to the chemist and he'd ask me to get him some things. When I got home, he'd say, "I'll pay for my things, how much are they?" But then he'd usually forget to pay. As I began to earn more money, I knew I was paying more, which would have been fine if he hadn't been guarding so carefully what was supposedly his. It was also getting to the point of absurdity—we couldn't get through a day without talking about his money or mine, and how he was going to chip in for this or that. It was really hurtful. Here I had gone into this marriage with my whole heart and all the money I made, and he was still trying to go Dutch treat. We were doing fine and making good money, but the pleasure was gone. There was nothing to show that we were in this together.

Then two things happened that really drove me crazy. The first was with this managed fund that we were investing in. We had the account together. We were both putting some money in every month, but he was usually putting in more than I was, although I kept adding more when I could. The market started doing very well, and one day I opened the statement and said something like, "Gosh, Richard, we're really making money here." He got funny, and said that most of the money, give or take, was his. He didn't see it as ours at all, even though we were both paying as much as we could and even though we were married. He just wanted to be able to take out his money and earnings and run. When I told him that according to the law, if we got divorced, half of it would be mine anyway, he didn't speak to me for three days.

The second thing was that we wanted to have a baby. Aside from the money fights, everything else was good, and we both wanted a child. Well, we had to go through fertility treatments, which I put on my charge card. By the time I got pregnant, the bill was up to about eight thousand dollars—but who cared? We had a wonderful son! What made me so angry was that Richard thought of it as my debt—his baby, my debt. Not his problem. It was my credit card; why should he help pay it off? It made me want to run, just take the baby and run. After a fight, we paid most of it off with our tax refund. I finally paid off the rest.

By this time, the arbitrary split had been thrown out the window. It is really expensive having a child, and how do you split those costs? Child care, clothes, nappies, toys, formula, birthday parties—it goes on and on. We're still trying to do home improvements, his share, my share. He *opened up another managed fund account, but he opened it in his name only. It's very discouraging. We are doing fine financially, but I feel totally on my own. I used to feel that the way to do it was just to plunge into the marriage and be generous, but now I think I'd have been better off guarding my own money and keeping tabs on everything. Last month his parents came to visit for a few days and I went out and bought all this stuff to make really nice meals, and the only thing he could say was something about how he wanted to pay for "most" of it. Most of it? What, his share and his parents' share, but not mine? By now the arguments are so familiar, they're like a running joke—only they're not funny.*

True Marriage: A Shortcut to True Wealth

You can construct all the formulas you want for financial harmony, but they won't necessarily work for long. Life is not a simple equation, and when it comes to money, we may have a common currency, but each of us has a different emotional currency. When you think about it, financial intimacy may be the most profound closeness there is. Many couples share a bed before marriage, some even share a home. We confide fears and painful stories of our pasts, and we certainly share our hopes and visions for the future. But talk about money? Possibly the last frontier of intimacy. A frontier that Katherine and Richard, even after nine years of marriage— a marriage that should be flourishing—have not yet crossed.

For a marriage or any partnership to work in the long run, you both have to go into it wholeheartedly—and not only with your whole heart but also with your cheque book. It's true that, with your prenup, you might have kept some assets out of the picture or might be able to work out an unconventional formula for managing your money that happens to work for you just fine, but that doesn't violate the underlying assumption of marriage, which is that the two of you will be richer together, in every way, than you would be on your own. Two people, contributing small sums of money, can build up a fortune much, much faster than one person. Two people working at it together can make a mortgage vaporise or send their children through school. Two people, even if one of them doesn't work outside the home for money, can together create a life with greater depth and texture and richness than most of us can on our own.

That's what marriage or living together, at its best, is about, and it implies a full commitment.

In some cases, your fortunes can grow by leaps and bounds if you both work, and learn to live on one salary. I have good friends who met and married when they were both thirty-five, knowing full well that the woman, a solicitor, would always make more than her husband, who works for the city. Their decision? To live on her salary, which would provide a comfortable but not luxurious life for them together, and invest every single penny of his. That was twelve years ago, and today they both know that within three years they will have enough money to live on comfortably forever if they no longer want to work. Their commitment was to each other and to their future, but it was their financial commitment to the marriage that built the fortune and made their dream materialise. No fine lines here of "yours", "mine", "ours". It was all "ours".

Or take the arrangements in which one party stays home and the other goes to work every day. Here's another chance to build great fortunes, if that's the direction the commitment takes. Only one set of professional clothes in this household, perhaps only one car. The stay-at-home spouse, according to the couple's agreement, cares for the house and the children, makes dinner, keeps everything running smoothly so that the working partner can devote his or her full energy to making money. Old-fashioned? Maybe. But if it's a whole-life commitment you're talking about, and it makes domestic and fiscal sense, this can be the road to riches.

In my opinion, the first law of money should be part of the marriage ceremony itself: *People first, then money.*

This is a lesson Katherine and Richard have yet to learn. If you're not together financially, then your marriage will not reflect a full commitment; it's that simple. And where there is divisiveness, it is much harder to create and sustain wealth, for conflict gives way to hoarding, counting, and, eventually, even deceit—all qualities that work against wealth. It takes courage (and, perhaps, a leap of faith) to enter into financial free fall with someone else, trusting that you will be better off by relinquishing your money for the sake of the greater good of your marriage. But if you can think of your money and marriage in the most expansive, generous way, then there will be plenty of room for both money and the richness that comes from love, from valuing achievements, both financial and otherwise. There's the money coming into the relationship, but there's also the love and energy that bring a lifelong relationship its vitality—the care spent creating and caring for the home, entertaining and planning to see friends, the actual work of raising children, shopping, cooking, paying bills, all of it. You can't put a price tag on every element that makes up a life. If you share joyously and willingly, if your commitment is financial as well as emotional, your partnership will be a rich, happy place to inhabit. Here are some issues to consider:

+ *Bookkeeping.* Who's paying the bills? There is nothing more frustrating, if you're sharing a joint cheque account, than to pay the bills and then have the phone ring off the hook because the cheques bounced, when, according to your figures, there should have been more than enough money in the account to pay for everything. You call the bank, only to find out that your distracted sweetheart forgot to deposit your last pay cheque, or perhaps forgot to record a couple of cheques, or made a large cash withdrawal from the ATM and spent every penny of it without ever saying a word. Each one of us has our own financial housekeeping preferences—some of us balance the bank statement every month, some never balance it. Some of us will pay the bills as soon as they come in, while others have no problem being late every month. Regardless of how you deal with your money, it is essential that you work out a plan that will meet the needs of both of you in handling the coming and the going of your money.

+ *Full disclosure.* Even if you decide to relegate the actual bookkeeping to one person, it is essential that you both know everything there is to know about your money—that you both know what it costs to live and what the bills come to every month; have a clear idea of the cost of food, clothing and shelter; have an understanding of what the children's expenses are, and everything about where your money is going. This is the only way for you both to be respectful of the money, and respectful and protective of each other, because it is unfair that the burden of bills fall on just one of you. My own feeling is that hands-on contact with the bills and the cheque book is important to bring you closer to understanding your money, so why not pay the bills together every month? If that doesn't work for you, one of you might do it one month and the other the next, or switch every six months. But see that you both touch, know about, and deal with your money.

- *Spending.* You must together reach an agreement about spending values. How often will you get a new car? What do you each have in mind when you talk about holidays? How much will the holiday season cost? Do you give presents for every occasion? Bottom line: You must talk about and compromise on or agree on what you need, what you want, and what you can afford.
- *Saving.* You must have a vision for tomorrow, and a means of getting there beginning today.

THE FORMULA FOR FINANCIAL SUCCESS: A STARTING POINT

It's true that what works for your friends or neighbours might not work for you, and any plan you start with will inevitably need some fine-tuning—if not today, then later on, when your circumstances change. Nevertheless, you have to start somewhere. Here are some principles that work for my clients:

Since we've decided to split the bills up proportionally, is it necessary that we have a joint account?

Remember Katherine and Richard? A joint cheque account or cash management trust (see Chapter 17) with both of your names on it is essential, for the simple reason that you are not going to split the bills but share them. You are joining lives, and therefore money, and this account is financially symbolic of that union. Unless you want to start calculating who drinks more orange juice or uses more toothpaste, you must have a place to house money to pay for those bills and items that you share.

How much should we each contribute to the joint account?

This will depend on how much money each of you is making. Let's say Melissa is making $100,000 a year, but Ted is making only $25,000. It would be very hard for Ted to contribute the same amount as Melissa. This is what I suggest: Add up all your joint expenses—the rent or mortgage, telephone, electricity, gas, food, movies, etc. Then add 10 percent to the total, because we always underestimate what it costs to live, day to day, week to week, month to month, and because the joint account is also meant to cover the relationship through any down times as well. You want to build this account up, not use it up, and create a slush fund, let's call it, for the bad times or unexpected bills that come your way. The idea here, remember, is to tap into the courage to be rich—and the richer your marital funds are, the richer you are, too.

Let's say that your joint expenses plus the additional 10 percent add up to $4000 a month. Melissa and Ted each should contribute the exact same percentage of what they are making toward paying these bills. In this case, after taxes, superannuation contributions, health insurance, etc., Melissa takes home $6000 a month and Ted's take-home pay cheque is around $1800. Add the two take-home cheques together. This comes to $7800 ($6000 plus $1800). Now divide the total of your joint expenses, $4000, by the total of your joint take-home cheques ($4000 divided by $7800). This equals the percentage, in this case 51.28 percent. That means that Ted needs to contribute 51.28 percent of his take-home pay, or $923 a month, to the joint account, and Melissa needs to contribute 51.28 percent of her take-home pay, or $3077 a month. This way, all the joint bills are covered and each one of you is paying the exact same proportion of your disposable income, which makes the equation totally equal. Remember, the *amounts* do not have to be the same to make something equal, only the *percentages.*

But it doesn't seem fair that I have to contribute more, even though I make more.

A larger dollar amount does not mean you work harder and therefore have more power or are entitled to more. The world, in fact, isn't a fair place—if it were, women wouldn't make less than men make. The measurement in a committed relationship is only this: Is each partner bringing everything he or she can to the relationship? That is the only measure that counts.

Maintaining equal power is a very important area of your relationship that you need to discuss now if you haven't already. The amount of money that you make when you are in a committed relationship is not what makes you more important or more deserving.

Many people do incredibly meaningful work, vital work, yet are totally underpaid, while others are paid exorbitant amounts for work that in the long run may not make a difference to one single soul. Do not—I repeat—*do not*, value yourself or your partner by how much either of you makes. Enter the relationship, and continue in the relationship, as equals—remember, *People first, then money.*

If we have a joint cheque account, do we need individual accounts as well?

Individual accounts in addition to the joint account are, in my opinion, a must. Grown-ups need discretionary income, and autonomy is an essential ingredient in any relationship—how degrading it would be to have to ask for money for a new lipstick or fishing tackle. You're partners, remember, and there are three entities here—yours, mine, and the big one, ours. But yours and mine count, too.

I make very little, but my spouse or partner makes a lot—and says it's okay if I use my money for my own needs and don't contribute to the joint household bills. Will this work?

This won't work. If you do this, the chances are good that as the years go by, it will backfire. When one person pays for everything, what usually ends up happening is that person tends to feel a sense of ownership toward everything, as well as a silent resentment toward the other person. In a joint life, you both have to pay. What's more, the person who is not contributing financially ends up feeling less and less powerful, and has less and less of a right to make joint financial decisions, which is everyone's right in a committed relationship. It is our nature to value our self-worth in dollars and cents. When you are working for money but not contributing financially, your inner radar will start to devalue your own opinion of yourself. It is far better to contribute on a fair percentage level, even if it comes out to just a few dollars a month, than to contribute nothing.

What if I decide to stop working for money, but stay home to take care of the children?

Then you will be doing equally important work. First you must ask yourselves: Is this financially feasible? In such a situation, I would recommend that you and your spouse add up all your expenses— everything from the mortgage to food to clothes for the children. How much is left over each month? If there's very little or nothing left over, and you both decide that this is the right course to follow anyway, then you must share equally in the responsibility of caring for and spending your money. If there is some discretionary money, it should be split fifty-fifty, regardless of who's bringing it in.

If I am going to stay home with the children, how do we work the money?

There is no simple formula for handling the money in this case, but the most important factor here is that you both agree that you will stay home with the children, because resentment on either side should tell you now that the arrangement won't work. You must agree, too, that any assets that build up belong to both parties, not just to the partner earning money.

You must work together to find your formula, whether it means seeking a higher-paying job for the partner earning money, moving to a more affordable place, or giving up certain luxuries. And you must find a way to ensure that you both know that the partner staying home is a full, equal partner, with equal rights.

How do you do this? In a perfect world, the solution would be that the partner working outside the home pays you, the stay-at-home partner, a "salary" equal to what you were earning while you were working outside the home, and you continue to apportion the bills as before. Most of us don't have that luxury, however. Another method is to attach a price tag to what you are actually doing. If you were not staying home with the kids and you had to hire a nanny or the equivalent, how much would it cost you? Let's say that amount is $1500 a month. Every month your spouse should write you a cheque for that amount of money. You should deposit it into your individual cheque account and then figure out, proportionately speaking, how much needs to go back into the joint cheque account. Remember, the discretionary amount is yours to spend as you please. It is not meant to cover expenses for the house or for the children; these costs come out of the joint account.

Why go through that exercise, when you could just have your spouse give you some discretionary money of your own? The answer is *Because people forget*. If you do it that way, eventually the person who is getting up every morning and going to work will from time to time forget the true worth of what you are doing. Money must change hands, one way or another, because neither of you should have to face the degrading experience of asking for or explaining every little bit of money you may want or need.

When a cheque is written every month, the tendency to forget is not so easy. Also, we ourselves forget what we are doing and what we are worth. This process serves as a reminder.

What if the one who was making less money starts making more?
Time to rework the deal.

The way we divided things up, my husband contributed the money for the car payment, but now that the car is paid off, he says he shouldn't have to put that money into the joint account anymore.
Big opportunity for getting rich. When something gets paid off or a former expense (day care, for instance) disappears, the money, which was benefiting the partnership anyway, should still be paid out every month—into the investment vehicle you both choose—and put toward your future.

What if I lose my job?
If you lose your job through sickness or downsizing, through no fault of your own, through bad luck, then the relationship must stretch to sustain you. Remember the extra 10 percent you were putting into the joint fund all along? That money is to help you both in times of trouble. This is true to the law and the spirit of marriage. Your part is to get back on your feet as quickly as you can.

Once our joint accounts and individual accounts are set up, how do we save for our future together?

The percentages calculated for what each of you would contribute to the joint account were calculated from take-home pay, which presupposes that your take-home pay has already had taken from it the maximum superannuation contribution. (Or, if you are self-employed, that you have funded your superannuation plan to the max.) As your circumstances improve, you'll want to invest in non-retirement-plan savings toward your future as well. Again, use a proportional approach to create money for your future, to be shared equally. If one of you makes much more money than the other and wants to invest more, it is up to you (or your prenup) to decide to whom that money will go in the event of a divorce.

THE SPIRIT OF MONEY, THE SPIRIT OF MARRIAGE

It is very important to know the enriching lesson that Richard, Katherine's husband, has not yet learned, which is that even though different percentages may be invested in your future, when the money comes out it comes out fifty-fifty unless you specify otherwise in a pre-marital agreement. Let's say, for instance, that over the past ten years you each have been putting 5 percent of your pay cheque into joint investment accounts. For you that may mean $100 a month and for your spouse or life partner that may mean $500 a month. You now have over $109,000 (assuming an 8 percent return) in this account. In reality, the one putting in $500 a month really contributed over $91,000 to that pot and the one putting in $100 a month would have accounted for roughly $18,300 of it. Regardless of what went in, what comes out has to be equal—even in the most acrimonious divorce. These are the fruits of your marriage, of your partnership. Half of that money is yours and half of that money belongs to your mate. The law does not necessarily say this pot has to be divided in half. But sharing equally goes beyond the legal system; in truth, it should be governed by the law and intent of marriage, the law of the heart. You were equal partners, and so you share in the partnership as equals. Know this up front and make it part of your commitment, which will be all the stronger for stating and following this course from the beginning. While you are together you reap the harvest of your marriage equally. Remember, when it comes to money it is not about doing what is easy, it is about having the courage to do what is right.

THE COURAGE TO TRANSCEND THE PAIN OF DIVORCE

When you got married, you and your mate gave your word to honour each other for better or for worse, forever. If you are now facing a divorce, you are breaking your vow, but you must still honour the "for worse" part of that promise, if only for your own sake. Your thoughts, your words, and the actions you take at this time will direct your way into your future. Remember, your thoughts create your destiny. If your thoughts and words are full of hate, anger, and rage, then those emotions will direct your actions, and they will be actions of poverty. No matter how hateful and angry you feel right now—and, by the way, hate and anger may be perfectly appropriate emotions for you to feel, depending on your situation— I ask you to recognise the power of your anger to impair your judgment, to negate the good in your past, to set the tone of your future. If, on the other hand, you can carefully and deliberately draw on your courage, faith, and grace during this time, you will be drawing on qualities of richness and taking those qualities with you into tomorrow. Dissolving a union can be one of the most painful experiences in life, and though it may seem hard to believe when you are in the throes of it, you will be much better off in the end if you do everything you can not to make the situation any worse than it already is. Whether you are the one who is being left or the one who is leaving, the way in which you behave during this period will live on with you, long after the pain of the divorce has faded.

This realisation surprised me, and it may sound shocking to you, but after working with many clients who've experienced divorce or the death of a spouse, I have come to believe that a death—whether forseeable or unexpected—is almost easier to cope with, over the long term. With death, there is no blame. Everybody loses with a death. A life is gone. The community surrounds you in mourning, and friends and relatives check in often to see how you are. If you have children, they draw closer to you. There is no ambiguity. The house is yours to sell or keep as you see fit, the car is yours, the superannuation fund, the life insurance policy, the possessions all are yours—everything that was "ours" is now yours. When you lose someone you love, the loss is great, to be sure. But you never lose the love. The love remains pure.

In a divorce, however, everything is different. If you are the bereaved party in the event of a divorce, you may be faced with a partner who is living a perfectly happy life with someone else. You may feel that for all you gave to the relationship, you got little back. Perhaps you are making do with less, while your partner is living on more. If you have children, your partner may take them away from you one night a week and every other weekend, and show them a great time. The children themselves are likely to be confused and angry. As for the community, not everyone is rallying around you unconditionally, the way they would have if your spouse had died; no one's dropping off supper for you. Rather, some of your friends aren't feeling very comfortable around you, and some of them are taking his side, thus compounding your loss. To rebuild your life from this point of disequilibrium will take great courage, and I want you to start, for your own sake, from the highest place you can.

CHARACTER LINES

I want you to think about this: Every action you take today will have an effect on your tomorrow. Actions become etched in our character, in our soul, whether they're actions based on anger, hatred, and rage, or when— despite the anger, hatred, and rage—we consciously and deliberately and purposefully "act" (and it may be the acting job of your life) from a higher place. Have you ever run into an acquaintance or friend you knew way back when, someone you haven't seen in a long time, and thought to yourself, My God, how old this person looks. I wonder what's happened in his life?

What you're seeing may be determined in part by genetics, but you're also seeing the outward manifestation of all the emotions that your friend has felt and expressed. You're seeing the external effects of his impure thoughts, his impure words, and especially his impure actions. You're seeing whether he's been mean in the past, and whether he is bitter today. You're seeing his character etched in the lines of his face. Maybe your friend has money, maybe not, but the life he's leading is anything but rich.

ACTING FROM CLARITY

There are many things you must do financially and legally to effect a divorce, but also things you must do emotionally—again, for your own good—to make sure that those financial and legal actions originate from a place of clarity, not a place of vengeance. Listen carefully to the language of breakup and divorce:

"I've never been so angry."

Acting from anger not only threatens to hamper your good judgment when it comes to making vital decisions, it can also increase your solicitors' fees. Working with clients going through divorces, I have noticed a direct correlation between the amount of the bills and the amount of anger the person has. What usually happens is that those who angrily refuse to settle end up in court, and end up paying a lot more. Ironically, those who go to court haven't a clue as to how their case will end up, because through the lens of their self-righteous anger, they can see only one side—theirs. If the court's decision is at odds with their expectations, they get angrier still. Even if they "win", there is no guarantee that their anger will subside, for what often happens is that a disgruntled ex-spouse may refuse to comply with the court order, and then the anger escalates to a whole new level. Please don't allow your anger today to cast a dark shadow upon your tomorrow.

On the other hand, if your estranged spouse is being unreasonable and there's no amicable way through the impasse, do not be afraid to go to court to have the judge determine the final accounting, pay off the debts, divide any remaining assets, and settle issues of child and spousal support, solicitors' fees, and so on.

"I don't care what happens."

So many times I hear these words from my clients: "I don't care what happens. I just want to get on with my life."

Remember that words are very powerful and that when you say you don't care what happens you are in effect creating a situation that almost surely will prevent you from getting on with your life in a rich, productive way. You may spend many more years divorced from your spouse than married to him or her; therefore the decisions you make during this crucial time will affect you for many years to come. Do not take this casually. Divorce is as serious a commitment to the future as marriage was. You must be involved in every decision, you must give a damn, for it is your life. Take control, cut through your numbness, and summon words of wealth: "I want to get on with my life, but I care deeply about what happens now, because what happens now will affect me and possibly my children forever." Say the words to your solicitor, to your ex, and say them with grace until they become true. They are words that others will respect, will help make the sentiment true, will help you to care, and will help assure for you a richer tomorrow.

"I don't care about the money. I just want him [or her] back."

So many times when divorce is imminent, the person being left refuses to face up to what is happening. She ends up thinking thoughts such as, "I can get him back if I do whatever he wants." When you give up your rights to money and make it seem so totally unimportant, you are not one iota likelier to save your marriage. All you are likely to do with this kind of thinking is impoverish your future. Logic like this will rob you of what little power you have left. Remember: Respect and power attract money; disrespect and powerlessness repel it. With thoughts and words like the ones above, you are about to serve yourself a double whammy. Not only will you start to repel money, money that is rightfully yours, but the person you are trying to bring closer will be repelled, too, by your lack of self-respect and your powerlessness. No one is attracted to weakness. Maybe you can put your marriage back together, maybe not. But please don't predicate your financial actions (or, for that matter, emotional actions) on a tenuous possibility.

"I know we're going to get back together."

Unfortunately, you don't. No matter how much you may want to get back together, there is no guarantee you will, and possibly little reason for hope. If you go into denial now, or let hope overshadow all reason, you may be setting yourself up for an emotional and a financial letdown. If your partner wants out, you have little choice but to believe it and to do everything necessary to protect yourself. Preventive action on your part will have absolutely no effect on a possible reconciliation, I can promise you that. If anything, should the possibility arise, your actions now—strong, powerful, clear, graceful, and, yes, rich—will better the chances for a reconciliation.

"I'll never get through this."

Watch your words. You will get through this, just as you got through other difficult times in your life. How you get through this, however, will largely be determined by whether you can reach for your courage, or whether you turn away from it toward your pain. During this transition period, you are going to have to make quite a few decisions, and it is vital that when you do so, your mind and body are as strong as possible. Act with strength, which itself will create strength. Eat well, exercise, allow yourself plenty of sleep. Even if the motions feel hollow, the actions are powerful, and powerful actions will nourish your courage.

"I hate the person who came between us."

Of course you do, if you're being left for someone else, even given the probable truth that the person who came between you didn't come un-invited. Nevertheless, if all your energies are devoted to hate, you will have little left for more constructive pursuits. If you think about this hate all the time, then you'll talk about it, and act on it, and you will be building a hateful, vengeful foundation on which to live the rest of your life. Try to pull away from the hate as much as you can, and instead expend your energies on caring for yourself.

"I'm going to take him [or her] to the cleaners."

Interesting expression, because it suggests he (or she) emerges clean, and where does that leave you? Dirty? Banish this thought, if only for the simple reason that the law won't let you impoverish your spouse. There's room to manoeuvre in some divorce cases, it's true, particularly when there's a lot of money involved, but the law (or at least the spirit of the law) has been created to protect you both. If your thoughts originate from a higher place—I am concerned only with getting what's fair; I want only what is rightfully mine; I do not have to settle—then you are starting with thoughts of power.

"I don't want anything. He [or she] can have it all."

Don't be a martyr. You were half of this marriage. You are entitled to half, you deserve half, and if you push away this money now, how are you going to learn to draw money toward you later on? Please let the laws and the spirit of marriage give you what is rightfully yours. Better yet, insist on it—with your solicitor, with your spouse.

"I'm not worried about the money. I know he [or she] will be fair."

When it comes to dividing up assets—which means giving up money—people behave very strangely, and a person you once thought the most generous in the world might seem to have been transformed overnight into someone entirely different. The person who must protect, nurture, and look after you now is you. Maybe you're right. Maybe he (or she) will be fair and decent all the way through, and I hope so. But protecting your own interests will not get in the way of your partner's decency.

"Not today."

Powerful words indeed. During the first years, your emotions are going to go up, down, and all over the place. One day you will feel great and the next you will be wretched. On the days that the blues hit you big-time, take a break. Do not make decisions on those days.

For the first six months, I always had my clients rate themselves on a scale of one to ten twice a day—when they get up and about eight hours later—a one rating being extremely happy and ten being miserable. If ever they felt they were a five or more, then they were not allowed to make any decisions regarding their money or divorce on that day. If asked to, they were simply to say, "Not today, thank you", let it go at that, and address the matter when they felt better. Check yourself twice a day, because sometimes a phone call, a song on the radio, a comment from a friend, or even two people walking down the street holding hands can set off a chain of emotions changing a one to an eight before you know what hit you. "Not today, thank you" is an expression of self-respect, coming from a position of power.

THE ONE WHO LEAVES
AND THE ONE LEFT BEHIND

This is not a contest to see who can get through this divorce with the fewest breakdowns. If you are the one who has been left, do not be surprised if your spouse seems to be doing much better than you are. Please remember that the chances are good that he or she has been thinking about this for a long time, long enough that the shock at the idea has worn off, whereas for you, the shock is brand-new and devastating.

Your job now is to rebuild your life and act in your best interests. Do not get pushed into doing anything during this time. Start doing your daily ratings immediately and take action only when you are ready. You have the power to set the pace of the divorce. You have the power, too, to drag it out, but that won't help you. Use your power to proceed, but only as you are ready to.

If you're the one leaving, your responsibilities are immense. Regardless of your feelings today, you have most likely just delivered a terrible blow to the person who was once the love of your life. For your own benefit, as well as your spouse's, proceed slowly and with compassion. Your marriage failed. Now it is your responsibility to conclude it as successfully as possible. How you end something as profound and important as a marriage is a reflection of how you live your life—financially, emotionally, and spiritually.

SEEKING HELP

No one can go through a divorce alone, even with the help from the guidelines offered here, and there is support available. The Family Court can assist you even before you start legal proceedings. To begin, you can attend a free information session. These sessions are conducted by a registrar or court counsellor. These groups are small and will tell you about the services provided by the court and how it works. If the divorce is relatively amicable, you may be able to settle the issues at stake with a mediator—or a mediator may provide a starting point. If the divorce is straightforward and you mutually agree on the division of your assets you can opt for a "do-it-yourself divorce"; these now account for 30 percent of all decrees granted. The Family Court staff can assist you with completing these documents but cannot offer legal advice. You can get help from legal advice services, community legal centres and citizens' advice bureaus. Otherwise you will need a solicitor, and the more you know about your situation, the easier (and cheaper) it will be to work with your solicitor. With respect to your solicitor, however, remember that he or she is there to represent you legally—not emotionally. However compassionate the solicitor may be, seek your emotional support elsewhere.

I urge you to seek therapy or counselling if you can possibly afford it and/or to consult with a member of the clergy. It is one thing to receive emotional support from family and friends, who will probably provide you with all the sympathy you need. But if you constantly let them see you at your very lowest point, it will be harder for you to restore the equilibrium of your relationships later, when you feel stronger. They may simply go on seeing you as a victim, and treating you like one, which would make it all too easy for you to continue acting like a victim. Plus, what if you need more than sympathy? A professional counsellor's impartiality may help make you stronger, both in the short and long term. If there are children involved, a counsellor may also help you in dealing with their pain and deciding whether they, too, need professional help.

DON'T FIGHT OVER THE ORANGE TOWELS: AN OVERVIEW

In the suite next to my office is a solicitor who deals with family issues and divorce, and her rule-of-thumb advice is to choose your battles carefully. If there is a lot of property to be divided, concede gracefully on the smaller stuff and you'll be on higher ground when it comes to the items that really matter.

In general, the Family Court is in place to see to the division of property and debts and to settle issues of spousal support, child support, custody, and visitation. The following are some of the points the courts ultimately consider:

+ The duration of the marriage.
+ The earning power of each party. How well is each of you equipped to maintain your present standard of living?
+ The marketable skills of the party seeking support; how long the party who has been supported until now has stayed at home; whether children will make it harder for the party seeking support to find work; what would be involved (time and expenses) to educate or retrain the stay-at-home partner for the current job market. The court's goal is that the party seeking support will eventually be able to support him- or herself.
+ The means of the partner who is being asked for support.
+ Child support and custody arrangements. In determining child support, the courts often look to the percentage of time the child or children spend with each parent and the respective incomes of both parents.
+ Age, health, and extenuating circumstances, such as whether you're caring for an invalid child or parent.

PENSION PLANS, SUPERANNUATION FUNDS AND STOCK OPTIONS

I learned firsthand how important setting the separation date can be when the husband of a very good friend of mine came home and announced, apparently out of the clear blue sky, that he wanted a divorce.

He asked her to move out as soon as possible. I couldn't figure out what happened, and why it was all so sudden and urgent. A few days later, as my friend was preparing to move, I happened to read in the paper that the company her husband was working for had just been bought out, and in two months all the employees were going to receive stock options and a generous pension plan. My friend's husband knew that if this took place after he and his wife were officially separated, there was a good chance that he wouldn't have to share that windfall with her. It was a tense two months, but she waited them out before she made her move.

Make sure you know how your and/or your spouse's superannuation plan works. When are the valuations of it made? If a pension plan is involved, consult a solicitor before making any move and obtain a copy of the benefit schedule for both your and your spouse's superannuation plans.

THE HOUSE

The hardest decision most divorcing couples face is who gets to keep or stay in the home that the two of you built. It is hard to give up not only a person but also the space that you felt safe and probably happy in for a long time. Who keeps the house and who moves out is a fuzzy legal area, in that the law does not mandate who must move out. Of course, when there are children involved, it's another story. The primary caretaker usually stays in the house with the children. If you want to be the primary caretaker, please see a solicitor before you do anything. If you've moved out, and there's a subsequent custody battle, many judges lean favourably toward keeping the situation as it is rather than disrupting the children's lives yet again. If there's any physical threat to the children, then you would have to seek a restraining order from the court that would prevent your spouse from staying in the house. Other than that, though, the decision will most likely be made between the two of you, or with the aid of legal counsel or a mediator.

With respect to the division of the value of the house, this is set on the date of property settlement, not the separation date. In other words, let's say you decide that the marriage is over, and you separate and move out. Two years later, the property settlement is final. If the value of the house has increased over those two years, you will get to participate in that increase in value.

If you are unmarried, the house issues will be resolved according to the property laws of your state. In most states this means that neither one of you has the right to buy out the other one; if you can't make a deal amicably, the court will sell the house and divide the proceeds. These are usually divided equally unless one of the partners can prove an agreement to the contrary. For these reasons, working out an amicable settlement in which one party buys out the other or they sell the place jointly is always the best solution.

DEBT

Make sure all joint accounts are closed or divided when you separate. Make sure, too, that you divide all debts and know who is responsible for each one. Before doing so, set up an account in your name and make sure that you qualify for credit, since sometimes your individual credit rating can be affected if you close out an account.

Contact all professionals and service providers (doctors, lawyers, dentists, etc.) and inform them in writing that if any work is being done for your spouse, you will not be responsible for the bills. Even if all these precautions are taken, it's still possible that creditors might come after you seeking payment for bills your spouse incurred. Thus the more accounts you can close, the better off you are.

CUTTING TIES

The hardest part of divorce, for many people, is money. People can move away from each other and start new lives, but often they seem unable to cut the financial ties quite as cleanly. Sometimes letting go of jointly managed money seems like the ultimate move, and they're not ready to do that yet. In other cases, guilt keeps the money together. Or the person who has always handled the money keeps handling it because it's familiar and easy, or because both parties are simply too lazy to separate the funds. Whatever the reason, it is wrong to remain financially intimate after you have severed domestic and emotional ties.

I have seen it time and time again: Apart from child support when someone continues to foot the bills after a separation, resentment builds up on one side and, on the other, there is an unhealthy dependence. At issue may be the house payment, let's say, until the ex-spouse can find him- or herself a new place to live, or a car payment. Whatever the case, power and respect are going out the window on both ends.

If you decide to pay for items for your spouse after you have separated, it is very important that a start date and a stop date are delineated. Set a time limit. The particulars of any financial arrangement between the two of you should be put in writing so that there is no misunderstanding. Remember, when one person is in shock—most likely the person who is being left—he or she is not going to hear things accurately or remember things clearly. Do not set yourselves up for additional misunderstandings. With your solicitors' help, put your temporary agreement in writing, both of you sign it, and both of you keep a copy.

TENDING TO MONEY ISSUES IMMEDIATELY

Once a separation seems inevitable, you must turn your attention to money issues as quickly as possible. If you prolong these actions, you may one day find that you are responsible for credit card debt that was incurred after you moved out, or that one of your joint accounts has been wiped clean of all its assets, or that the home equity account that was there in case of emergencies now has a loan against it for twenty thousand dollars, for which you are responsible. Do not be afraid to separate your accounts immediately. If you should end up getting back together, you can always open these accounts again.

FINANCIAL CHECKLIST

What follows is an overview of everything that should be done immediately when it becomes clear that a separation is imminent:

- Consult with a solicitor regarding divorce laws in your particular state.
- If you don't already have one, open up an account in your name only.

- Close all joint accounts. Don't freeze accounts, because one or both of you may need access to the funds for any number of reasons. With your solicitors' approval, split the money from joint accounts equally.

- Make copies of all the financial documents that show your true debts, assets, and expenses, including household and credit card bills, bank records, expenses for the children—every cent you spend to live month to month.

- Start keeping track of all debts incurred and money paid to each other after the date of separation. This includes money spent on joint bills, improvements to the home, moving expenses, children, insurance premiums—everything that could pertain to the two of you. If you decide to pay support to your spouse while you are working things out, make sure that all these sums are documented and that you have an agreement in writing as to what these funds are for.

- Sit down and really figure out what you are worth as a couple. First determine the worth of everything you own together—household furnishings, real estate, cars, everything. You can do this by hiring appraisers or by getting estimates from real estate agents. It is essential, too, that if you have investments you work with a tax specialist who can inform you of the tax consequences of every move you make.

- Gather documentation about all your assets—any investments, superannuation, bonds, managed funds, savings or cash management trusts, etc. In addition, a tricky and relatively new area is that of stock options, which are given to employees at great discounts but may not be exercised until years later. If your spouse has any stock options, you must see a solicitor at once, as they may be considered a joint asset when it is able to be exercised, however many years down the road.

- After you determine what you have in assets as well as your expenses and income, try to sit down with your spouse and see if you can work out something that is equitable. Don't do this before you have all your documentation, however, because you can't negotiate without the facts, and don't agree to anything without consulting a solicitor.

LEGAL SEQUENCE

- Know your legal rights and responsibilities either by doing research at your local library or bookstore or by consulting a solicitor.

- Now this is where courage really comes in, because this is the point at which you truly separate—which is to say, make the separation legal, the requirements for which differ from state to state. During the separation, one of you will file *for divorce*, and this will start the formal divorce proceedings.

- One of you may need to file a *request for child and spousal support,* and for anything else that may apply to your situation. The Child Support Agency both assesses and collects child support. In most cases these payments are deducted from the non-custodial parent's wage by their employer, and sent to the Child Support Agency who then deposits these payments into the custodial parent's bank account. Self-employed people make their payments directly to the Child Support Agency. You can also make your own agreement, and put it in writing, as to how much will be paid and how often. Instead of paying a lump sum your spouse can agree to pay your rent or mortgage payments or school fees, for instance. This agreement can be registered with the Child Support Agency who will enforce it on your behalf. Spousal support is not an automatic right. If your spouse does not agree to pay this support, you can apply to the Family Court for a maintenance order. These orders are usually for a limited period, until the final property settlement has been granted. You may also find that, if you have custody of the children, you are entitled to a Sole Parent's pension. Your local Centrelink office can tell you if you are eligible.

- Once all this is done, it's time to negotiate the settlement. If the marriage has been very short, without children, and there are negligible assets (or debts) to divide, you can apply for a divorce using a "do-it-yourself" kit, or employ a solicitor to file on your behalf. If your case is amicable and relatively uncomplicated, look into settling it in the easiest and least expensive way possible.

- If the way in which the property will be divided is clear-cut to you both, you are in full agreement about custody arrangements, and you are certain to behave like adults, then a *mediator*—a negotiator who acts impartially, with no allegiance to either party—may be all you need to propose a marital settlement for the solicitors to draft.

- In cases where custody arrangements or property division are complicated, or when emotions are running high, you each will need a solicitor—and possibly even a *judge.* The solicitor's role is to represent your interests, suggest appropriate settlement terms, convey settlement offers, advise you as to what the court is likely to do in your situation, and help with the division of property and debts. The solicitor, in other words, will fight your battles for you and insulate you from your estranged spouse.

- You do not need to wait for property settlement to be concluded to be granted a divorce. A decree nisi is granted when arrangements have been accepted by the court for the welfare and care of children under 18. A decree absolute (the final order) is granted one month later.

- Once the terms have been settled on—who gets what and when—either by the two of you or with a court order, a property settlement can be concluded. If you cannot come to an agreement, you will end up settling your dispute in court.

BEWARE THE BUYOUT

In some instances, the spouse who is required to pay spousal support may instead offer you a one-time, lump-sum offer of *settlement,* which in effect is a "buyout" of any future obligations, excluding child support. Emotionally, a once-and-for-all settlement can be a clean break. Financially, however, a settlement is a gamble, because the spouse required to pay is using today's dollars to settle what might be a significantly higher amount tomorrow. If you are considering a settlement, consider all the factors, not just by today's standards but also by tomorrow's.

COURT: THE LAST RESORT

The court system, when it comes to divorce, is set up to make sure that the division of property is handled fairly and to ensure the welfare of any children involved. When you go to court, the outcome is solely in the hands of the judge. This means that you are putting the fate of your future, your home, your children, and retirement plans in the hands of a stranger. If you can somehow try to work it out between yourselves and reach a clear resolution, you may be better off. If, however, you cannot resolve your differences, then don't be afraid to put the matter in the hands of the court.

Even if you are committed to taking your spouse to court, an out-of-court settlement may be reached days or perhaps minutes before the case is to begin—and this is the time when big mistakes are often made. Many divorces are settled out of court, no matter how hellbent both parties are on having a judge hear their case. Imagine this scenario. You are about to go into the courtroom, nervous and high-strung as can be, probably shooting daggers at your ex from a few feet away, and vice versa. Your lawyer, who has been talking in hushed tones to the lawyer representing your ex, approaches you and says your ex is willing to settle the case right now if you give in on these few points, but the decision has got to be made right away, because once the proceedings begin it is too late. You agree and instantly feel a wave of relief . . . until two months down the road, when you realise that you may have made a mistake. Do not make decisions that will affect the rest of your life when you feel pressured. If you have come all this way, unless you know the precise ramifications of everything you may be agreeing to, do not accept a last-minute settlement.

FREE AGAIN

You are single again. Now you need to make sure that all your documents—the deed to your house, the title to your car or boat, your will or trust, insurance policies, every investment or asset that was previously held jointly—reflect your new status. Please don't let this paperwork slide, for financial decisiveness will help the healing, the closure, and make you feel stronger for having put your financial past behind you. With this financial clutter behind you, you'll be freer to put your energies into starting over.

THE COURAGE TO LIVE AFTER A DEATH

To have someone you love taken from you forever creates a pain so deep that there is little anyone can say or do to help. Hard as it is to believe in the days, weeks and months after a death, healing is a function of faith, courage and time. Having faced the financial aftermath of death many times with my clients, I have come to believe that we never quite know the meaning of life until we draw close to death. Often only then do we seem to learn what has true meaning and what does not. Everything is put into perspective, and in our grief, most of us put thoughts of money at the bottom of our list of priorities. Which can be a terrible mistake. The death of a partner is an event that forces us not only to deal with a new emotional reality but also to accept a new financial reality.

SUZE AND KATIE'S STORY

I was sitting at my desk in the bullpen area with the other brokers at Merrill Lynch, waiting for a new client. I was nervous, I remember, because I was still new to the business and didn't yet have many clients, and the man I was expecting, whose name was Allen, had a substantial sum of money to invest. The receptionist called when he arrived, and I went out to greet him. As I approached the reception area, I saw a burly man of about fifty-five with a kind face. I introduced myself, and he reached out to shake my hand. He asked if he could possibly have a glass of water, and I told him I would get it for him and be right back. As I was walking away he said, "By the way, what time is it?" I looked at my watch and said, "Five after one." I was gone only a few minutes, and when I returned with the water, he was resting in the chair with his eyes closed. "Here is your water," I said, but he didn't reply. In a louder voice I said, "Excuse me, Allen. I've got your water," but again he did not respond. I shook his shoulder, and with that he fell forward onto the floor. I realised that he must have had a heart attack and screamed for help. The receptionist frantically called an ambulance, and in seconds, another broker who was trained in CPR started administering mouth-to-mouth resuscitation. The paramedics arrived, huddled over Allen, then looked up and said that they were sorry, but he was gone. I remember thinking, *Gone where?* I couldn't comprehend what they meant with him lying right there in front of me. His last words had been a question: "What time is it?" Did he somehow know that this was his last moment on earth and want to know the hour of his death? Deeply shaken, with the fact of this stranger's death coursing through me strong as life, I knew all I could do was go home.

About a month later, Allen's widow, Katie, came to see me to ask me what had happened. She wanted me to recount the last minutes of her husband's life. Which I did over and over again. It was as if she wanted to prolong those final moments forever. Clearly, she was having a hard time coming to terms with his death and with the fact that she was supposed to carry on alone. Alone not only emotionally but financially as well. I asked her if she knew anything about money. She said no. All she knew was that they had a savings account at the local bank that she had been using to get her money, but there was not a lot left in there. She knew, too, that Allen had had a life insurance policy, but she had not looked into that yet. She was hoping that since Allen had come to see me, I could tell her more about their finances. But now she learned that he had never even had the chance to do that. She didn't know what she was going to do, and she asked if I could help her.

This was one of the most heartbreaking days of my professional life,

for there really was very little that I could do. I felt so powerless. I remem-
ber thinking that now was not the time that this woman should have to
learn about money. She could barely deal with her grief as it was, let alone
take on a task that to her was absolutely intimidating and terrifying. I felt
a helpless anger rising up at the man she called her husband. I wondered,
If he could see her, would he see not only her hurt but also her confusion?
Would he realise that it didn't have to be this way? I knew that she was not
totally without blame herself, that she could have asked to learn about
their finances, forced the issue, but how many of us voluntarily do any-
thing that scares and intimidates us? And there is nothing so formidable
to most of us as death and money.

I am sorry to say that this was not the last time that I encountered someone in precisely this situation. Over the years I have been called upon
many times to pick up the financial pieces scattered after a death. Some
people were lucky; when their spouses or life partners died, they had a
friend or someone they could trust to help them on their new financial
course. But many bereaved souls had sought the advice of a so-called professional when they were most vulnerable and ended up losing everything, or nearly so. By the time they found their way to me, many people
had already handed over their life insurance proceeds, portfolios, their
futures to con artists posing as concerned professionals or to commission-
hungry salespeople. It is hard enough to have the courage to go on living
after you have lost your emotional equilibrium, but it is almost impossible
when you have also lost your financial stability. Hard as it may seem to you
now, in the early stages of your grief, I ask you please to keep your financial realities in mind as you come to terms with the death of your loved
one. The actions you take at this time will have important effects later,
when the death and your grief are not so new and raw.

IF I SHOULD DIE BEFORE
I WAKE . . .

The death part of life's equation cannot ultimately be prevented, but we
most certainly can prevent the financial confusion, and at least some of
the emotional uncertainty, that so many of us seem to face when death is
introduced into our life.

I strongly believe that in order to assure yourself a smooth passage through this lifetime, you must, out of respect for yourself and your loved ones, plan carefully for your death as early and as thoroughly as you can. Whether there is very little money at stake, or a lot, those who survive your death deserve to grieve without the further burdens of fear and confusion about what will happen to them after you are gone.

In my earlier books, *You've Earned It, Don't Lose It* and *The 9 Steps to Financial Freedom,* I wrote about estate planning—everything you need to know about wills and trusts, protecting your assets, and protecting your heirs. Please take the necessary measures to see that your loved ones are provided for in the most caring (and financially efficient) way you can, and please do it now.

I beg you, too, not to wait to learn about your finances. Discuss with your spouse or partner everything you need to know about your estate—including insurance, the children's best interests, the location of all documents, and a list of whom to notify. I urge you to make your preferences clear—whether you wish to be buried or cremated, where you would like your remains to rest, what kind of service or ceremony you would like to have. It is so overwhelming when someone dies that having some of the details worked out and a sense of purpose for those first painful days will provide some relief.

AFTER A DEATH

The shock of losing someone you love is devastating and paralysing—you must take care of the business of death, which at the time can seem as complicated as the business of life. Here is a checklist of matters that will require your immediate attention, whether you feel like attending to them or not. If you have a friend or a relative who can help you, please ask for help. Even though you may think you are aware and totally capable, you are most likely, whether you know it or not, in shock. Your numbness may prevent you from collapsing under the intensity of your pain—but it also can impair your ability to make the best and most appropriate decisions.

The first job that you will be faced with will be making proper arrangements for the burial or cremation of your loved one.

Before you do anything else, if you are not sure of his or her wishes, please check to see if there is an organ donor card on the back of his or her driver's licence. If there is, please contact the nearest hospital authorities so that these wishes can be carried out. Now you must contend with the remains, surely one of the most painful tasks, but I want you to take care and pay attention, for these first moves can become emotionally and financially costly if you or someone close to you is not vigilant and well informed.

+ If the death took place in a hospital, you will be asked the name of the funeral home that you would like them to call. They will do so and take care of transporting the remains to the home.
+ If the death took place at your home or anywhere other than a hospital, then you will have to contact the funeral home or cremation society of your choice, which will then make arrangements to transport the remains.
+ If you want the burial or cremation to take place in a different state from the one in which your loved one has died, again, either you or the hospital will place the call to the out-of-state funeral home or cremation society you want to use, and the funeral home will take care of the transportation arrangements for you.
+ If you don't know which funeral home you want to use, ask your friends, your clergyman, or an administrator at your local place of worship for a recommendation. Most churches or synagogues will have a list of funeral homes for you to call. If you do not have this outlet, and none of your friends can make a recommendation, call your local hospital for assistance.

THE COSTS AND THE DANGERS

When you are trying to live through a loss of great magnitude, it is all too easy to lose touch with reality—the reality of life and the reality of money. Especially money, since money seems so irrelevant in those first few days after a death. Nevertheless, there are costs of death that are unavoidable. Beyond the funeral and during your period of mourning, how are you going to pay for the everyday expenses that will continue to come your way? So often we find that every penny we have is in a superannuation fund, in a life insurance policy, or locked up in equity in our home, where we can't readily get to it. We are left with very little cash to draw upon. If you haven't before, you will now have to try to estimate your monthly expenses and take that figure into consideration before you make any choices regarding funeral and burial services. For instance, let's say you have $8000 in a savings account and your monthly expenses total $3000. If you spend $8000 on the funeral, you'll be unable to pay your bills.

Even if you have a life insurance policy, the insurance company may not release the funds for many months. This is particularly the case if the cause of death is unclear or appears to be a suicide. I have a friend whose brother died in a car-racing accident. It just so happened that he had raised his life insurance policy from $50,000 to $250,000 the month before his accident. Because of the timing, the insurance company did not release the insurance proceeds until they had thoroughly investigated the possibility of a suicide. In the intervening months, his widow was left in terrible financial straits.

In other words, before you start spending what you have, it is essential that you have a clear picture of what you are going to need to get by for the next few months, and where that money is going to come from. My advice, as always, is to have an understanding of your finances long before you find yourself in a tragic situation.

THE CEMETERY PLOT

Unless you have planned for this ahead of time, the funeral home or cremation society also will discuss with you whether you need a burial plot, and can assist you in making the arrangements to purchase one.

PLANNING THE SERVICE

When it comes to planning the service, carefully consider your options. You needn't try to prove your love by choosing the most expensive options available. Dignity, remember, costs not a penny. If you know what kind of service your partner would have wanted, so much the better. One often hears of people who choose the music they'd like to have played at their funeral services, and the survivors cherish that music forever. If you don't know of any clear preference, your options are many. The service can be held at the funeral home or a place of worship. The burial can be public or private, or you can hold a private burial at once and a memorial service later on.

Again—a lot of choices. But so often, a "nothing but the best" attitude prevails, where "best" translates to most expensive. There is nothing honourable in a send-off you can't afford, so I ask you please to aim for restraint. Public and private good-byes can be dignified, holy and simple at the same time.

KNOW YOUR RIGHTS

To make sure that you are not taken advantage of during this time, the AFDA (Australian Funeral Directors Association) has established a code of ethics which states that a funeral home must provide you with a full disclosure in writing of its practices, services and fees. This includes: the cost of caskets, obituary notices placed in newspapers, and embalming; any payments made on your behalf for flowers, funeral escorts, honorarium to clergy, limousines, copies of the death certificate, memorial cards, and musicians' fees; and any additional service fee that the funeral home may charge you. If you wish, you can obtain this list from a number of funeral homes so that you can compare costs. If you are not happy with the funeral arrangements for any reason, please talk to the funeral director first and, if the problem is still not resolved to your satisfaction, contact the association.

VETERAN'S BURIAL

If your partner or loved one was a veteran, you may investigate whether he or she is eligible for a payment of $500 towards funeral expenses.

To be eligible for this payment, the veteran must have met one of the following criteria:

+ Died in a hospital where the medical expenses were being paid by Veterans' Affairs
+ Be in needy circumstances, that is, defined as having only $5000 in assets after funeral expenses are paid
+ Be totally and permanently disabled

- Be a double amputee or blind
- Be an ex-prisoner of war.

CAUTION

Because obituary notices tell the time and date of most funerals, they make your home a target for burglars. As sad as this may seem, please have someone stay in the house during the service to make sure that you do not come home to yet another loss.

THE BILLS GO ON

I would also suggest you ask whomever you have chosen to help with the arrangements to collect your mail for the next few weeks and to keep it all in one place. It would also be helpful if he or she could see if there are any bills that need to be paid immediately and keep track of when the rest of the bills come due. If you are corresponding through the mail with respect to any financial matters related to the estate, please make sure that copies are made of any outgoing mail. It is always important to be able to document everything that you said or that someone said on your behalf during a time of sorrow. Later you may remember these early days only as a blur of pain and confusion.

CALL A SOLICITOR

The way your spouse has set up his or her estate will determine the extent to which you will need a solicitor to help you get on with your life. If everything the two of you owned was in Joint Tenancy, and you are the sole beneficiary of the life insurance proceeds, or superannuation funds, or if everything was held in a trust for your benefit, then settling the estate will be quite easy. Once the appropriate places are presented with a certified copy of the death certificate and whatever other papers those particular institutions may want to see, everything will simply switch over to your name. If, on the other hand, your partner had many separate accounts, had only a will, had the house title in his or her name only (even if the intent was that it should pass on to you)—if, in other words, the paperwork of death is in chaos, then the process will be a longer one. Either way, you should contact a solicitor within the first few days. If you do not have a solicitor already, please find one who specialises in estate planning to make sure that everything is in order or to help you organise what must be done.

Whether you have a solicitor or not, there are many ways to save yourself some money, because there are certain things that will need to be done that you could do by yourself or with the help of a friend. For example, a friend could call the insurance companies and the bank or brokerage firms to find out what paperwork needs to be done to report the death. The most important part of your immediate job will be helping to locate and describe all of your loved one's assets and liabilities—debts, outstanding loans, everything your loved one owed to the world.

THE "LEGALESE" OF DEATH

- *Executor:* The man or woman the deceased has designated to carry out the terms of the will.
- *Co-executors:* The people (more than one) who are designated to carry out the terms of the will.
- *Administrator:* The title of the person whom the court assigns to oversee your estate or your spouse's estate if there is no will.
- *Trustee:* If the estate is held in trust, then this is the person who is responsible for carrying out the terms of the trust.

FINANCIAL CHECKLIST: SPOUSE

The duties that a spouse or life partner must carry out vary from that of the executor, etc. Below is a list of what you must do as a life partner, spouse, or next of kin, whether or not you are also the executor.

- Order at least 15 certified copies of the death certificate. You will need these in order to collect insurance proceeds and to change names on bank accounts, deeds and other assets. Please do this right away. The funeral home usually will get the number of certified death certificates you request. Otherwise, they can be obtained, for a fee, from the Registry of Births, Deaths and Marriages, where death, birth and marriage certificates are kept. It's easiest to have the funeral home handle this, and I recommend that you request them to do so immediately—you need certified copies of the death certificate for many purposes, and it will prove time-consuming to request them from the Registry later.

- If you do not already have one, please open up a bank account in your own name.
- If you do not have a credit card in your own name, you may want to wait to notify the credit card companies where you have cards listed in both of your names. It is not unheard of for credit card providers to lower your credit limit if the limit was based on the deceased's income. (It's always a good idea to have a credit card in your name alone, so that over the years, you will build up a good credit rating.)
- Do not pay off any credit card debts that were not yours before you check with your solicitor or executor. Some solicitors or advisers might advise you not to pay off most of the deceased's debts, because it's unlikely that creditors will spend the money to come after the estate to recoup small amounts of debt. I disagree with this advice, because I believe that honouring the debt, if possible, is honouring both the dead and the living. If there isn't enough money in the estate to pay off all debts, check with your solicitor before you begin paying the debts.
- Review any insurance coverage that the deceased may have had with banks or credit card companies. You may be surprised to find out that some things slipped through the communications cracks. For instance, offers for life insurance often come in the mail via a bank statement or credit card bill, at just a small cost every month. Your spouse may have impulsively signed up for such coverage. This kind of thing happens more often than you think. You may have more than you know. Call every credit card company and bank that your partner or next of kin had accounts with and ask whether there is also an insurance policy in the name of the deceased.

- Consider whether you will have enough money to live on in the coming months or will need money from the estate before it is settled (the granting of probate can take from one week to several months). If so, please go through six months of your and your late spouse's records, and estimate your monthly expenses. If there is not enough money in your existing accounts to cover your projected expenses, consider what investments you can cash in now. Most financial institutions will release funds to you when they receive a certified copy of the will, a copy of the death certificate and an indemnity signed by the beneficiaries.

- Contact your local Centrelink office to see if there are any benefits that you qualify for. You may qualify for benefits if:
  - you are 50 years of age or older.
  - you are disabled.
  - you care for a child who is under age 16 or disabled.
  - you care for an aged parent.

  If you do not fit into any of these categories, it is still a good idea to check with Centrelink as there may be other benefits, such as Newstart, that you are eligible for. Your children may also be eligible for Austudy.

- If you and your spouse both were collecting the pension or benefits you will need to advise Centrelink within 14 days. However, Centrelink pay the combined amount of both pensions for an extended period, usually fourteen weeks after the death of one spouse. There is also a lump sum payment available for funeral and other expenses, so check with your local office.

CHANGING YOUR WILL/ BENEFICIARY FORMS

Do not forget that your own will or trust should be changed now, for most likely you have left everything to the person who has just died. Make sure that you change the beneficiary designation on your superannuation, life insurance polices, and any other investment or retirement plan.

EXECUTOR DUTIES

In many cases the executor is the surviving spouse or life partner. If this is the case with you, then the following obligations also pertain. If not, then just make sure all the actions above are completed.

Please note that an executor is held personally and legally responsible for all of these actions. This is not a job that should be taken lightly. The duties of the executor primarily fall into the following categories:

+ Paying all outstanding bills, including taxes to the Australian Taxation Office (ATO)
+ Tallying and securing all assets in the estate until they are ready to be distributed among the rightful heirs
+ Supervising the settlement procedures and managing the estate during this process
+ Distributing all the assets to the designated beneficiaries at the appropriate time

LEGAL CHECKLIST: EXECUTOR

+ Your first job as executor is to locate the will or trust and all assets, including life insurance policies, retirement, bank and brokerage accounts, and stocks and bonds. If no will can be found, then call the deceased's solicitor, if there is one, to see if he or she has a copy of a will. If nothing else, a solicitor may know if one was ever written. If no will is found, the estate passes by what is known as *intestate succession,* which means that the assets in the estate will be distributed by a formula determined by law. In this case, there will be a court-appointed administrator.

  If the estate is small, less than $15,000, or if all assets are in joint names, there is no need to apply for probate. If you do need to apply for probate this is usually done by a solicitor but you can do it yourself. In either case you will need to supply your solicitor, or the Supreme Court in your state if you are applying yourself, with the following documents: the death certificate, the will, a copy of the funeral notice and a list of assets and liabilities of the deceased.

- The executor must protect the estate. This means that heirs are not allowed to remove any of the assets that have been left to them until the probate court has granted final approval for distribution.

- During the probate procedure, the executor must keep careful track of all expenses as well as income (receipts, statements, etc.) that the estate pays out and receives.

- If the surviving spouse has not already obtained certified copies of the death certificate, you should obtain at least 15 copies.

- Notify all the insurance companies of the death, including life, disability, car, and homeowner's insurance companies. Notify all the banks, brokerage firms, investment companies, super-annuation funds, and any other institution where the deceased had accounts or deeds, or even accounts that were in both spouses' names.

- Often individual bank accounts in the deceased's name will be changed first to the name of the estate. If a *joint tenancy* is involved, that money and title of the account will go directly to the surviving spouse or partner. For example, Jane and John have a bank account held in joint names. If John was to die, Jane would get the account immediately. However, if John had an account in his name alone, and John's brother was executor of John's will, the account would first be transferred to John's estate while the will was being settled, even if John left everything to Jane. The account would be transferred to Jane's name upon settlement.

- Before any accounts are closed down, please make sure that the financial needs of the surviving spouse are going to be met. It is best to clear it with the solicitor before closing down any existing accounts.

- Make a complete inventory of the safety deposit box. After probate is completed, the executor will distribute the contents according to the will.

If the estate is to be distributed through a trust, it does not have to go through probate, and the trustee named in the trust will carry out the actions designated in the trust.

DEATH'S TOLL

What lives on after you die? The legacy of your work, your kind and generous acts, and the people you love, who will suffer the emotional toll, and possibly the financial toll, of your passing for a long, long time. How can you help? The care with which you prepare for your own death is a supreme act of love toward those you will one day leave behind. It can help your survivors a great deal emotionally, for dealing with chaos after a loss makes the loss itself more painful and frightening. It can also help your survivors a great deal financially, because with careful estate planning, you may save your loved ones thousands of dollars in probate fees, and legal fees. Won't you take the actions necessary to protect the people you love, emotionally and financially? Will you please do it right away? Seeing to it that the people you love will always be safe is an expansive action, and once you've done so, you'll be the richer for it, closer to clarity, and all the more ready to receive all that you can, for the rest of your life.

CHAPTER 13

STARTING OVER

It may feel like small comfort to you now, but sooner or later every single one of us will be faced with the prospect of starting over. At a time in your life when you believe that everything is going great, something happens—a death, an illness, a breakup, a divorce—that leaves you emotionally and perhaps financially exhausted. And starting over from a place of loss is even harder than starting for the first time. When you were just starting out in your adult life, you were equipped with hope, dreams, expectations and strength. All of these are stripped from you when you're starting with feelings of loss and emptiness. Will any of us be spared the painful test of starting over, one way or another, one day or another? Unfortunately, I don't think so. This test seems to me utterly universal.

As a financial planner, I can never leave emotions out of a client's financial picture. For example, if someone is terrified of the stock market, I could never, in good conscience, put their money in the market, for it would leave them feeling powerless and afraid. If someone believed with all their heart that the only way they would feel safe was by owning an expensive life insurance policy, then I would have to take that into account as well.

I know, too, when someone comes to see me about how to start over, that I will be faced with a weak emotional pulse—and a weak financial pulse. If you are starting over, you already know that you must replenish your strength in order to go on. It is also a treacherous time financially, and you must be very, very careful with your money.

Facing the "what"s and "what-if"s of starting over requires immense courage.

What if I can't make it? I've never handled money before.
I've never had to work before. What if I can't pay my bills?
My husband left me with just a small settlement, and it's all I
*   have. What should I do with the money?*
What if the insurance money doesn't last?
What do I do now?

Even though your own questions may be different, the common denominator in these situations is fear—fear of not making it, fear of failure, fear of tomorrow—and these fears come at a time of life when you are at your most vulnerable. That's the bad news. The good news is that, even though you might not believe it, I have seen men and women in this very predicament who were ready to give up instead rise up and create for themselves, possibly for the first time, a new life they learned to love. A life they can call their own. How did they get there from here? By drawing on the faith and courage that reside in each and every one of us.

W E N D Y ' S   S T O R Y

I remember thinking at the time, If this is a test, okay, I will take it.

It started, I guess, when I was diagnosed with Lyme disease, a serious and recurrent case, which was unbelievably debilitating. My husband, Alex, and I were frightened, yes, but it didn't seem like a major thing. I could still work, we kept telling ourselves, and we'd be okay. Then Alex's factory went bankrupt. He had worked there his whole life and now, suddenly, there was no more life insurance, minimal superannuation, no holiday pay or long-service payout—his whole career erased, and our future, too. I was the office manager of a small company, but I only had a small superannuation fund. I thought it couldn't get any worse, but it did.

167

The epitome of health—active, fit, health-conscious—my husband had a heart attack five years ago. He was fifty. We had been married twenty-five years. We live in the country, and the hospital was a couple of hours away. It was a nightmare. Alex was in the hospital for almost five months, and his stay was a series of mistakes—one thing led to another, kidney failure, his lungs. I did everything I could to be there all the time, so bills—for the motel, for petrol—were piling up on my credit card. I would drive home as often as I could to take care of things at the office. I still had my job.

We thought he was going to get better, and we were really worried about the bills, the costs building up. The main thing was that I stayed with him. At the time, money wasn't even an issue. We knew we'd be okay.

Then, one afternoon when I was at work, the call came—Come to the hospital at once. I had left Alex just that morning and he had seemed fine, but by the time I got to the hospital it was too late. I could not believe it; he was not supposed to die, that was not what they said was going to happen. I didn't even get to say good-bye. I went to the hospital and then went back home in shock, all alone and devastated.

A few weeks later, the bills started pouring in, which did not make matters any better. The funeral was expensive, plus there were the credit card bills; before this happened I had never had a credit card bill I couldn't pay.

The credit card company said they could set up a payment plan, but I didn't have the money. A social worker said that I should file for bankruptcy, quit my job, and get a disability pension for the Lyme disease. But I couldn't, the thought of it horrified me; we had worked so long and hard for what we had. It would seem like cheating everyone out of what they were owed. I thought if I gave up now, I would give up on everything, that I would never have anything, and then what? I felt crazed and scared, but I was determined to make Alex proud of me. I went back to work and took on two extra bookkeeping jobs. My doctor said, You can't do this, you'll overtax yourself, don't worry, it will be okay; then he patted me on the head. I got so angry. I said, You come and live in my shoes. Don't send me home and tell me everything will be okay, because it won't unless I keep on going.

I was still working the three jobs when my parents died, within months of each other, and that was hard because we were a really, really close family. I felt utterly alone, and I was. I finally understood what was *meant by the saying that the only friend you will always have is God. I just knew I could not give up, not now. I kept up the three jobs. I paid off as much as I could, but it was never enough, and the finance charges kept building. I kept thinking, I have to get this paid, just get it all over with. Finally I went to the bank, because I decided to refinance my house, which was the last thing I wanted to do—I love it, it's over a hundred years old, and it's the only thing I have. They gave me a loan for $45,000. That helped a lot. There's one small bill I'm still paying, but they are okay about it, and now I am working only two jobs, which makes it easier. I have a little more time for myself, and I can see my friends again.*

Now that I feel I can breathe again financially, I'm beginning to think about the future, and I have started putting fifty dollars away each month, sometimes more, in a managed fund. That was a turning point. Now I feel as if there is hope again.

People keep saying how courageous I am, but I realised long ago that courage is a choice. You choose. If you keep thinking there isn't anything you can do, then there won't be, and I didn't want to get to that point. I reaffirm this thought in many different ways, many times every single day: Yes, I can; I'm so tired; No, I am not; What if I can't make my house payment; Yes, I can.

You can't replace people, bring them back, but the things you do should at least honour them and yourself. If you simply give up because you don't have the initiative, you're not honouring anyone. If only for the love of yourself, you have to do it. My husband wouldn't have wanted me to give up. You either give up or you go on. I chose to go on.

After a loss, we rejoin the world of the living.

By opening herself up, Wendy, against the greatest possible odds, is starting over. She is close to owning her house outright again, her debt is nearly gone, and she has honoured her past. She is building up her nest egg, honouring her future. Her thoughts, words and actions have begun to make her life easier, when instead, had she taken different actions, she could have been left destitute—emotionally and financially. She met her suffering with grace, clarity, and, yes, courage.

By any financial measure, Wendy is creating what she needs, and by following her course, she will have more than enough. By the measure of the soul, she has been immensely rich all along.

169

YOU FIRST

When you look back upon this time, you will see that, during the months after a loss, in many ways you were simply going through the motions of life.

I can't tell you how many times I have sat across from someone who has just suffered a loss and must start over. I would review his or her situation and say, "Okay, we have to do thus and such, and then we will do this and that and finally this." My clients would agree with me, acting as if they totally understood what I was saying, and then I would take the necessary actions based on our conversation.

What would inevitably happen is that six months to a year later, these same clients would come back and say, "Can you tell me why we did what we did with the money?" It became obvious to me that they had not heard a word I had said during the early stages of their grief. It was as if they had been present in body but not in mind. I would explain the reasons for the actions we took again, and this time, my clients would finally get it.

Many of us emerge from a divorce or a death with some assets, which we must protect, perhaps for the first time in our lives. After seeing the ways in which people tend to jeopardise these assets in their grief, their anger, their exhaustion, or their confusion, I have come up with a rule that has never once failed a client of mine:

THE ESSENTIAL LAW OF MONEY
AFTER A LOSS

Take no action with your money
other than keeping it safe and sound
for at least six months to a
year after a loss.

You have just been through a hard time, with the legalities and expenses of divorce, or the hard tasks you've had to take on after a death. You are not equipped now—emotionally or financially—to make the big decisions that have to be made about investing your money yourself or entrusting it to someone else.

If your money is in a secure place, a place that has made you feel safe and comfortable up until now, I want you to leave it there and to wait to take any action with your money until your emotional equilibrium is restored, along with your sound judgment. If you feel your money is not currently safe, make those financial changes that will get your money to a safe place and then do nothing else for the time being.

If you are not sure whether or not your money is invested safely, seek the advice of a financial adviser, one who comes highly recommended by a friend who has money under management with that person. If you have no friend who can recommend someone, what you want for now is a fee-based planner, one who does not sell products of any kind. When you go to see this adviser, you may want to take a friend or relative with you for support. The first thing you should say is, "I am not going to buy anything for at least one year; I just want to make sure that the money I have is safe and sound. I want to put any money that is not safe now into a cash management trust or term deposit and that is all. No new purchases of any kind are to be made on my behalf."

Do not let your money be a burden or cause you needless worry at this time. Live your life, nurture and replenish yourself, but when you're just starting over, leave your money alone.

This sounds like easy advice, doesn't it? Maybe. But you will have to be vigilant to adhere to it, for you will be surprised at how many people might come knocking at your door to offer to "help" you with your money.

YOUR SUDDENLY ATTENTIVE ADVISER

How many times did the adviser or broker your spouse was using to manage your joint money ever talk to you before your world fell apart?

What will happen is that a financial adviser builds a relationship with one of you. Seldom does the adviser take the time to talk to both of you equally. Understandably, it's more convenient for him or her to have a single contact. A separation or death gives an adviser the opportunity to establish a new rapport with the spouse who previously was merely a name on joint documents. Believe me, this opportunity is not lost on the adviser. Remember, this person is very aware of what is going on not only with your money but also in your personal life. If there is to be a divorce, and therefore a dividing of the assets, the adviser is going to be one of the first to know what you each will be left with. If there is a death, the total picture of your finances is right at his or her disposal. So do not be surprised if you get a cosy call from an adviser with whom you have never really had a relationship to ask you to come in and see him or her to go over what to do with the money in your portfolio. Stand back. You're not ready. Not for six months to a year.

WHEN LOYALTY IS NOT A VIRTUE

Just because your late spouse or ex-spouse was using a certain adviser does not mean that the same adviser is right for you. First you have to face this situation and know that this is your life, and everyone in it from this point on must be someone with whom you feel safe and comfortable. Ask yourself these questions:

+ Why was it that you never had a relationship with this particular person to begin with?
+ If you did have a relationship with him/her, did you like and trust the relationship?
+ Did you feel as if he/she had your best interests and concerns at heart, or just those of your spouse/partner?

Bide your time. These questions will answer themselves in due course.

ONLY THE LONELY

It's not only burglars who read the obituaries. Cold callers, hungry brokers, needy financial types all look to the papers to see if they can expand their business. A sympathetic call when you are feeling vulnerable is a self-interested call—and you are not the "self" in question here. Please say that you are grieving now and ask that callers who appear out of the blue call back in a year. They won't.

INSURANCE PROCEEDS

If you are entitled to any life insurance proceeds, regardless of the amount, take the payment in full, even if the insurance company tries to persuade you to take it in instalments, or offers to invest it or hold on to it for safekeeping. Insurance proceeds are tax-free, so you will not incur any penalties by taking them in a lump-sum payment. You may need to deposit some cash into a cheque account right away to cover immediate expenses. Then put the rest into a cash management trust or anywhere you know it will be safe. Leave the money there until you are more emotionally stable, so that you can intelligently decide what to do with it—six months to one year later. This account will also serve as a place to access funds if you need them for your living expenses.

TAKING STOCK

Over the next few months, try to make as few changes in your life as possible, but begin asking yourself some essential questions. How do you feel about where you are living? Are you frightened by the amount of money it takes just to live? Are there easy areas in which you could cut back? In time, clarity will set in, and you will know what you must do, however painful, whether it's selling the house, taking a job or a second job, or cutting back on what you can do for your children. In time, you will be able to do it.

People first, then money. When you are the one starting over, the "people" in the first law of money probably refers to you, even if you're the kind of person who is always taking care of everybody else. Let me be the one to remind you to grant yourself the time to recover, to assess this new beginning, to grasp the terms and necessities of your new life. So much of fear is simply not knowing. It's my hope that the information in this chapter diminishes some of your anxiety and encourages you to turn to the future, not with fear but with hope and courage. Take your good memories with you, and treasure your past even as you create a new tomorrow. Treasure your money, this legacy from your past, too, so that it can sustain you well in the new life I know you will create.

PART IV

BUYING
A
HOME

SEEKING SHELTER

It's the age-old dream: owning a place of one's own. For most of us, home is all-important—a place to feel safe and comfortable today, a place for security tomorrow. Large or small, new or old, one day the house we live in will be ours scot-free. Even if that "one day" is thirty years from now, the dream is well worth going after. Unfortunately, many of us pursue the dream before we're financially ready, or we chase after it in an overly ambitious way so that the house we buy ends up owning us. Others among us assume the dream is out of reach—when it may not be. If you harbour the dream of owning the perfect house, here is what you need to know in order to achieve it.

STARTING OUT

In 1973, I was living in my first grown-up home, a two-bedroom apartment I shared with a friend. We were paying $220 a month for this great place, and I loved it. It was a brown shingled house divided into two apartments, and we lived in the one on the ground floor. The dining room opened, through two big glass doors, onto a little porch not visible from the street. I used to love to lie there and soak up the sun, and I felt I could easily live in that apartment my whole life. One night, my roommate's brother came to visit, and we got to talking about a house he had bought a few years before. I thought, Wow, that must really be something, owning your own home. But thinking how expensive it must be, I didn't pay much attention, until I heard him say that his mortgage payment was only $153 a month. All of a sudden I sat up and said, "Wait a minute. Are you telling me that you own a house twice the size of this apartment and all you're paying is one hundred and fifty-three dollars a month, while we're paying two hundred and twenty dollars a month just to rent?" "Yup," he said. "And that one hundred and fifty-three dollars includes insurance and rates."

Granted, this was a long time ago, when real estate in some areas of California was acknowledged—even then—to be dirt cheap. Back then, if one had the deposit, it would have been absolutely crazy to do anything other than own a home—all the more so with the benefit of hindsight. Today, many of us still believe the conventional wisdom that was true a generation ago, that real estate is the best investment around. But the fact is, this isn't necessarily true anymore. There are important factors to consider before you even begin to look to buy. Beyond the calculations of what you can afford for a deposit and a monthly mortgage, you must take into account the recent price fluctuations of real estate in your particular area, the price of rentals, your job stability with respect to income and location, the possibility that your living-space requirements are going to grow or shrink in the near future, your physical ability to maintain a house, and the current interest rates for mortgages. All of these factors must be weighed against renting before you take a single step toward buying.

PLAYING THE REAL ESTATE MARKET

In some areas recently there has been a boom in the price of residential real estate. If this holds true in the area in which you want to buy, consider the possibility that perhaps you are better off renting until the real estate market cools, as it will sooner or later, than buying at the height of the market. If, on the other hand, real estate has recently been stable in your area but is beginning to inch up in value, you might want to act as fast as you can, while houses are still fairly priced. How do you know when the real estate market is too high, ready to take off, or about to decline?

This is a very difficult question to answer for certain, but you can definitely get a sense of what's happening with prices in your area. The best way to do this would be to call many—at least five—local real estate agents and ask them directly. Are houses selling within a few days or weeks of being placed on the market? Are the buyers paying more than the sellers are asking? Are more people than usual putting their houses on the market in the hopes of selling high? If the answer to all of these questions is yes, then you are in a booming market. A real estate agent can also tell you just how much the real estate market has been going up over the past few years. This information is usually available in your local newspaper, as well, and you can learn a lot simply by reading the real estate ads and articles.

What does this information mean to you? Well, if you are seeing increases in real estate prices of 2 to 5 percent over a year ago, that's not a big deal; real estate prices in your area are just plodding along, keeping their value, holding steady. If you want to buy and the numbers work, you can probably pick up a house for what you would like to pay for it, maybe a little less. If you see that prices have declined from where they were a year ago, this should indicate that you might be able to pick up a great deal. Go in way under the asking price, knowing that you have the upper hand—and knowing too, no matter how good a deal you think you got, that a year from now, you probably could get a better one. When, on the other hand, you start seeing increases of 10 to 20 percent from a year ago, you know that you are dealing with a booming real estate market and that if you buy now you are going to pay a pretty penny. This doesn't mean that the market cannot go higher still, for of course it can, but at least be aware that if you want to proceed, it is going to cost you. Once you've determined that now is the time for you to buy, the next step is to figure out what you can afford. But first, a word of caution.

THE SIREN SONG OF THE REAL ESTATE SECTION

Once the idea of owning a piece of real estate gets in your blood, watch out. It can overtake you. It is at this moment that most people make their first big mistake. Before they calculate what they can afford, they idly look at ads in the Saturday papers, noting the prices of houses with enticing descriptions. Then they take drives in the areas that they want to live in and visit houses that are open for inspection. They talk to the agents just out of curiosity, to learn the asking prices of the houses. Before they know it—and before they've worked out their own numbers—they've made a date with a few agents just to take a look at what's on the market. This is the usual sequence—and if you allow yourself to follow it, it can end up being one big trap.

The first question the real estate agent will ask you is how much you want to spend. Because you haven't actually taken the time (and don't even quite know how) to figure out what you can afford, you offer as your answer the approximate amount of the house that you called about in the first place. Even as you're saying it, it sounds like a lot to you, but perhaps you're too embarrassed to say so, and certainly you don't want the agent to think you can't afford something nice. So you think, Well, I'm only looking anyway, and what harm does it do to see what's out there? You are about to tempt fate, and before long could find yourself in one of the following three scenarios:

- You fall in love with a home that carries a hefty price tag. Even though it costs more than your gut feeling tells you is affordable, your eager sales agent will try to figure out a way to make it work financially for you. Even if you summon the courage to say you don't have the minimum deposit stipulated by your mortgage provider, don't be surprised if the agent finds a creative way for you to make the deal work anyway.

- Let's say this agent has spent days with you, calls you all the time to give you updates on houses you've seen or to tell you about a house newly on the market, or sends you notes of greeting, just to check in. You start to feel guilty about having wasted this person's time, and feel you must come through in the end and buy something. This guilt can get you in over your head.

- Even if you resist the domestic temptations put before you at the outset, you have peered into the expensive forbidden garden. It will not be easy to get those gorgeous homes out of your head. If you go to see houses priced in your realistic price range, nothing will look as good. You will be constantly comparing what you can really afford to houses you've seen and fallen in love with. You will ask to go back one more time to look at that beautiful house you saw when you first set out. On this visit, you'll spend a little more time imagining yourself there—whether or not the house is compatible with your financial reality. With the aid of a little creative financing, you think, Well, maybe I can do this after all . . . but can you?

HOW MUCH CAN YOU AFFORD TO SPEND?

Before you make a single call or take down one phone number on a house that looks inviting, take a look at your finances.

First, figure out how much money you have for a deposit.

Conventional wisdom has it that when purchasing a primary residence, the deposit should be 20 to 25 percent of the sale price. If a house is selling for $250,000, for example, then the financial institutions that might finance the mortgage will expect you to come up with $50,000 ($250,000 multiplied by .20). So let's work backwards.

How much cash do you have available to you right now to use toward your deposit? This money might come from:

+ Savings accounts
+ Stocks, bonds, or managed funds
+ Cash management trusts
+ Term deposits
+ Financial gifts you are about to receive
+ Debentures, deposits that will mature shortly
+ Funds you have in credit unions/building societies
+ Money in your cheque account
+ Annual bonus
+ Tax refund

Now total the money presently available to you, or that you know will be available when it comes time to buy the house. Multiply that amount by 5 to figure out how much of a house this deposit will buy for you if you want to stick with the 20 percent-deposit rule. If you had $20,000 for a deposit, for instance, you would multiply $20,000 by 5, which will give you $100,000. This is the *most* you can spend on a house if you want to go with a traditional deposit of 20 percent. If you have $50,000 for a deposit, multiply $50,000 by 5 and you know you will be able to buy a house for $250,000. Remember, though, we're just talking about a deposit here; we have yet to figure out if you can afford the mortgage. We'll get to that in a bit, but first things first.

Let's say that after you add up everything, you have only $10,000. You know, then, that the most you can spend on a house is $50,000, and there is not even a kennel in your area that sells for that price. You have two choices. First, decide whether there are any other sources upon which you could draw:

- An insurance policy that can be cashed in
- Superannuation that has been rolled over but is not preserved
- A loan or gift from your parents or a friend

Now add any of these possible amounts to the $10,000 you already have. Let's suppose you can add $15,000 from superannuation money that can be drawn (factor in that you will have to pay income taxes on that money in the year of withdrawal; that could be 30 percent if you are under 55), plus a $5000 gift from your parents to help you out. Now you have a total of $25,000. Multiply that by 5 and you can purchase a house, using the conventional deposit formula, for $125,000.

Let's say that there are still no homes available in the area for $125,000, but you're determined to own a house. Your other option would be to pay less than 20 percent as a deposit. In some cases, the lender will give you a mortgage even if you have as little as 5 percent as a deposit. But this is another potential trap; pay less now and you might find yourself paying more later. If you buy a home and put down less than 20 percent of the final sale price, you will have to pay an extra insurance premium known as mortgage insurance.

MORTGAGE INSURANCE

Mortgage insurance can be a great moneymaking scheme—at least it is for many banks, so you must take care. If you pay less than 20 percent deposit, even 2 percent less, you will pay for it—with mortgage insurance.

Simply put, mortgage insurance protects the mortgage lender against financial loss if a homeowner stops making mortgage payments. Lenders require insurance on low deposit loans for protection in the event that the homeowner fails to make his or her payments. When a homeowner fails to make mortgage payments, a default occurs and the home goes into foreclosure. Both the homeowner and the mortgage insurer lose in a foreclosure. The homeowner loses the house and all of the money put into it. The mortgage insurer will then have to pay the lender's claim on the defaulted loan.

It is crucial that the family buying the home can really afford it—not only at the time it is purchased but also throughout the time period of the loan.

THE COST OF MORTGAGE INSURANCE

Although there are only a very small number of companies providing mortgage insurance, you must apply for it through your bank; you cannot shop around for the best rate. Mortgage insurance is a once-only premium that is payable at the time of taking out a mortgage; it is only required when you put down a deposit of less than 20 percent. If you are buying a house for $200,000, mortgage insurance will cost you around $2800. Make sure that you keep your credit history squeaky clean for five years before applying for this insurance as mortgage insurers don't want to take on anyone they consider to be high risk. For the same reason, mortgage insurers prefer people with a very stable work history.

Overall, putting less than 20 percent down allows more people to get into the real estate game, possibly for the first time—but don't get too excited yet, because having the money for a deposit is just one of the hurdles to overcome.

BEYOND THE DEPOSIT

Many people become so focused on the deposit, they fail to look at the substantial costs beyond it, as if the deposit will, so to speak, slide them right into home base. Please don't make that mistake. Instead, think about the money you'll need months and years beyond the deposit, to make certain that a house won't be all you have.

ALAN'S STORY

At first, it seemed like all our dreams were coming true. I was offered a position as an associate professor at a city university. My wife, Helen, and I were very excited; we had spent all our lives in the country, but this was the big time—the bright lights! The salary was higher, too, which was a good thing, given the higher cost of city living. But Helen would be able to find work fairly easily, since she's in hospital administration, and the university would help us find an affordable apartment, so we'd manage fine. In January, we sold our cars, got rid of some of our furniture, and packed up the rest. Helen had found a good job at a city hospital, and we made our move.

Helen and I and our two sons settled into a rented two-bedroom apartment in the inner city. But the adjustment to a much smaller space was harder on the boys than we'd expected; they felt cramped and would grow stir-crazy. Helen and I both liked our jobs, though, and wanted to stay in the area, but we agreed that we needed a house. We began looking in the suburbs—the real estate agents would meet us at the railway station and drive us around—and finally we found a house we liked. We had almost enough in savings for the deposit, but we managed to pay a little less. We got a mortgage, and we were thrilled, because the mortgage payment was about what we'd been paying in rent. We went through the whole settlement thing, which was surreal—we just kept writing cheques to strangers—hired some movers, and moved. It was like a movie on fast forward.

Settling in felt great. Helen and I were unpacking the kitchen things and watching our sons running around in a backyard again. We moved in the autumn, and the leaves were turning beautiful colours. The kids liked their public school, and everything seemed like it was going to work out fine. We hired a teenager from the neighbourhood to bring the kids home from their after-school program and stay with them until one of us got home, which went off without a hitch most of the time, although once in a while Helen or I had to leave work early. We were both commuting to the city, and we hadn't quite figured the commuting cost into our calculations (actually, we hadn't calculated much beyond the deposit and the mortgage payments), but, okay, we could basically afford the commute. For the first few weeks we walked to the train, which was only a few blocks from where we dropped the kids at school. But when the weather started to get colder,

*that walk plus the distance to the local shopping centre became more diffi-
cult. Anyway, how do you live in the suburbs without a car? So we bought
a used car, which meant more money going out every month. Also moving
house twice in less than a year was really expensive, and we were pretty
strapped. So we got another Visa card, figuring we just needed a little time
to catch up.*

*In the meantime, we needed to replace the dishwasher; then we bought
a dining-room table and chairs from a secondhand shop. We got the boys
a trampoline for Christmas, plus we paid for Helen's mother to fly up for
the holidays. Everything was adding up: water bills, which we hadn't had
to pay at the apartment, really high electricity and gas, and council rates.
I kept feeling that we were falling more and more behind. Here we were,
both making more money than we had before, living in a house no bigger
than the one we had in the country, but suddenly we're $12,000 in debt to
the credit card companies.*

*So we're paying the mortgage and everything else, but barely. I mean, if
the refrigerator goes, which it very well might, we'll sink. I didn't anticipate
all these costs beyond the initial biggies, and now I don't see a way out.*

If you're like most of us, you will start out trying not to buy more house
than you can afford, but your thoughts will tell you one thing, your words
will tell others something else, and your actions will head you in a different direction altogether. When you are considering any major purchase,
our law of financial harmony, which requires the unity of your thoughts,
words, and actions, must come into play. Otherwise, your mind will come
up with all kinds of excuses to make it okay for you to spend more than
you know you should. Excuses like these:

*"As we get older, we'll be making more money, and it will become
easier to meet those payments."*

The future of your job and your income is not solely up to you. If you
work in the finance sector and the market falls, it is possible you could be
out of a job before you know it. If you are working for a corporation, they
may suddenly downsize, plunging your once-bright future into darkness.
Even if you are self-employed, changes in the economy can affect you and
your income drastically. Financial developments overseas may increas-
ingly affect us all. Never gamble on what is to come.

"We'll just cut back on everything else in order to afford this house."

Even though you may want that perfect home so much that you're willing to make sacrifices to own it, do not underestimate how very difficult it is to cut out other ways in which you might want to spend your money—travel, hobbies, your children, even renovating the house. Given everything else you will want to do with your life, spending more than you can easily afford on housing will be enjoyable for only a short period of time. The hardest part of owning a house comes long after the deposit has been made. The hardest part is being able to afford the payments month in, month out, for the next fifteen to thirty years, while still enjoying a full, rich life doing the things that you love. I've seen plenty of clients who were house rich, cash poor, and miserable.

CRUNCHING THE NUMBERS

After you've figured out how much house you can afford based on the amount of money you have for the deposit, you now must make sure you can afford the monthly mortgage payment, as well as rates, insurance or strata levies

Start with the amount of money you have for a deposit. Subtract from that figure the amount you need to cover the purchase costs (stamp duty, legals, mortgage insurance, loan application fee). Next, subtract this balance from the purchase price of the house and that will give you the amount of the mortgage you will need.

For example, if you can afford a house costing $250,000, and you are able to put down a deposit of 20 percent ($50,000), you will need a mortgage of $200,000 ($250,000 minus $50,000 equals $200,000). You can find out how much your repayments will be by ringing any of the bank's home loan lines which are usually open seven days a week, or use the chart below as a quick reference guide. Find the going interest rate to the nearest half of a percent and then find the closest mortgage amount and go down the chart to find the amount of the monthly payment.

For example, on a 15-year, $200,000 mortgage at a 6.5 percent interest rate, the monthly payment would be $1742; the monthly payments for a 30-year mortgage would be $1264.

15-Year Mortgage

	$100k	$150k	$200k	$250k	$300k	$350k	$400k
6%	$844	1266	1688	2110	2532	2953	3375
6.5%	$871	1307	1742	2178	2613	3049	3484
7%	$899	1348	1798	2247	2696	3146	3595
7.5%	$927	1391	1854	2318	2781	3245	3708
8%	$956	1433	1911	2389	2867	3345	3823

30-Year Mortgage

	$100k	$150k	$200k	$250k	$300k	$350k	$400k
6%	$600	899	1199	1499	1799	2098	2398
6.5%	$632	948	1264	1580	1896	2212	2528
7%	$665	998	1331	1663	1996	2329	2661
7.5%	$699	1049	1398	1748	2098	2447	2797
8%	$734	1101	1468	1834	2201	2568	2935

Be conservative when choosing an interest rate to base your calculations on. Interest rates may now be 6.5 percent but ten years ago they went as high as 18 percent. It never hurts to budget for a slight increase in interest rates.

Once you calculate your monthly mortgage cost, you need to add the cost of home insurance. Call any insurance company or your bank to obtain an estimate of this cost.

Write the insurance figure here: $_____

Next, ring the local council and water board to find out how much your rates will be. Your real estate agent could also provide this figure for you. Your real estate agent can also advise the cost of strata levies.

Write that combined figure here: $_____

Add up all these figures (if given as yearly estimates) and divide by 12 (e.g. $2500 ÷ 12 = $208) to determine how much it will cost you per month for rates, insurance or levies.

Write that figure here: $_____

Add this figure to your monthly mortgage payment to determine the total cost of your monthly payments. In the above scenario, based on a 30-year mortgage, you would add $1264 for the mortgage, plus $208 for insurance, rates and levies = $1472.

Here's a worksheet for you to fill in:

Take the price of the house	$_____
Monthly mortgage payment	$_____
Home insurance	$_____
Rates—council	$_____
Rates—water	$_____
Strata levies (if applicable)	$_____
Total monthly payment:	$_____

Now let's see if you can afford this monthly payment. First, add up your current income from all sources:

Take home pay (salary after tax)	$_____
Family allowance	$_____
Interest and dividends	$_____
Miscellaneous	$_____
Total	$_____

**Subtract your total monthly payment
from your total monthly income (after tax):** $_____
That is the most basic calculation of the impact your new home
will have on your monthly earnings.

Now let's go one step further so you can really see what your financial life will look like if you were to buy this home. Figure roughly your monthly and seasonal bills to calculate how much more it will cost you to live in this house than it does for you to live where you are now. Estimate as best you can the following monthly costs. Be as accurate as possible. Call service providers in the area; see if your agent can provide you with information. If you're guessing, better to err on the high side than to underestimate. Consider also the cost of other necessities such as public transport, food, clothing, medical bills, education, as well as the cost of those things that give you pleasure that you couldn't bear to go without, such as movies, CDs and sport.

Electricity, gas $_____
Firewood, if there's a fireplace $_____
Pool maintenance, if there's a pool $_____
Extra petrol, if you'll have a longer
drive to work $_____
Gardener, landscaping costs $_____
Other $_____

Add up all these costs and subtract the figure
from your remaining monthly net: $_____
If you still have money left over, then you can afford to buy this house. Welcome to the dream.

BYPASSING THE CONVENTIONAL ADVICE

Other advisers might tell you that it's not necessary to go through all this trouble to see if you can afford a house. Just go to the bank and see if you can prequalify for a loan, they'll say. Let the bank do the work for you, and then you will know for sure. The problem I have with this advice is that every single person who has lost a home to foreclosure or bankruptcy originally qualified for a bank loan. Got the loan, moved in—and then something went wrong.

The conventional formula used by the bank tells you that your housing should cost no more than 25 to 30 percent of your *gross* income. In my opinion, this formula simply does not hold up. Gross income is almost irrelevant. Most of us never see anything close to our gross income. So do your calculations as described and concentrate on your *net* income. In short, you cannot adhere to a single formula when you are gauging how much housing you can afford. The object here is not just being able to buy a home. The object is to keep the home you buy forever.

FALLING IN LOVE . . . AND KEEPING YOUR HEAD

There's something about the prospect of owning a home that makes otherwise rational people giddy with longing. Your relationship with your house will be an important and long-term one, so it's important not to "marry" it in the throes of early passion. Rather, get to know it well first. Go back time and again before you say "I'll take it." Visit it at different times of day to see where the sun hits, what it feels like in the morning, afternoon, and night. Go on weekdays as well as weekends. See it with your kids, so you can feel and hear what it will be like to live there together. Walk around the house, drive by it, and listen. See if you can hear the neighbours, their children, or barking dogs. Talk to your neighbour's neighbour and ask them if your shared neighbour is loud. Do the kids blast music? Ask about break-ins or robberies in the area. It is important that you do not simply take the seller's word at face value. Neighbours will be more candid and objective, and they are the people whom you will be living among for a long time to come. I have known many people who bought a home, loved it, but ended up selling, finally unable to tolerate noisy neighbours. And make sure that you like the area. The grocery store, dry cleaner, restaurants, movie theatres, schools—the places that you are going to frequent. For instance, if there is a school nearby, you may have a herd of kids hanging out on your block for hours after school and on breaks. Drive around at rush hour, check out access to the freeways, and time how long it will take you to get to work every day. Look, too, at the surrounding areas, what would happen in case of major rain, floods, etc. Make sure the whole package works.

Now turn your attention to the house itself, not just the view from the pretty bay window you're falling in love with, but everything about the house. Don't be shy. Flush the toilets, test the water pressure. Turn on the hot water in the kitchen and bathrooms and see how long it takes to become hot; it should take only a few seconds. Check to make sure that each and every appliance works. Find out how old the water heater, gas heater, air conditioners, and stove are. Most appliances last about seven to ten years before they need to be replaced. If any of the appliances are under warranty, find out if the sellers have the paperwork; would they mind leaving it for you if you buy the house? Look at the placement of power points and make sure that they all work. Check to see if the house has an up-to-date electrical system or if it's still wired with older circuitry. And turn on everything at once to see whether you blow a fuse or the circuit breaker trips. Make sure you ask when the roof was last replaced, and visit the house after a heavy rain to see if there are any leaks. A roof is a huge expense. And take one more good look: Does this house have everything that you want? I have a friend who fell in love with a town house that she saw, simply because of the fireplace. It was absolutely beautiful, and that was that, she bought the house. After she moved in, she realised that she didn't have much of a backyard or a deck, and what good's a beautiful fireplace all summer? Look at the house and really make sure that it has everything you need. You will find the perfect house if you just take your time.

LISTENING TO YOUR REAL ESTATE AGENT, LISTENING TO YOURSELF

When you find the perfect house, the next step is to make an offer to buy it. Your inclination will be to ask your real estate agent for advice. However, you must remember that despite all appearances to the contrary "your" real estate agent doesn't really work for you but for the seller. The bottom line: The agent is paid by the seller.

A real estate agent makes a commission from the sale of the house. Commissions vary from state to state and with the value of the property. If there is a real estate agent who represents the seller and another who represents you, usually they will split the commission. Regardless of how the agents divide the pie, it's the seller who pays the commission, which comes out of the sale price of the house. If the sellers get $200,000 for their home, for example, approximately $5000 of that comes off the top and goes to the agents involved in the sale.

As the buyer, you of course want to get the best possible price, but you must understand that the better the deal you get, the worse the deal for the agent. You pay less; they earn less. You pay more; they earn more. In short, the agent's best interests are the seller's best interests as well. This is an important fact to keep in mind. When it comes time to make an offer, stick with the figure you want to offer without worrying that you are insulting the seller or the agent.

So without talking to your agent, think about what you are truly prepared to pay for this house. Do not lose courage here, for often we begin to feel we are going to lose the house if we don't offer the right price. If you do end up losing it, trust me, it is a blessing in disguise. Back in 1976, I found what I thought was the perfect house, and I put in a bid on it. Someone else bid more, and I lost it. I was terribly upset, until a week later when I was driving around another pretty area and saw a sign for an open house. I went in and fell in love all over again, only this time the house was less expensive and was situated on much more property. That's the house that I live in to this day, and every so often I still think how glad I am I that I didn't get the other house. If you try and do not get what you want, just move on; there are many, many houses out there.

LAW OF MONEY

If you are not overly attached to what you want, you will attain it.

Come from a place of plenty when looking for a house, not from a diminished place. Set the price in your head, check it out with your heart, and then tell the agent what you want to offer. If the agent says he cannot make an offer at that price, ask him why not. Chances are he will say he has been instructed not to put in a bid under a certain price. Depending on what that price is, you may feel okay about changing your bid. If, however, you feel that this is simply a sales tactic, just walk away, let it go, don't engage on that level; if it is meant to be yours, it will come back to you.

Years ago, I used to love to go along with friends who were looking to buy a house. One Sunday I accompanied two of my friends who were both looking, and before long we saw a home that was offered for sale by the owner. When we went in, my friend Woody absolutely fell in love with the house. We had already done the numbers, so Woody knew exactly how much she could afford to spend. We asked the owner how much he was asking for the house, and he named a figure that was $30,000 more than Woody could afford. She looked at him and said, "Too bad. If you would sell it for thirty thousand dollars less, I would take it on the spot." He apologised, but declined, so we left. As we were about to get into our car, the owner came running out of the house. "Wait a minute," he said. "Okay, okay, I'll accept your offer." So Woody bought the house she fell in love with at first sight.

About a month later we went out again with Paula, another friend, who was still looking for her dream home. Once again we came across a home that was for sale by the owner, but this time we had to make an appointment to see it. We made a date that was five days away. During those five days, Paula drove by the house a thousand times, and she was becoming more and more attached to it. "If the insides are anything like I imagine them," she said, "I've found my dream house." Sure enough, the house was adorable inside and out. Now the only thing left was to make a deal. The owner was asking more than Paula could afford to pay. Remembering what had happened with Woody a few weeks earlier, she said, "Too bad. If you would sell it for twenty thousand dollars less, I would buy it on the spot." With that she thanked him, we said our good-byes, and we left. We got into the car, and as I put the key into the ignition, Paula said, "Wait!" "Wait for what?" I asked. "He's going to come running out of the house—watch!" she said. We sat in his driveway for a few minutes, and then I said, "Uh, Paula, I don't think this is going to happen." She got a sad look on her face and said, "God, I wanted that house so much. How come he didn't come running out after us like that other guy did with Woody?" The answer to that question was that Paula was too attached to getting the house; Woody was not. When Woody walked out, she never imagined that the owner would come running after her. She liked the house but knew what she could spend, and that was that. Paula, on the other hand, had spent days driving around, falling in love with this house, before she ever set foot in it. Whether he was consciously aware of it or not, I would bet that the seller could feel it. As most overly attached buyers do, Paula ended up going back to him and paying full price for the house—she paid the price of wanting something too dearly.

IT DOESN'T HURT TO ASK

Sometimes you really want to buy, and the seller really wants to sell to you, but you're still thousands of dollars apart. For whatever reason—be it that he owes money on the mortgage or needs money to buy his new home— the seller is unable to come down in price. Sometimes in these situations, you can enlist the help of your real estate agent to chip in some money. An agent's commission is not fixed in stone. Often, to bring a deal to completion, the agent will cut a percentage point or more from his commission. With real estate prices in many areas astronomical, 1 percent can mean a nice saving for the buyer. If you are a buyer and the seller refuses to come down to your top offering price, ask the real estate agent if he will throw in some of his commission to make it happen. It doesn't happen every time, but sometimes, under the right circumstances, you can get lucky.

THE INSPECTION

My friend Woody took a risk when she made her offer—and had it accepted—after seeing her dream house just once. What if the house harboured some hidden structural damage or was being devoured by termites invisible to an untrained eye? What if it contained dangerous levels of asbestos or flaking lead-based paint? For this reason, an engineer's inspection is essential. In the best-case scenario, you would bring in an expert to inspect the house for structural soundness, pest problems, environmental risks, and the like before you made your offer. That way, your offer could take into account any expensive repairs you'd need to undertake once the house was yours, which could end up serving as a bargaining tool.

Unfortunately, in most cases you will likely be worried about someone buying the house out from under you while you are taking the time to conduct your inspection. Which means that in most cases, you will have your inspection conducted after your offer's been accepted but before contracts are exchanged, and you can negotiate further if the inspection reveals major problems. Check in the Yellow Pages or ask friends or a conveyancing solicitor to recommend a building inspector.

THE CONTRACT OF SALE

Now is the time to negotiate the terms of the contract of sale. It is customary to retain a conveyancing solicitor, or other licensed conveyancer, to do this for you but you can do your own conveyancing with the help of a kit. This contract sets forth the terms of the transaction, including a description of the property, the purchase price, the deposit, the settlement schedule, whether or not the deal is conditional upon your obtaining mortgage financing, and the seller's representations concerning the property. The seller's conveyancer draws up this contract. Be sure you understand your rights and obligations before signing. Don't be afraid to ask your solicitor or agent to explain whatever you don't clearly understand.

CITY HOUSE/COUNTRY HOUSE

These chapters will give you a basic understanding of what is involved in buying a house, but for many—especially those who live in urban areas—a home of your own more likely will mean a *unit* or a *townhouse* than a ranch or split-level with a yard and picket fence. When you buy a cooperative apartment, or what's commonly known as a *company title,* you are purchasing shares of a cooperative corporation that owns the building; thus, strictly speaking, you don't actually own your apartment, you own shares of the corporation allocated to your apartment, together with a lease that allows you to occupy the apartment. When you buy a strata title unit, just as when you buy a house, you are purchasing a piece of real estate—albeit one that's part of a larger building or development.

Much of the information and considerations of these chapters apply equally whether you are buying a Torrens title house or a strata or company title unit. However, there are some important distinctions. First, company titles are harder to finance as they are harder to sell. This is because all the shareholders must agree on the new purchaser. However, because of this, units with company titles usually cost less to buy. Second, because company and strata titles are situated within a building, the inspection prior to signing a contract should focus not only on the unit to be purchased but on the financial and physical condition of the building overall. It is a good idea to have a strata search carried out at this stage as well. This will identify any problems or conflicts with tenants that may exist. Third, with a company or strata title, your monthly costs also include *maintenance charges* and *insurance,* in addition to your monthly mortgage payments. There may even be assessments to be paid monthly, if the building or any of its systems is undergoing repair or restoration. These additional monthly charges should be factored in when you crunch your numbers to determine what you can afford.

CHAPTER 15

THE MORTGAGE MENU

GETTING THE BEST MORTGAGE

You find the perfect house, and before you know it, your offer has been accepted. Unless you have prequalified for a loan, your next step is to find someone who will lend you the money. You can find a mortgage for yourself or you can enlist the help of a *mortgage broker.* A mortgage broker is someone who will find you the best loan to finance your home and make the process as easy as possible.

How do you find a good mortgage broker? Chances are that there will be at least one real estate agent—maybe two—involved when you buy your home. An agent will very likely recommend a mortgage broker to help you get a loan. You see, once your offer has been accepted by the seller, the agent switches hats, so to speak, and begins to work on your behalf, in order to make sure the deal goes through—and that the commission does, too. So the agent has a vested interest in helping you get your mortgage.

There is a tremendous difference between a mortgage and a good mortgage. This is why it is so important that you learn how mortgages work, so you know all the right questions to ask. If there is no agent involved or the agent doesn't know a broker, ask your homeowner friends for recommendations.

Why get a mortgage broker? A good mortgage broker can offer you a variety of loans from many different lenders. They're usually very up-to-date on the nuances of each lender and what each particular lender is looking for in order to qualify people for loans. Also, the mortgage broker will put together and present your entire loan package, so that you get through all the paperwork and documentation that will be required with as little hassle as possible. Many people wonder if it is more expensive to use a mortgage broker than simply to go to a bank and do it themselves. In the past mortgage brokers always charged a fee, usually 1 percent of the amount borrowed, and many of them still do. However with deregulation there are some brokers that don't charge this upfront fee; they receive commission from the lending institution, usually in the form of a small annual commission for the life of the loan. The advantage of using a broker is that they can often obtain finance for people who have trouble qualifying for loans, and they sometimes offer very attractive rates of interest. However, whenever commission is involved, you need to be sure if the broker is really working in your best interest, rather than recommending loans that are in their interest. Very few brokers will recommend a loan if they do not receive a commission.

It is not a bad idea first to check out rates or deals for yourself; you can find a list of interest rates that are currently being offered by various banks in *Your Mortgage* magazine. This magazine is published quarterly and contains home loan comparison tables that cover virtually every possible feature, fees and terms available. Look through the advertisements and you will find a multitude of ads from private home loan companies that you have probably never heard of before. In the past banks, building societies and credit unions were the main providers of mortgage finance. Since deregulation this area has opened up and, because of exensive advertising, companies such as Aussie Home Loans and Rams have become household names, but they are not the only private loan companies. There are many little known companies that offer some tremendous deals and they are worthwhile checking out. In most cases the loan application costs are similar to those of banks.

The Internet can be another great source of information, and applying on-line for mortgages is getting more and more common. Once you have gathered your information, you can compare your notes to what your mortgage broker or loan officer is quoting you. The whole process of approval, start to finish, should not take more than three weeks. If it does, then something is wrong. Either your broker or loan officer is not doing his job or there is some other problem, but after three weeks find out why you've not yet been given an answer.

I do recommend reputable mortgage brokers, but I also recommend that my clients know and understand the mortgage process. As complex as it seems, it is comprehensible. Please read the sections below before you begin to look, and then again before you buy.

MORTGAGE: THE MENU OF CHOICES

This part of the decision-making process is probably the hardest, because nowadays there are more choices available. Some factors you will want to consider:

- How long are you planning to live in this house?
- Are interest rates at the time of purchase high, medium, or low?
- Are interest rates projected to go higher, go lower, or remain stable?
- Will you struggle to make the mortgage payment or make it with ease?
- Are you approaching retirement, or do you still have more than fifteen years to go?

The answers to these questions will play a big part in what kind of loan you should get in the first place. So please keep them in mind as you read through this section.

There are hundreds of variations when it comes to a mortgage. However, the primary types of mortgages that you will be considering are as follows:

1. Fixed-rate mortgage
2. Variable rate mortgage
3. A fixed and variable combined mortgage
4. An interest-only mortgage

FIXED-RATE MORTGAGES

This mortgage is just what it sounds like. The interest rate is fixed for a set period. Since the interest rate is fixed, so are your monthly payments. This means that you know from the start how much your monthly payments are going to be—they will not change for the duration of the fixed period. Each mortgage payment is made up of interest and principal. In the first years, the greatest percentage of your mortgage payments is made up of interest, with very little going to pay off your principal, because lenders always want their interest paid first.

Just to give you an idea, on a 30-year, $150,000 mortgage at 7 percent, the payments would be $997 per month.

The first year, 13 percent of your payment goes to principal; 87 percent goes to interest.

The tenth year, 25 percent of your payment goes to principal; 75 percent goes to interest.

The twentieth year, 50 percent of your payment goes to principal; 50 percent goes to interest.

The twenty-fifth year, 70 percent of your payment goes to principal; 30 percent goes to interest.

The thirtieth year, 99.5 percent of your payment goes to principal; 0.5 percent goes to interest.

The period of time that you will have to pay back your loan can vary. For years, the most conventional time frame in Australia was 25 years. A surprisingly unknown fact among home buyers even today is that you can get fixed mortgages for periods of less than 10 years. The time frame for the payback period makes a difference in two ways:

1. *The longer the length of the loan, the lower the monthly payments.*

    Monthly payments for a 30-year mortgage are lower than monthly payments for a 15-year mortgage, which are lower than those for a 10-year mortgage.
2. *The longer the length of the loan, the more interest you pay.*

    The interest payable will be greater for a 30-year mortgage than for a 15-year mortgage. The longer the loan, the more you will pay in interest in the long run.

Overall, you will end up paying far more for a 30-year loan than you will for a 15-year loan, and you will pay more for a 15-year loan than you will for a 10-year loan.

See pages 203–5 for a detailed comparison of 15- and 30-year mortgages.

Fixed mortgages are best utilised:

+ when interest rates are low and you expect to stay in the house for more than 5 to 7 years. In most cases if you repay the mortgage prior to the fixed term you will pay a 3 month penalty.
+ if interest rates are currently low and you are approaching or are in your retirement years and are or will be living on a fixed income. Whenever you have a fixed income, it is preferable to have fixed expenses whenever possible.

VARIABLE RATE MORTGAGES

A variable rate mortgage is the opposite of a fixed-rate mortgage. Rather than being fixed for a set period, the interest rate can move either up or down over the length of the loan. To entice you to go the variable route, a bank usually starts the loan at a lower rate than comparable fixed-rate mortgages, so that, at least in the first year, your monthly payments will be less than they will be later on. This can be appealing for cash-strapped home buyers. After your initial entry interest rate, which is set for 6 months to 1 year, depending on the terms of your loan, the interest rate will adjust. In most cases, it will adjust upward, and when that happens: ouch.

In fairness, back in the eighties and early nineties, when interest rates were high and then came down, variable rate mortgages moved downwards, so they were a big boon for many borrowers, but as of the writing of this book, interest rates are extremely low, so in years to come they are more likely to go up or remain right around where they are, rather than go down.

If one bank is offering a lower starter rate on a variable rate mortgage, is that always the right way to go?
In addition to the interest payments, another consideration is the fees. These are the monthly management fees, statement fees and

account keeping fees that are often added to your account monthly by banks but are not disclosed in the actual interest rate. For instance, one major bank advertises a standard variable rate of 6.55 percent, but in a comparison done by a private mortgage insurer which included all fees and charges, they discovered that on a $100,000 loan the actual rate is 6.75 percent; this is the true rate and even such a small amount can cost considerably more over the term of the loan. Legislation is under review by all state governments to make disclosure of the true rate law.

Do all lenders calculate interest in the same way?

No and this is where many people get caught. There are two ways lenders calculate interest: on a daily basis or a monthly reducing balance. If you make a standard loan payment once a month, both loans will cost you the same. If, however, you choose to pay your mortgage fortnightly or, even better, weekly, then a daily rate loan will end up costing you less. You see, a daily rate loan is calculated on the actual balance owing each day and if you make weekly payments that balance is being constantly reduced. If interest is calculated on a monthly basis, then you gain no benefit by making weekly or fortnightly payments. Take a standard $100,000 loan repayable over 13 years: with a daily rate loan you can reduce the term of the loan by one year, compared to paying the same amount off a monthly reducing loan, and that is without making any extra repayments.

GUIDELINES

Questions to ask before signing up for a variable rate mortgage:

1. If interest rates increase, how much notice will we be given of a rate change?
2. What are the account keeping, statement or other regular charges?
3. Is the interest charged daily or monthly?
4. Does it have an early payout penalty?

Make sure you get the answers to each of these questions, then go back and read this section again to make sure you understand how the loan really works.

. . .

Variable rate mortgages are best utilised:

- By people who know that they are going to stay in their home for a maximum of 5 to 7 years.
- When interest rates are high and projected to come down.
- When your cash flow is currently tight but you expect it to increase as time goes on.

Bottom line: Whether you should choose a variable rate over a fixed mortgage will ultimately depend on what interest rates end up doing during the time you are living in your home. Try to do a few projections using various interest rate scenarios. If you are computer-literate, there are many programs on the Internet that will help you analyse the different possibilities. One site is realestate.com.au where you can find a loan calculator. Make sure you run the numbers, or have someone else do them for you. Make sure, too, that you work out the numbers in a worst-case scenario and think about what would happen if that scenario came true.

FIXED AND VARIABLE COMBINED

A few years ago, a new kind of mortgage—a fusion of a fixed mortgage and a variable rate—popped onto the scene. This mortgage is a bit like hedging your bets and would suit anyone in doubt as to which way mortgage rates are going to move. It gives you the security of a fixed term with the flexibility of a variable rate.

Fixed-and-variables are best utilised:

- If you doubt that you will be staying in your home for more than 5 to 7 years.
- If you are on a fixed income and would be unable to meet mortgage repayments if there was a sudden increase in interest rates.

Look into these mortgages if you are fairly certain that you're buying a starter home, or if you know you will want to stay there for only about 5 to 7 years.

INTEREST-ONLY MORTGAGES

If you are trying to buy a property that is out of your financial reach, it is not unusual for a real estate agent, or mortgage provider, to suggest that you apply for an interest-only loan for the simple reason that you can borrow more because all of your repayments go towards interest, and nothing comes off the amount you borrow.

These loans are also recommended at some property investment seminars where they are trying to entice you to borrow as much as 95 percent against the value of your home. This is in the salesperson's best interest and not yours. The logic behind this argument is that lower repayments mean that you can buy more property and over the long term when property prices increase you can sell your property and take your profit. Good in theory, but as we all know you cannot predict the future. What happens if property prices fall and you owe more than you can sell your property for? You could be wiped out entirely.

THE LENGTH OF A LOAN

In deciding which kind of mortgage you should apply for, you will also have to decide whether you are going to apply for a 15- or 30-year mortgage. There are other durations as well—you can choose any term—but the term of the loan makes a vast difference to how much interest you pay. For the sake of this example we'll focus on the 15 and the 30. What's the difference between these two? Simply put, with a 15-year mortgage, your house will be paid off in 15 years rather than 30. Potential downside: Because the time frame is shorter, you will have to pay a few hundred dollars more a month.

Twenty-three years ago, when I bought the house that I live in now, I didn't know that a 15-year mortgage existed. I was buying a home, I was told to get a 30-year mortgage, and what did I know? Nothing, so I did what I was told. It wasn't until I had already owned my home for 10 years, with 20 years left to pay on it, that I learned that if I had taken a 15-year mortgage to start with, I would have had only 5 years remaining on my mortgage. Yes, you may be thinking, but it's a lot more expensive to have a 15-year mortgage; I probably couldn't have afforded it. Not true! In many cases the difference could be as little as $150 a month, and in most cases it's not more than $300 or $400. For instance, my mortgage at the time was for $48,000. The difference between a 15-year and a 30-year mortgage was only $115 a month. If I had known that for $115 more a month, I could own my home outright in just fifteen years, I would have found a way to make it work.

Not only that, but with a 15-year mortgage you will save a tremendous amount of money overall. Let's say that you have a 30-year, $150,000 mortgage at 7 percent. Your monthly payments are $998 a month. Over 30 years, you will have paid $359,280 for that mortgage ($998 multiplied by 360 equals $359,280). A 15-year mortgage would cost you $1348 a month, $350 more a month. However, in 15 years, you would have paid a total of $242,683, or $116,597 less than you would have with your 30-year mortgage. That's a lot of money.

Below is a chart so you can see the difference in monthly dollar amounts between a 15-year and a 30-year. Also included are the total overall dollar amounts of a 15-year mortgage versus a 30.

Mortgage amount	15-year/6.5%	30-year/6.5%	Monthly difference	Total savings of 15-year loan over 30-year loan
$50,000	436	316	120	$35,372
$100,000	871	632	239	$70,745
$150,000	1307	948	359	$106,118
$200,000	1742	1264	478	$141,490
$250,000	2178	1580	598	$176,863
$300,000	2613	1896	717	$212,235
$400,000	3484	2528	956	$282,981
$500,000	4356	3160	1196	$353,725

Why don't more people take out 15-year loans? My guess is that many of us think first of what we can comfortably afford today, and think, too, that over the years we'll make more money, and then if we want we can pay the mortgage off faster later. The problem with this approach is that very few of us are disciplined enough, even if we start to earn more, to put more money monthly into our payments.

In my opinion, a 30-year mortgage can be a waste of good money. If I still haven't convinced you, consider this: with a 7 percent, 30-year mortgage, after 15 years of paying month in and month out, you would still owe roughly 75 percent of your original balance. If you had chosen a 15-year mortgage, you'd own the house outright.

CHOOSING YOUR INTEREST RATE

Run the numbers every way you can to see which of the loans available to you is the best option. Your broker can help you with this or, again, turn to SmartCalc on the Internet. Remember, it's not that *the bank* is granting you a loan. *You* are taking out a loan. Even though millions of us do it every year, buying a home is a big, big step, and most home buyers meekly do what they're told. It takes courage here to take charge, but it's worth it financially, and making the soundest decision, for yourself, will grant you true pride of homeownership.

CHAPTER 16

YOUR HOME AND YOUR FUTURE

TAKING TITLE

If you are buying the house with another person, then the way in which you take title—that is, the way ownership is recorded on the deed—will be very important. There are two main ways that people take title to a house: *joint tenancy* and *tenants in common*.

JOINT TENANCY

This is the way in which most married couples or partners take title to their house; however, marriage is not a prerequisite in order for you to be able to take title in this form. When taking title as joint tenants, the parties involved are considered to have equal ownership of the entire property. In the event that one of them dies, regardless of the beneficiary instructions of the deceased's will or trust, the surviving spouse or partner automatically receives ownership of the deceased person's half of the house.

One great part of titles that are held as joint tenants is that the deceased person's half passes directly to the survivor or survivors without having to go through the probate court procedure (and expense).

Bottom line: This is an incredibly efficient way to own property together and to have it change hands upon a death.

TENANTS IN COMMON (TIC)

This is the way to take title if you want to make sure that upon your death, your portion of the house goes to your designated beneficiaries as governed by your will, and not to the person or people who own the property with you. Property under TIC ownership can be owned by two or more people. When you own real estate under this title, you really own only a designated percentage of the property. Unlike joint tenancy, where in essence you each own the entire house, with TIC, your partner could own 60 percent and you could own 40 percent. You also could sell your 40 percent anytime your heart desires, and to whomever you desire. When you take title under TIC, the beneficiary or beneficiaries to whom you leave your portion via your will will have to go through the court procedure to take ownership of their share of the property. If you're in a second marriage, say, and want to leave your share of the house you're living in to your children from your first marriage, TIC is a way to pass your share to your children through a will or trust.

SETTLEMENT COSTS

Okay, you've made it this far. In order for the house you're buying to become truly yours on paper, you have to go through a few more financial acrobatics and come up with some more money. In addition to the deposit, you are also going to have to pay additional fees on settlement. I have to tell you, these are not cheap. Some of these costs can be absorbed into your loan, others like stamp duty have to be paid before settlement, but one way or another you are paying for them. On average, settlement costs run to approximately 5 percent of the cost of the house.

Settlement costs include the *loan application fee* (if not already paid), *building insurance,* a *valuation fee* (sometimes included in your application fee), *legal fees, title search, stamp duty on the mortgage* and *mortgage insurance* (if you are paying less than 20 percent as a deposit), among other expenses. Your lender should supply you with an estimate, which should give you a good idea as to what these settlement costs are going to add up to. If you do not get one, call the lender and ask for it. Here is a list of the approximate upper limits of settlement costs and fees that you can expect:

- *Loan application fee.* This should cost up to $600. This is the fee the lender charges you simply to apply for the loan.
- *Valuation fee.* Your house must be valued independently, so that the lender can make sure that the amount of the mortgage is in keeping with the true value of the house. This costs about $250 but is often included in your loan application fee.
- *Title search.* The lender wants to make sure that the title to the home you are about to buy is free and clear of any liens from the previous owner. Title searches are usually included in your legal fees.
- *Legal fees and disbursements.* Conveyancing fees cover the paperwork and searches carried out to ensure that all is in order with the purchase. Disbursements are the costs spent on your behalf to cover fees for certificates from councils, title searches etc.
- *Pest and building inspection.* Some lenders may require a pest inspection certificate, and it is a good idea to obtain one for your own peace of mind.
- *Stamp duty.* This is government duty which is based on the purchase price of your house, and is the most substantial amount you will have to pay. Stamp duty taxes come under state legislation and vary from state to state. As a guide, a $250,000 property in NSW will incur stamp duty of $7240.
- *Stamp duty on mortgage.* At the time of writing this stamp duty is being reviewed by all state governments and may be replaced or modified when the GST comes into force on 1 July 2000. At the present time this fee is based on the size of the mortgage. The cost for a $100,000 mortgage is $341.
- *Strata search fees.* If you are buying a strata title property it is wise to have this search carried out to ensure that there are no

maintenance problems with the building, or future work planned that you will be required to contribute to, and also to see if there are any problems with tenants.

♦ *Building insurance.* All lenders will require a certificate of currency prior to settlement to show that the property is adequately insured. This could cost between $150 and $300, depending on the value of the property.

When all is said and done, the closing costs on a property of $150,000 can add up to about $7000. Make sure that you have your lender outline in great detail what they think every one of these items is going to cost you. Factor these costs, too, into your overall financial picture.

CAUTION

As I mentioned earlier, many people will find themselves including some of the settlement costs in the mortgage itself. For instance, if you had a $150,000 mortgage, the lender might suggest that you let $5000 of settlement costs be tacked on to the mortgage and that you pay it out monthly. Sounds like a great idea, but if you do that, you have just increased your $5000 in settlement costs to $11,520. How? Well, let's say you have a 30-year mortgage at 6.5 percent and you plan to keep the house for all 30 years. That extra $5000 adds about $32 a month on to your payments, which over 30 years adds up to $11,520. Another way to look at it is that if you invested that $32 a month over the next 30 years at 8 percent, you would have $47,692. Either way you look at it, there's a lot of money at stake. If you have the cash, pay for settlement costs up front, especially if you plan to stay in the house for the entire life of the mortgage. If, however, you plan to stay there for only 5 years, I don't have a problem with financing your settlement costs.

YOUR HOME AND YOUR FUTURE

Most of this chapter has been devoted to what you need to know in order to make wise decisions when it comes to buying and financing your home, which is the investment most of us hold closest to our hearts. But there are still lessons to learn, even after you become a homeowner. To my mind, the most important of these is how best to use your home to secure your retirement years. Your home can prove to be one of your greatest financial and emotional friends, if you learn how to make it work for you. Whether you're starting over, whether your working years are ending (perhaps sooner than you expected), or whether you just haven't planned as well as you should have, if you happen to own a home and you'd like to remain in it for a long time, I want you to consider as your first priority paying off your mortgage in full, as quickly as you can.

Many of us have been told for years that you would never want to pay off your mortgage because you could be investing that extra money and getting real growth on it, rather than having it simply remain as equity in your house. This points is valid, especially when you have more than enough money to meet your monthly expenses and have the money to do all that your little heart desires.

With respect to investments geared toward growth, rather than good money just sitting in your home, well, some of us would rather be safe than sorry. True, growth investments such as stocks can go up, but they can also go down. The bottom line is this: If you are in a situation where you are having trouble meeting your monthly expenses, one of the best alternatives available to you, if you possibly can, is to pay off your mortgage right now.

Let's say that your mortgage was originally a 30-year, 7 percent fixed-rate mortgage for $150,000, with payments of $998 a month. You have been paying off this mortgage for about 10 years, which leaves 20 years to go. Even after all these years, the balance remaining on your mortgage is $128,718. You're happy living where you are, and you really don't want to move or have to sell your home just to make ends meet, but you're having a hard time, you're barely squeaking by. You have four choices: You can go back to work; you can make sure that the money you do have is making the highest safe return possible; you can reduce your expenses; or you can do a combination of any or all of the above.

The first option is always a possibility but not always a reality. Depending on your skills, your health, your desire, your ambition, the current job market, and your age, sometimes going back to work may not be as easy as it sounds. Plus you just may not want to, and even if you do go back to work for now, there may come a day when you're not able to work. Remember, there is a big difference between having to work and wanting to work.

In the second place, when you are approaching or are in your retirement years and have very little money, it is essential to place what you have in investments that are safe and sound. In reality, all that you have saved will, most likely, be required to generate the income that you use to pay your bills, so you cannot take the risk and invest it for growth. Investments that give a nice secure dividend or interest rate will be your best bet. But secure investments cannot do a lot to give you a significant increase in income. For instance, let's say that you had $200,000 invested in term deposits, paying you 5 percent interest, and you change that to debentures paying you 5.8 percent. The difference would be $1600 a year. Granted, that's $133 dollars more a month, which can help, but it won't pay the mortgage.

Your third option is to reduce your expenses. If your largest monthly expense is your mortgage payment, getting rid of it would certainly free up a good portion of your available income. If you still have time before retirement and are able to send in more money every single month, please make sure that you do so, so that your mortgage will be paid off in full by the time you retire—one of the richest feelings there is. If you think money is going to be tight when you retire, if you want to continue to live in your home, and you do not have any current credit card debt, I urge you to increase your mortgage payments right now. To find out how to be home free by retirement, call your lender and ask them to give you the extra monthly amount that will be needed to have your house paid off in X number of years, X being the number of years until you retire.

If you are facing retirement and don't have years to pay off your mortgage, here is what I would suggest.

THE COURAGE TO OWN YOUR HOME

If you have retirement savings in superannuation and other investments, you probably plan to use those savings to help you pay out the mortgage. However, if you have enough money available to you to pay off that mortgage in full right now, then I must tell you that is the best thing you could do to increase your cash flow. Let me show you why, assuming this money is not in a superannuation fund and you have access to it and that there will not be a heavy tax burden to liquidate it.

Let's assume that you have a mortgage balance of $128,718 with a monthly payment of $998, and you have 20 years remaining on the loan.

Let's also say that you have $200,000 in a term deposit earning 5 percent, but that is essentially all you have besides a little sum of money in a super-annuation fund

Most people do not like to touch the cash they have in reserve, because money in the bank makes us feel safe. But sometimes you jeopardise your safety by holding on to what you have rather than using it wisely. So let's say this is true for you, that you feel safe with that $200,000 in a term deposit, for you know that with its 5 percent interest rate, it generates about $10,000 a year, or about $833 a month before taxes. But think about this.

What if instead you took $128,718 out of your term deposit and paid off your mortgage in full? That would leave you with $71,282 in cash, which at 5 percent would still give you income of $297 a month. Even though your income from the interest would drop from $833 to $297 a month, your monthly expenses would have dropped by $998, since you no longer have a mortgage payment. The result will make all the difference, once you think about it, and if you are eligible, you would qualify for a higher social security benefit because of the drop in income from your term deposit.

Perhaps you're thinking that having only $71,000 in cash to your name does not make you feel safe. It is important that you remember that this money has not disappeared but is in your home. And it may be safer there than in your accounts.

Another scenario: You want the security of knowing you will have access to cash sometime in the future, should you need it. You can put your home to work for you by applying for an equity line of credit. The time to do this, however, is preferably when you still are working and have an income, for it is hard to qualify for a loan when you do not have money coming in. If you do get an equity line of credit, make sure you get one where you can write cheques when you need the money, not one where they give you a lump sum of cash. What we want here is a source for emergency cash only; if you never have to use those funds, it shouldn't cost you anything. It is only when you need money and write a cheque against that line of credit that you start paying interest on the money you used. If you do this, then in case of an emergency you have access to some extra cash and you do not have to feel afraid. Also, chances are good that any payments for whatever money you do use from the line of credit will be far less than your mortgage payments were.

Look for an equity line of credit with the lowest up-front fee and ongoing costs

HOME FREE

In the long run, if money is expected to be tight, the sooner you pay off your mortgage the better off you will be. The other aspect to doing so is that nothing will make you feel more secure than owning your house outright—knowing that you have a place to live that no one can take away from you. All my elderly clients have said that it was the best thing they ever did. For that matter, many of my younger clients worked hard to pay off their mortgages early as well, for the emotional payoff that comes from owning their home outright.

When you're younger, is it better to invest that extra money for growth rather than use it to pay off your mortgage early? It depends. If the idea of owning your house outright makes you feel safe and powerful, then that's the way for you to go. If you have the discipline and the tenacity to invest your money for growth, follow through on your instinct with focus and determination. I have found that the people who follow a course toward wealth and financial freedom have the courage to be rich, the courage to plan for tomorrow.

PART V

THINKING AHEAD

THE COURAGE TO CREATE YOUR FINANCIAL DESTINY

Think of the lengths we go to keep our lives safe. We want recommendations when we hire baby-sitters for our children; we buy the best locks we can to keep our houses secure. We insure what we own; we practise preventive medical care. We even make sure that a beloved pet who has to be tended to while we go on holidays will be sent to a clean, cheery kennel. Yet what do we do to safeguard our money? Surprisingly little. Can you tell me how your superannuation money is invested and how much it is earning? Can you tell me what the fee is on any managed fund you may have? Are you absolutely certain that you are doing the right thing with your money? If you have a financial adviser, are you confident that you have picked the right person to whom to entrust your financial future, and do you know how much he or she is earning from your money every year?

If it is your intention to be the master of your financial destiny, you must begin paying more attention to your money. Not all financial advertisements or advisers have your best interests at heart, so you must learn the difference between the myths that you are being told and sold, and the reality of how money works. It is never too soon to begin, it's true, but it's also true that it's never too late to start.

LAW OF MONEY

If you expect your money to take care of you, you must take care of your money.

There are only three ways to make money. One is to go out and work for it. However, few among us can work forever, and there will likely come a time in our lives when working for a pay cheque may not be an option. The second way to make money is to inherit it or to win the lottery. Again, not something that we all can count on. The third way, and the only one that is available to all of us for an unlimited amount of time, is to invest what we earn during our working years wisely, so that the money we work so hard for goes to work for us.

True richness begins when the money you earn begins to earn money itself.

CASH MANAGEMENT TRUSTS

Who should pay attention? Everyone, whatever your age. It is key that you know what to do with your cash, how to build a foundation of liquidity, and how to avoid becoming a target of salespeople when you have money just sitting in an account.

When I first started working in the money business, most people simply kept all their money in a passbook savings account at a bank. They were happy with the 2 percent a year that their savings earned, and felt safe. The other bank account that everyone had was a cheque account. This was where everyone kept the money to pay the monthly bills. Cheque accounts did not pay any interest—and in most cases, you would have to pay the bank a monthly service fee just to be able to write those cheques.

Then, brokerage firms and investment companies saw an opening in banking and began to market a more aggressive way to bank money, by combining a savings and cheque account in one account known as a *cash management trust.* A cash management trust was simply a managed fund that offered investors stability and a higher interest rate than passbook or cheque accounts, and in many cases, at a cost far less than the monthly expense of having a cheque account.

For instance, if back then you had had $20,000 in your savings account at your bank earning 2 percent, you would have earned $400 a year in interest. If you also kept $1000 or more in your cheque account to pay bills, not only did you not make any interest on that $1000 but you paid $10 a month in bank charges, so your cheque account cost you $120 a year.

When cash management trusts really started to hit the scene, in the early eighties, interest rates were unusually high. If you had had that $20,000 in a cash management trust, you would have earned 18 percent a year, or a total of $3600, compared to the $400 you'd have earned in your savings account. Many of these funds also served as cheque accounts for people who wrote just a few cheques a month. Add to this the $1000 in our example that you always kept in your cheque account that did not earn a cent of interest; in a cash management trust, you would have seen interest on that money, too. In the end, between the $400 interest that you earned on your passbook savings account and the $120 cost of your cheque account, you would have netted $280 on your $20,400. If you had opened a cash management trust with both your cheque and passbook accounts in one place at 18 percent interest, you would have earned $3780 that year. That would have been $3500 more in just one year.

Even though interest rates paid for cash management trusts today are less than one-quarter (4 percent) of what they were in the early eighties, the principle still holds true. Most savings accounts today pay about 2 percent. Consider, too, the hidden charges of banking—service charges for your cheque accounts, fees for ATM withdrawals, and so on—and then ask yourself whether a cash management trust is the right kind of account for you to have. I'd be willing to bet it is.

Questions you need to ask yourself: The money that you want to keep liquid, safe, and sound—is it earning only 2 or 3 percent in interest? Could it be earning more? How about your cheque account? Are you still paying $10 a month or more in bank charges and not earning any interest on that money? If the answer to these questions is yes, or if you don't even know for sure, then you need to put the law of money into effect: What are you doing for your money? What you can do right now is to start checking out cash management trusts.

To find the funds paying the best interest rates, check a financial magazine such as *Personal Investor.* Every month they list the best-performing trusts.

A cash management trust usually offers both a cheque account and a telephone withdrawal facility. To use the telephone withdrawal facility, all you do is ring the fund manager's office before 12 p.m. and your money is deposited into your bank account that day. If you call the fund manager's office after 12 p.m. the money is deposited into your account the next day. This redemption time can vary with different fund managers. Some fund managers also offer the option of linking your cash management trust to your American Express card. This means that if you are travelling overseas and you need more cash, you are able to make withdrawals using your American Express card.

Banks offer cash management accounts, and you have access to this money immediately and you can use a card anywhere in the world, but there are differences between the two. A cash management account will usually charge fees for each transaction, and if your balance reduces below a certain level the interest rate reduces to normal bank rates around 2 percent.

THE BEST USES FOR
CASH MANAGEMENT TRUSTS

People will often ask me, "Suze, I have some money I'll need a few years down the road, but in the meantime, what's the best way for me to invest it?" They're saving to buy a house in two years, let's say, or their child is going to university next year, or they want to buy a car in six months, or they know they'll need a new roof in about a year. Whatever the case, they want to make the most of their money in the interim. When I suggest a cash management trust, they always look at me and say, "No, you don't understand. I want to make the most I can on these funds until I need the money, and cash management trusts only pay around four percent." With that, before I say another word, I ask them to take this little test.

I ask them how much money they have to invest right now. Maybe $10,000 is the answer. Then I ask them to choose between two investment options. In the first, I can guarantee an 80 percent return on the money the first year, but it will lose 40 percent in the second year. In the second option, I will guarantee a 5 percent return on the money the first year, and in the second year it will earn 5 percent again—pretty much the way a cash management trust works.

Almost without fail, they choose the first option, for if they think they earn 80 percent the first year and only lose 40 percent the second that will still be a 40 percent gain, which is still more than the 10 percent total gain in the second example. Right? Wrong. An 80 percent gain on $10,000 is $8000, for a total of $18,000 that first year. The second year the loss is 40 percent of that $18,000, or $7200. $18,000 minus $7200 is $10,800. With the second option, 5 percent of $10,000 is $500, for a total of $10,500 after the first year. And in the second year 5 percent of $10,500 is $525, for a total of $11,025. This example tends to illustrate for people that sometimes if you just plod along steadily you can still come out ahead—much like the fable of the tortoise and the hare. This doesn't mean you should always just plod along with all of your money, not by any means. But when you have a limited time frame in which to invest, such as a year or less, then you really have only a couple of safe choices, and those are cash management trusts or term deposits.

GUIDELINE

Money you know you will need within the next six months to two years belongs in a cash management trust.

"SAFE AND SOUND" MONEY

After you have taken care of the money you know you're going to need in the not-too-distant future, the next eventuality you need to plan for is the unexpected. The goal of creating emergency funds is to make you feel safe, and this money, too, belongs in an investment such as a cash management trust. Some will feel safe with $100 in a "safe and sound" account; others will need to have $10,000 or more. Conventional wisdom says one should have three to six months' worth of living expenses set aside in a safe place, and, for the most part, I agree with this. But there is no set formula for "safe and sound" money, because your relationship with your money is personal and unique to you. So you need to ask yourself this question: How much money do I want to have safe and sound for an emergency?

Write down the first number that pops into your head. $_____

Okay, that's your figure. Either put that sum of money away in a cash management trust right now, or if you do not have that money available to you at this point, you must begin to create it. (This is assuming that you have already paid off all credit card debt.)

Let's say that you wrote down $5000, and you have nothing to start with. The next time you pay your bills, and every month thereafter, I want you to write a cheque for at least $50 to deposit into an account to work toward that goal. The sooner you get to this goal, the sooner you can go on to creating even more. Again, as soon as you have enough, try to keep this money making the most interest it can, for it will help you reach your goal that much sooner. For instance, let's say that you are able to put away $100 a month. This $100 a month put into an account earning 5 percent interest will take only 3.7 years to grow to $5000. If instead you kept the money in an account earning only 2 percent, it would take you three months longer to reach that goal.

The reason I want you to have this "safe and sound" money? Because when you feel safe, you feel powerful, and power, remember, attracts money. The safer you feel, the more powerful you are, the more money will come your way.

THE RISKS INVOLVED IN A CASH MANAGEMENT TRUST

Once you have accumulated a nice sum of money, you must make sure that it stays secure. You see, one danger of having more than five or ten thousand dollars in an account is that it is possible that you will receive a call from someone representing the bank or brokerage firm where the money is kept, offering to help you invest it so that you can get a better rate of return. Many banks now have in-house financial planners to help their clients invest. Obviously the bank or brokerage firm will make more money in the long run if you invest it in certain ways rather than others. So these companies keep an eye on accounts with a consistent stash of cash, in the hope that if they call you, you will be open to listening to their ideas. Please be careful if this happens. Just keep in mind, and say so, that your goal with these funds is to keep them safe and sound in case of an emergency.

MARGARET'S STORY

When I was eighteen and going to college, my dad got me a cheque account at his bank, which was great—my own cheques, with my own name on them. That was that, I never thought about it again. Banks are there to take care of your money, right?

When my dad died about two years ago, he left me forty thousand dollars, which was the most money I'd ever seen. I'm single now, I work at a magazine and don't make that much money, so I thought this would be a great nest egg; I would just keep it forever. I don't know anything about money. I just wanted to keep it in the bank, so I opened a savings account at the same bank, my dad's bank.

The money had been in there for about five months when I got a call from a man who said he was representing the bank. He was concerned, he said, that I had so much money sitting in a savings account when it could be working harder for me and earning more. He asked if I wanted to come in and talk to him, so I did. I remember thinking how nice it was for the bank to be so concerned and to offer this service. He said that he could put the money into managed funds, where it would grow at a great rate and be totally safe, and also that it wouldn't cost me a cent, that there weren't any commissions or fees. I said, Great, let's do it.

About six months later, I was out with a friend, and started to tell him about what had happened and all my bank was doing for free. He said that was impossible, that nobody can guarantee a great return and nobody does this stuff for free. So we went and called the bank, but the guy didn't work there anymore. The man I got instead looked up my invest-ments in the computer and said he would never have put my money in those managed funds. The first guy had put all the money into these two funds that I now learned had an upfront fee of 5 percent. They were spec-ulative equity funds, whatever that means, but I learned it meant that my money wasn't safe at all. In fact, I had lost six thousand dollars by then, and I got out of those funds that very day.

Margaret was lucky. A friend tipped her off that she had not done the right thing, but far too many of us do not have such knowledgeable friends. It may also be true that the people we have helping us might not know themselves what is right, even if they have our best interests at heart. Or it may be that they care more about their commissions than they do about our future. Whatever the case, when your money is at stake, it is your responsibility to know and understand exactly where it is; why it is where it is; what it is costing you to be there; and what the return on your investment is amounting to.

At thirty, Margaret was well advised—even by her unscrupulous adviser—to invest some of her nest egg for growth, though she was ill advised to invest it all, as well as on how to invest it. This is not a morality tale to keep you from investing, which is the last thing I'd want to do. It is a morality tale to compel you to invest wisely and well.

INVESTING FOR YOUR FUTURE

Once you have your "safe and sound" money, you have also acquired the habit of creating money, systematically, month after month. Now it is time to put that money to work for your future.

Very simply, over the course of your lifetime, a lot of people are going to try to tell you many things about many different kinds of investments. It is going to be your job to know if these investment recommendations are good for you, bad for you, or merely good for the people who are trying to sell them to you. There are a handful of investment options that come up time and again. Regardless of how your bottom-line numbers read, I want you to understand each one of them inside and out, because sooner or later, someone is going to dangle them like sugarplums before your eyes: annuities, bonds, bond funds, stocks, managed funds, insurance bonds, gold, gold funds, real estate, and superannuation. I'll address some of these investment options in the coming pages.

There is a reality inherent in most investments, and a myth, and I want you to understand the difference in each case. And you must also know and understand what is in the investment for you—and for the person selling you the investment.

KEVIN AND SUZE'S STORY

Recently I was on a plane, sitting next to a wonderful man named Kevin, who was telling me all about his youngest son, who had just become a financial planner for a small financial outfit in their home town. Kevin went on to tell me how he had turned over all his and his wife's money to their son, and how safe they felt, since they knew that they could trust their son not to take them for commissions. When I asked what kind of investments he had put them into, I felt sick to my stomach. In my opinion, Kevin's son hadn't made the wisest investment choices for his parents' money. Not even close.

I tried to be gentle as I explained to Kevin what was involved in this investment. But first, I tried even harder to explain the investment from his son's point of view, because his son, I knew without a doubt from talking to Kevin, would never have knowingly done anything in the world to hurt his parents.

You see, when you become a broker, you are learning the business from the ground up, and what you are learning is what your brokerage firm teaches you. And what is that? They are teaching you how to sell investments that make the most money for the firm but don't always make the most sense for the investor. All investments presented in a certain way can seem perfectly suited for a particular investor, even if they don't in the real world. Most brokers are not bad people. I know; I worked with many wonderful people at Merrill Lynch and Prudential-Bache, and by no means is this to suggest that every broker—and every investment he or she advises—will work against your best interests. Investing your money wisely and well will, indeed, make you rich. It is, however, a reminder that, bottom line, you and you alone are responsible for your money and your investments.

CHAPTER 18

How Does Your Superannuation Grow?

You've heard the phrase *Pay yourself first*? What this means is that tending to your future is the highest financial obligation there is—and the best way I know how to do this is by investing in superannuation as soon as you possibly can, and adding to it year after year, all the way through your working life. This act of self-service will reward you richly.

I have had young people tell me they can't afford to save extra in superannuation; they don't make enough money yet. To this I say, You can't afford *not* to think about your future *now,* in your early adult years, for even the smallest contributions made during these years can grow into huge sums later on, and later on comes sooner than we expect—for all of us. I have also had people say to me that their employer is investing the max in their superannuation at work, so why bother topping up? Because a little less money for you to live on today will mean a lot more money later, it's that simple.

I don't recommend contributing your own money to your superannuation fund if you intend buying a home in the future, and you will need to access this money for a deposit. Once you've done this and if all of your other needs are taken care of, you should start adding your own contributions into superannuation as soon as possible, because there are tax benefits to be gained from this investment and the sooner you start the more you will accumulate. The only other time I would *not* recommend topping up your superannuation is if you know that you can receive a better after tax return on investments you could make on your own.

People often tell me they feel too old to join a superannuation fund— what difference will it make now? Such reasoning lacks courage, for there is no room for wealth in defeat. If you're playing catch-up, joining a superannuation fund is the place to start.

HOW SUPERANNUATION WORKS

There was a time when superannuation was relatively clear cut, but since the introduction of the Superannuation Guarantee Levy many of the rules have changed. Even though it seems complicated it is important that you understand how your superannuation works as it can make a difference to your financial future. Below are questions and answers to help you better understand superannuation.

Are all super funds the same?

No. There are two types of funds: *defined benefit* and *accumulation fund*. A *defined benefit fund* is one where you receive a set payout figure on retirement. This figure is based on the age you retire. For instance, if you retired at 55 you could receive four times your annual salary, and if you worked until 60 you could receive five times your annual salary. The advantage of this type of fund is that you know exactly how much you will receive when you retire and your money is not subject to the ups and downs of the financial markets. These funds are common for government employees and some private companies. If you are a defined benefit fund the investment performance of the fund is of no real concern to you, as it does not affect your end benefit.

The performance of an *accumulation fund*, on the other hand, does make a difference. A poor performing fund can make a big difference to how much your final payout will be. *Accumulation funds* are the most popular, and work this way: whatever you or your employer contributes, minus fees, is invested and how those investments perform will affect how much you receive on retirement. The timing of these investments is important as well. While shares are a good long-term investment and may serve you well in your 30s and 40s, you need to pay careful attention to where your money is invested as you move closer to retirement. Following the Stock Market crash of 1987, some people discovered that 50 percent of their retirement benefit had been wiped out overnight. And, it wasn't just the people who liked to take risks that were affected; some people who put their money into superannuation funds with their bank, thinking banks are safe, lost money as well. You need to choose carefully the superannuation fund and nominate where you want your money invested. This is something that you need to know.

If my employer contributes to superannuation at work, do I still need to have my own super fund?

Since the introduction of the Superannuation Guarantee Levy, employers must contribute a percentage of your salary to a superannuation fund. The following are the percentages that your employer must contribute to superannuation on your behalf:

1999/2000	7 percent of gross salary
2000/2002	8 percent of gross salary
2002/2003	9 percent of gross salary

While this may seem like a lot of money to some people, your superannuation may have to provide for you for a period of twenty or thirty years. Australians have been very fortunate in having a system where they could count on a government pension in their retirement years, but statistics show that the number of retirees will be more than double what they are now in twenty years time— there will not be enough people in the workforce to pay for these pensions. A pension will no longer be an automatic right, and it is your responsibility to provide for your own future.

Let's say that you accumulate a lump sum of $300,000 in your superannuation fund; that may seem like a large amount, it could be the largest sum of money you will ever have in your life. If you invest $300,000 at 5 percent, you will receive an annual income of

$15,000 before tax. That's not a lot of money, and keep in mind that not everyone invests the whole amount; most people usually dip into their lump sum when they retire to buy a new car or major appliances, take a trip or give some money to their children.

How much can I contribute?

Quite a lot and there are tax advantages to saving this way. Whatever your employer contributes on your behalf is taxed at 15 percent (you can pay up to 30 percent if you're a high income earner), and that is considerably less tax than most people pay on their salary. The maximum tax-deductible contributions your employer can make on your behalf for the year 1999/2000 (these figures are indexed) are shown below:

Under 35	maximum contribution is $10,929
35 to 49	maximum contribution is $30,356
50 and over	maximum contribution is $75,283

You can make your own contributions by taking "salary sacrifice". "Salary sacrifice" means that you take less salary and ask your employer to contribute the difference to your superannuation fund. These contributions are also taxed at 15 percent (unless you are a high income earner) and if your marginal tax rate is 34 percent you've saved money even before your investment starts working for you. But to do this your employer must make this offer to you in writing.

You can also add your own after-tax contributions, but whether you will receive a tax deduction depends on your income. If you earn less than $27,000 a year, you can claim a rebate up to $100. This rebate reduces between $27,000 and $31,000, finally cutting out when your income reaches $31,000. Contributions into superannuation that come from after-tax dollars are not taxed.

Can I contribute to a superannuation fund for my spouse?

Yes. If your spouse earns up to $10,800 a year, you can contribute up to $3,000 to her or his superannuation fund and receive a tax rebate. This rebate is $540 on contributions of $3000, and 18 percent on lesser amounts. If your spouse earns between $10,800 and $13,800, you can still contribute but the amount of the rebate will be less.

Where can I join a superannuation fund?

Some employers allow you to elect which superannuation fund your contributions go to; others have their own superannuation fund that the money is automatically paid into and there is little you can do about it. You can also join your own superannuation fund, and these are available from insurance companies, investment companies and banks.

Once I join a superannuation fund, what can I invest the money in?

You can invest it in a variety of ways. Your selection will depend on what the firm you joined has to offer. Please take this into consideration before joining a fund. For instance, if you wanted to invest in a particular area such as shares, and you opened a superannuation fund that only invests in cash type investments, you would be unable to do so. There are many superannuation funds that offer a wide variety of investment choices, and they allow you to move your money (this is called switching) from one fund to another. This type of fund is ideal, as it allows you to move your money into more secure investments as you get closer to retirement age.

Will I have to pay tax on my money while it is in superannuation?

No. The superannuation fund pays tax on contributions and investment earnings at the rate of 15 percent, unless you are a high income earner. If you earn over $78,208 (1999/2000), you will pay a surcharge of 1 percent tax on contributions for each thousand, until you reach $94,966. These figures are also indexed. So, for instance, if your income is $100,000 a year, you will pay 30 percent tax on your superannuation contributions between $75,856 and $92,111, but this is still a lot less than the top personal tax rate. Either way, you do not pay the tax yourself, your superannuation fund pays it out of contributions.

How many superannuation funds can I have?

You can have as many as you want.

Is there an advantage to having more than one superannuation fund?

In my opinion, in most cases there is a disadvantage in having more than one account. You see, most superannuation funds charge a yearly fee. That annual fee can vary according to how much you have in each fund, but they add up, particularly over a number of funds. If you are paying a $25 fee on your superannuation fund, that may not seem like much, but multiply it by a number of funds and your investment return diminishes.

Can 1 or 2 percent difference really add up to that much more or less in actual dollars?

Absolutely. Let's say that you put $2000 a year in a superannuation fund that averages 10 percent a year for the next 30 years. You would have a total of $328,988. If you had made just 9 percent a year, or 1 percent less, you would have only about $272,614 and at 8 percent a year you would have $226,566. Over time a little less return really can make a huge difference.

Are there any other disadvantages to having many superannuation funds?

Yes. When it comes to keeping track of all the accounts and what the investments are doing, sometimes it's easier to get just one statement with everything on it. It will also be easier for you to have a single account when it comes time to withdraw your money on retirement. And, people have been known to forget about a fund when they have too many and forget to claim their money.

What do I do then with all the small superannuation funds that I have accumulated from the different jobs?

You do not have to leave your superannuation in your employer's or industry fund; you can roll it over into your own fund. Or, if one of the funds you currently have is a good one that suits your investment criteria, you can roll all of your other funds into it. You need to be careful if you are planning to roll over a personal superannuation fund as the penalties incurred for early withdrawal can be savage and may not be worth it. Ask for a pay-out figure before making any decisions.

Will I have to pay tax on superannuation if I roll over?

No. Just as the name implies, your money simply rolls over from one superannuation fund to another, so no tax is payable.

How much can I have in superannuation?

The *reasonable benefit limit* is the same flat rate for everyone and this is indexed to weekly earnings every year. For the financial year 1999/2000, the reasonable benefit limit was $485,692 for a lump sum, or $971,382 if you wish to take half as a lump sum and half as a pension. Amounts accumulated over those figures are called *excess benefits* and are taxed at the top marginal rate. Keep in mind, though, that you have to save a lot of money to accumulate nearly a million dollars, and that these figures are indexed.

When can I access this money?

Contributions from the Superannuation Guarantee Levy and personal superannuation funds cannot be withdrawn until you retire, and you must be at least 55 before you have access to them. These are known as *preserved contributions*.

Recent legislation increased the age of preservation for many younger Australians and if you were born after 1960 you will be unable to access your preserved benefits until the following ages.

If you were born between 1 July 1960 and 30 June 1961, your preservation age is 56.
If you were born between 1 July 1961 and 30 June 1962, your preservation age is 57.
If you were born between 1 July 1962 and 30 June 1963, your preservation age is 58.
If you were born between 1 July 1963 and 30 June 1964, your preservation age is 59.
If you were born after 1 July 1964 your preservation age is 60.

Generally your superannuation contributions are preserved if:

+ they are part of the superannuation guarantee levy.
+ you contribute to a personal superannuation fund.
+ your company contributed (including "salary sacrifice") after 1 July 1996.
+ all contributions after 1 July 1999.

However, if you are under age 55 and you withdraw contributions that are not preserved, you will have to pay tax at the rate of 20 to 30 percent, depending on whether these benefits were originally taxed or not.

Can I access this money in an emergency?

The early release of superannuation is subject to stringent guidelines by the Insurance and Superannuation Commissioner. You can apply for early release of part or all of your superannuation under the following circumstances:

- To meet medical expenses for yourself or a dependant.
- To meet medical transport expenses for yourself or a dependant.
- If you are disabled.
- If you need palliative care.
- For funeral expenses.
- To meet mortgage repayments if you are in danger of losing your home.

It takes four to six weeks for your request to be assessed by the Insurance and Superannuation Commissioner's office, and then usually three to four weeks for your money to be released from the fund manager, so even in desperate circumstances it takes time to access this money and tax would still have to be paid on these withdrawals.

What tax do I pay on retirement?

Tax on superannuation has been complicated by the many different amendments that have been made over the past 15 years or so. There are four different categories and all are taxed in different ways.

- *Pre July 1 1983 component.* Ninety-five percent of this money is tax free. Only 5 percent is taxable at your marginal tax rate plus Medicare levy.
- *Post 30 June 1983 component.* Firstly, there are the contributions you have paid 15 percent tax on, and secondly the contributions that have not been taxed; the other consideration is your retirement age. These tax rates are as follows:

233

Retirement age	Post 1983 taxed component	Post 1983 untaxed component
Under 55	20 percent tax	30 percent tax
55 and over	Nil up to $93,731	15 percent
Over 55 and in excess of $96,657	15 percent	30 percent

The amount of $96,657 (1999/2000 figure) is indexed to weekly earnings.

+ *Undeducted contributions.* These are your contributions made after 30 June 1983 that you received no tax deduction for. There is no tax on these contributions.
+ *Excess benefits.* Any amounts over the reasonable benefit limit are taxed at the top marginal tax rate plus Medicare levy.

What happens to my money in superannuation if I die?

If you nominated a beneficiary when you joined the fund, the money will automatically go to that person. Failing that, the trustee will pay the entitlement to the most appropriate person, such as the contributor's spouse or children.

THE END RESULT

Let's say that beginning at age 22 you invest $2000 into superannuation for the next 15 years, a total investment of $30,000. And let's say that after that you cease work so you just let the money sit there until you turn 65. At the end of the 15 years, at age 37, if your money earns 9 percent, you will have $58,722 in this account. By the time you turn 65, if your money continues to earn an average return of 9 percent, you will have $655,757. All this money was created from investing $2000 a year, starting at age 22, for just 15 years. No matter how much you make later on, this will be a wonderful nest egg. I urge you to start now.

MAKING SENSE
OF INVESTMENTS

What do we think, say and do with our money? Too often, we base our thoughts, phrase our words, and take action based on myths that have been passed down from parent to child, financial adviser to client, real estate agent to home buyer, car salesman or insurance agent to consumer; from colleague to colleague, neighbour to neighbour, or friend to friend. The problem is that when financial reality hits—perhaps in our forties, fifties, or even later—these financial myths explode, making us wish that we had been paying closer attention to our own financial reality all along.

Things are going to be different in the next century from the way they were in the century that's just behind us. Most likely, you are not going to have a benevolent employer to take care of you throughout your working life. What will happen to social security, and the promise of that system, is anyone's guess—although the people who are guessing don't, for the most part, have high hopes that the system will protect you in the way you wish it would. If you have an employer now, this employer is proba-bly asking you to help fund your own retirement. If you are self-employed, as more and more of us are today, you already know that you must fund your own retirement. Statistically, you are projected to live longer in the next century, too. Tomorrow, in other words, is becoming much more urgent for all of us. And for many of us, tomorrow may be closer than we think.

So the question that presents itself is: How are you going to live tomorrow? It is a question that we all must answer today.

ANNUITIES

This is the great blanket investment to cover you when you're about to retire or are retired, right? Not so fast. Even though this is an investment that many financial advisers love to sell you, and one that lots of people, regardless of age, love to buy, more myths surround it than almost any other investment I know about. In some cases, annuities make sense, and in others they do not, but sooner or later someone will try to peddle you some, so I want you to read this section very carefully. Getting into an investment is easy. Getting out is a different matter entirely.

GRACE'S STORY

When my father died, everything was left to my mother in an insurance policy. He left her $56,000, which was pretty much all she had. So my brother, my mother and I went to a financial adviser, who put her into an annuity with something called a ten-year-certain period of time. He said this would give her the highest possible monthly income. The adviser was really persuasive on this point, so we went ahead.

Shortly thereafter, my mother started feeling really unwell, and it turned out she had cancer. The doctors couldn't tell exactly how long she had, but they thought it would be a matter of months. My mother died two months later, and of course she left the money to my brother and me, and again we had to sort everything out. We decided we didn't want the annuity anymore, since we didn't need the monthly income, so we called the adviser again. This time he wasn't so congenial. He said that if we cashed it in, we would get only $38,000. This was just two months later! Our so-called investment had gone down by 32 percent! We found out where some of that money went when my brother read the fine print more carefully. The adviser had made a commission of $3000. But the more upset-

ting part was why he had put Mother into an investment that lost so much
money. We still don't understand it.

Grace is right not to understand, for investing her mother's money in an
annuity makes no sense from her standpoint. From the financial adviser's
standpoint, however, it made a great deal of sense. Let's define an annuity,
and how various ones work, and then I will explain when they make
sense and when they do not.

WHAT IS AN ANNUITY?

An *annuity* (regardless of what kind of an annuity it is) is a contract, or
policy, between you as the policyholder and an insurance company,
which invests on your behalf and provides a regular income stream. The
minimum investment in most annuities is usually around $5000, and can
be purchased with ordinary money or eligible termination payments.

Eligible Termination Payments (ETP)

When a person leaves their employment, for whatever reason, they can
receive an ETP. An eligible termination payment includes:

- A payment from the employer for permanent disability, an ex
  gratia payment that does not include annual leave or long service
  leave, and a golden handshake.
- A payment from a superannuation fund
- Payment in lieu of notice
- Compensation for wrongful dismissal

WHERE DO YOU BUY AN ANNUITY?

An *insurance company* can sell you an investment called an annuity. As
with other investments, you can buy an annuity through a brokerage firm
or financial planner, and in some cases through banks and investment
companies.

COMMISSIONS/FEES

Annuities pay high commissions, which is why brokers love them so. Usually the fee that the person "earns" by selling you an annuity is around 5 to 6 percent of the amount of money you invested. In some cases it can be lower.

OWNER

The person who purchases the contract, or policy, is known as the *owner.* This person can make any changes he wants subject to the terms of the policy, anytime he wants—he owns the policy. Two people or more can own a policy as well, as co-owners, provided the annuity is not purchased with ETP money.

DEATH BENEFIT/ANNUITANT

In order for an annuity to qualify as a legitimate insurance contract—which is what allows it to enjoy certain tax advantages—someone has to be insured. This person is known as the *annuitant.* The annuitant has no power whatsoever over the money, unless, as is often the case, the owner and the annuitant are the same person. There is no additional death benefit involved with an annuity, which makes it very different from other life insurance policies that you may be familiar with.

The annuitant becomes important because the amount of income that you can receive will be determined by the annuitant's age. In other words, if I bought an annuity and named my mother as the annuitant, she would qualify for much more money each month than I would if I named myself the annuitant. This is because the monthly payments are partly based on the annuitant's life expectancy. The older the annuitant, the shorter their life expectancy, the shorter the amount of time the insurance company will have to pay out those monthly payments, and so the larger each payment will be.

DIFFERENT KINDS OF ANNUITIES

Today, for all practical purposes, the main kinds of annuities fall under the following categories:

+ Immediate annuity
+ Deferred annuity
+ Allocated annuity
+ Complying annuity

IMMEDIATE ANNUITY

An *immediate annuity* is a contract with an insurance company that guarantees the annuitant an immediate fixed income for the rest of his or her life. Annuities can be taken out on joint lives and payments continue until the death of the last surviving person. For this promise, however, you must sign over all the money you have deposited in the annuity to the insurance company with full knowledge that you will never be able to touch it again, apart from receiving the monthly income. There are tax advantages to a policy like this, in that each monthly payment is considered a partial return of principal, so that a portion of your payment is not taxed. In addition to the interest your funds are earning, the return of some of your principal enables the company to pay you a higher monthly income than you could probably get elsewhere on a guaranteed basis.

Annuitisation

The amount of income you will receive is based on your age, the current interest rates, and the maximum amount of time you have chosen for the company to have to pay out that stream of income, even if you were to die. The income options range from the highest monthly amounts of *life only,* to lower amounts known as *term certain.* Here's how they work.

Life Only

If you were to choose *life only,* the company would pay you a certain amount of money every month, starting immediately, for the rest of your life. These fixed payments would continue like clockwork for as long as you are alive, even if you were to live another hundred years. You cannot outlive the income stream of an annuity, no matter what option you chose. If, however, you opted for life only, and you died the month after you had started to receive this income, too bad—the payments stop, and your beneficiaries get nothing. The reason that this option gives you the highest monthly income is that they know that once you die, they're off the hook. These monthly payments are determined by a number of factors, including your age, your medical history, and the current interest rate environment. An insurance company can usually project your life expectancy with a fair amount of accuracy. If they're wrong, and you die sooner than projected, they win big-time. If you live to your full life expectancy, then they are within the limit of their projected figures. If you live far longer than expected, well, they figure that doesn't happen very often, so it's not a financial disaster for them.

If an annuity is purchased in joint names and one party dies, the annuity would continue to be paid but the income would be less. Usually the income reduces to 60 percent of the original agreed rate.

Capital protection

The most obvious drawback to an immediate annuity is the financial loss if you were to die shortly after purchase. You can now incorporate a guarantee period. With a guaranteed period, in the event of death of the annuitant, the income is paid until the expiration of guarantee period, or a lump sum can be paid. The income stream from this annuity would be less, as the risk for the insurance company is higher.

The other option is *term certain*. What this option means is that they will pay you your designated amount every month for the agreed term. This is usually five to ten years, but can be as little as one year. If you die before the annuity term runs out, the remainder of the income will be paid to your estate, or, if the annuity is in joint names, to the survivor.

It is possible to commute part or all of this annuity prior to the expiration of the term. A penalty may be imposed, as the investment company may need to dispose of long-term securities purchased to fund the annuity.

A term certain annuity also has an option that allows you to receive a part of your capital at the end of the term selected; this is known as the RCV (residual capital value). This option will reduce the income, but if a term certain annuity is purchased when interest rates are high, you can still collect a regular income and retain your original capital.

Who Might Want to Buy an Immediate Annuity?

- Those looking for a guaranteed monthly income with some tax benefits
- Those who have no beneficiaries to whom to leave their money

- Those who immediately need a higher income than a straight interest-bearing investment can provide
- Those who want to take advantage of a high-interest-rate environment. The perfect time to have purchased an immediate annuity, for example, with respect to interest rates, would have been in the eighties, when interest rates were high, not in the late nineties, when interest rates were relatively low.

Caution

Please note that a lifetime immediate annuity is my least favourite of all annuities. Purchasing an immediate annuity, especially in today's low-interest-rate environment, is not something I recommend. If interest rates go up—and as of this writing I do not think they can go down much further—you are stuck at these low rates for the rest of your life.

TAX AND ANNUITIES

Financial planners often use the taxation benefits as one of the major selling points for purchasing an annuity. In the case of an immediate annuity purchased with ordinary money, your tax is reduced because a part of the income you receive is a return of your capital—this would be the case with any other investment if you drew down capital. The real benefits are only seen when an annuity is purchased with ETP money.

By rolling over into an annuity, you can avoid lump sum tax. As well as that, the Taxation Office grants a 15 percent tax rebate on the assessable amount, provided that the annuity is purchased with ETP money, you are over 55 and the ETP is not excessive.

BOTTOM LINE ON ANNUITIES

As we've seen, there is much to know about this one investment that so often is presented to us as if we would never want to invest our money anywhere else. There are reasons why they sometimes make sense, but there are many more reasons why they do not. Please be careful; even though this is an investment that most likely will not devastate you, it is not, in most cases, an investment that will give you the biggest bang for your buck. When in doubt, get a second or a third opinion. Make sure the people you are getting the second or third opinion from know at the outset that they will not be selling you anything, that you are just asking for advice. Remove any sales motivation from the transaction. And take the time to look around to see whether you can do better.

PART VI

THE
COURAGE
TO BE
RICH

CHAPTER 20

THE COURAGE
TO CONNECT
TO THE WORLD

Let us infuse our lives with this thought. It is our job on this earth to make the world a nicer place when we leave it than it was when we entered it. Think of all the good you can do in a lifetime—create a happy world for yourself, with the happiness radiating to those around you; raise a decent, responsible and productive child; tend a plot of land; be a loving friend; participate in your community; do a good and ethical job in your life's work; help strangers in need; vote and volunteer for what you believe in; give money to charity.

In every action, we are making an offering to the world. If you litter, you are making an offering, and if you pick up litter, you also are making an offering, though one of a very different kind. Yelling at a child is making an offering to the world, and taking time to be patient with a child is an offering, too. Expressing curtness in the simplest daily transactions is an offering, as is showing kindness in those very same deeds. Thousands of times a day we tell the world who we are—our thoughts, words, and actions resonate and affect others as well as ourselves. In this respect, we can live a rich life or a poor one, and it won't make one bit of difference whether we have lots of money or none at all. Have you ever offered help to a stranger, with no forethought, just because you happened to be there when that stranger needed help? And didn't that rich act of kindness bring you satisfaction and a sense of well-being all day? That's living rich, beyond the bottom line; looking a stranger in the eye and wanting to help is tantamount to seeing and reflecting God.

There's more than simply kindness called for, though, if you are to live a life both courageous and rich.

We go through life, you see, relying on thousands of givens—that when we go to sleep at night we'll surely wake up in the morning; that our car will take us where we want to go; that aspirin will cure a headache. The very rhythms of our lives are ordered by such givens, which propel our course from one day to the next—and they inspire the biggest given of all: that we are safe and sound. When it comes to the all-important subject of our money, however, most of us are unable to create or summon, let alone believe, the givens that truly will keep us safe: that we have done all we can for our money, so our money will do all it can for us; that there will always be enough; that we have put in place the course toward wealth. This is what the courage to be rich is about—creating the givens and believing them. Once you can believe in yourself and your money in the same way that you believe the sun will rise each morning, you will be rich. And once the doubts have been dispelled and replaced by new financial givens and convictions, you will be free to live a different kind of life, a rich life.

We have seen how to use money to elevate our relationships with other people. We have learned how to value money, how to spend it wisely, how to invest and protect it. These all are generous acts, set as they are in the context of our immediate lives. Now we must learn to draw upon our courage to send our money farther into the world, to relinquish our money, and to make our offerings.

THE SPIRIT OF GIVING

LAW OF MONEY

When you open your hands to make an offering, you draw the world back inside you.

In the Hindu tradition, there exists a goddess called Laxsmi, the goddess of material and spiritual abundance. Whenever you see her image, she is pictured atop a lotus blossom, the flower of enlightenment. Gold coins pour from her hands into the ocean of existence below her. The idea, of course, is that in order to rise up, materially and spiritually, we have to free ourselves by making offerings, by allowing some of the money we're holding to pour back into the world. Our responsibility in life is always to keep money flowing, for in the flow is purity and, ultimately, richness. Hoarding stops the flow. An unwillingness to give stagnates the flow, obscuring true richness.

What can your money give you? In many ways, it gives you your place in the world. But in order to give the richness and abundance of the world a place within you, to enable the world to dwell within you, you must in return give money away.

I am asking you to consider giving money away every month, not only for the sake of the world but for your own sake. Whenever there is a flow of money in, even the merest flow, then money must be sent back into the world generously and expansively.

The reason for this is that you can never become rich if thoughts of poverty determine your actions. If you hate paying bills and feel oppressed and poor, then you will be showing to yourself and others a demeanour that is also clenched and poor. If, however, you write a cheque to charity—in any amount—every single month as you pay the rest of your bills, then your demeanour will instead be expansive and open, ready to receive. Consider it a private transaction between you and a cause you believe in, on behalf of the cause and on your own behalf. You will feel lighter as you mail your cheques, and you will think richer thoughts. You were able this month to do something to help.

As a result of that thinking process, you will also be more open to possibility and, as a result, more will come your way. Don't give in order to receive, but know that a gift will always be returned. Making a donation monthly is the way to connect with the world and to add to and participate in its flow of abundance. You have, therefore you give, and then—sooner or later, in one form or another—you will receive all that you can possibly hold, all that you are meant to have.

HOW MUCH SHOULD I GIVE?

Every religion and charitable organisation seeks, accepts, and relies on offerings or donations, and those offerings, from each and every one of us, keep money and goodness flowing throughout the world. Our world would be unimaginable without such offerings. Yet how many of us actually sit down and figure out what we can responsibly afford to share with the world and, given how much we have, how much we're required to give back? This is a decision that we each have to make for ourselves, and it's not solely dependent on either heart or pocketbook but on a harmonious collaboration between the two. But no matter how much or how little you have today, you must give money away each and every month.

The traditional formula for giving is tithing, which Merriam Webster defines this way: "to pay or give a tenth part of [one's income] especially for the support of the church". Ten percent. But is the standard 10 percent always the right amount to give? Is 10 percent what God really wants?

The poorest people (emotionally speaking) I've worked with, regardless of how their actual numbers read, are those who give nothing or too little—and also those who give too much. Recent statistics show that Americans are not a nation of givers, or at least not a nation of tithers. In 1995, 69 percent of American households donated money—certainly a majority. Among households with income less than $10,000, the giving rate was the highest for any economic group: 4.3 percent of income. Among households with income in the $40,000 to $50,000 range, the level of giving fell to 1.3 percent. Jumping to households whose income was

$100,000 or more, the level of giving rose again, to 3.4 percent, but it was still less percentage-wise than that given by those making less than $10,000.

Although these numbers reinforce the conventional truth of philanthropy—that people who have less give more—they do little to tell us how much you or I should give, because each of the 69 percent of households that give is an entirely different household, with different needs, concerns, values and obligations. Having worked with so many people and their money, I have come to believe that there is no predetermined formula, that you must decide the amount to give on your own, but that amount must be a respectful amount. I am all for giving as much as you can, not a penny less, and not a penny more.

LESLIE'S STORY

Not that we were doing that well before, but after I lost Sam, my husband, three years ago, things went from bad to worse. After the medical bills and the funeral expenses, I never caught back up. I make thirty thousand dollars a year, but the thing is that I also have twenty-five thousand dollars in credit card debt. I've always been a spender, but now I've stopped and am spending only on necessities—still I'm just trying to stay afloat. Sam and I bought a new car shortly before he got sick, and it's been repossessed. I put our house on the market and, once it sells, I'll move in with my daughter to save money, but I'll be lucky if I get enough money out of it to pay off the mortgage.

In desperation, I made an appointment with a solicitor I found in the phone book to ask about declaring bankruptcy, but that's as far as I got; I ended up cancelling the appointment. It's such a small town, you know, I'd be mortified if anyone found out.

I don't know what I'm going to do. I look at my bills, and I don't know how I can live any more cheaply. I shut off the lights every time I leave a room, and sometimes I build a fire in the fireplace to heat the house so I can save on my gas bill. I never eat out or go to the movies. I cancelled my cable and go to the library rather than buy books. The only good thing is that I still manage to give two hundred and fifty dollars a month to my church. I haven't missed a payment yet!

GIVING TOO MUCH

I can't tell you the number of letters I've received telling stories like Leslie's, of people who haven't a penny to their names, are close to declaring bankruptcy, yet are still tithing 10 percent a month, month in and month out. Is this what God wants? I have to tell you I do not think so.

I have not travelled the world as widely as some, but wherever I have gone, I have been struck by one thing above all else. God's dwellings—his churches, temples, synagogues, mosques—exist everywhere, and they are beautiful everywhere. Even in the poorest regions of our world, God dwells in splendour, or at least in splendour relative to the conditions His subjects live in. But doesn't every doctrine in the world tell us that God dwells not only in His own house but in the house and heart of each and every one of us? Would God want you to give more than you are truly able to give? Do you really believe that God wants you to live with the anxiety that comes from not being able to pay your bills? For your children to live in squalor, while His own house is gilded? If you are not making it financially, it is possible that in the end you will be asking God to work twice as hard to take care of you. And it is not only God who will see your pain and suffering, but your family and those who love you as well.

Nowhere in the scriptures is it written that in order to be spiritual you must remain poor, although far too many of us still struggle with the notion that there is something intrinsically evil about wanting money, or pursuing it. In fact, the opposite is true: The more you have, the more good you are able to do, for your loved ones, for your community, out in the larger world. Keeping yourself poor to enrich others is doing a disservice to yourself and, therefore, to God.

I myself believe that God wants you to give enough to feel expansive and rich, without ever giving so much that it makes you poor.

LAW OF MONEY

—

*You must give to feel richer,
never to become poorer.*

When you give more than is respectful to yourself, when you put your own financial safety in jeopardy, then you become a burden on this world rather than a gift to it. For in the end it is possible that your God, your community, and possibly your children will have to take care of you. Is this the kind of offering that you want to make to your world? Is this passing down a message of true generosity? When you can't be generous to yourself, you aren't being generous to or respectful of the world. When your gift imposes a burden on yourself, then it is not a generous or respectful gift. When you are in debt and give anything more than a small but respectful monthly offering, then you are giving away not your own money but your creditors' money.

What is a respectful amount? For each one of you it will be different. For some, if you are in a situation like Leslie's, it could be five or ten dollars a month; for others it could be far more. Make your offering from the heart, an offering that is not so easy that it is an almost thoughtless gesture, but one that will allow you to pay your bills. For those of you who do not have debt, make an offering that will expand who you are and how you feel about yourself, not one that diminishes all that you have become.

JULIA'S STORY

I always knew I wanted to be a solicitor, and actually, I was lucky when I went to law school, because back then there were so many fewer women attending—and everybody wanted to (or had to, anyway) hire female solicitors. I was the first woman to make partner at my firm. I guess I've always been pretty hard-driving, a workaholic, but to a great extent it's because I have to be. I travel a lot, I'm hardly ever home, but I don't feel deprived, because I love my work, so devoting so much time to it doesn't feel like a sacrifice to me. And how could I complain anyway, when I'm so well compensated? I make two hundred thousand dollars a year, and don't spend that much of it. I have a lot invested in the market and superannuation.

When I went to see my accountant last year to prepare my taxes, she asked about charitable deductions I might have made, and I felt so embarrassed. I had given very little. She didn't say anything directly, but she gave me this kind of reproachful look. She explained that charitable donations were great deductions and I ought to look into them, and left it at that. But I knew what she was thinking. Here I am, making all this money, and I hadn't given more than the five hundred dollars I gave in honour of my uncle when he died. It's not that I'm a greedy or selfish person, I don't think, it's just that I'm so busy all the time, I never stopped to think about it in any kind of organised way. It was never an issue in my life.

For all her money and despite her high-powered career, Julia is anything but rich. By her own admission, she has a single-track life, and she's right—she is lucky to both love her work and be well paid for it. But look how easily embarrassed she was by her accountant's reaction to her stingy pattern of giving. What that tells me is that beneath that high-powered, intelligent exterior is a person living uncomfortably with shame. A person made smaller by the knowledge that she hasn't adequately shared her gifts with the world—for whatever reason. Doesn't Julia's story remind you of one of the stories from Chapter 2 of this book? I bet if she looked deep within herself and into her past, she would find the source of the shame that results in her hoarding and holding on too tightly to what she has.

If you are ashamed of what you give, you are diminished by your actions. If instead you expand to give what you can, you are enhanced.

GIVING TOO LITTLE

When you don't have vast sums of money, it gives you a very powerful feeling, and is a rich and courageous act, to write a cheque and make an offering of a respectful amount, whether that amount is ten, fifteen, twenty dollars, or more. You come away knowing that you could happily afford your donation and also that giving, regardless of the amount, is an expansive action. This sense of well-being that comes from giving and the hope implicit in that gesture are surely reasons why, in our culture, those with the least give the highest percentage as offerings or donations. But what happens when you have more?

GIVING THE RIGHT AMOUNT

When you have more, as your income grows, it can become much harder to write commensurately more expansive cheques, to add the right number of zeros to the amount, to stick with the same generous percentage as your monthly offering. For instance, when you are making $25,000 a year it is a lot easier to write monthly cheques for 10 percent, or roughly $200 a month, than it is to write monthly cheques of $2000 when you are making $250,000 a year, or $20,000 a month if you are making $2,500,000 a year. Suddenly, that 10 percent seems enormous.

PAMELA'S STORY

I have to say, I'm the last person who ever expected to make any money. I'm an artist, and I always thought being an artist meant being poor. And it did for a long time. All through my twenties and thirties, I was poor. But after an influential critic singled out my work in a group show, it began to sell, then really sell. After two decades of toiling away in virtual obscurity—I was "discovered" overnight! I was picked up by an important gallery and given my own show. It was incredibly exciting—living out the dream I'd nurtured way back in art school. A lot of the pieces sold even before the opening! At that point, the money started rolling in.

At first I just spent it. I bought a house, a car, clothes, until that started feeling pretty empty. It actually felt kind of weird, having so much more money than I ever expected I would. I didn't like this "art star" thing. It came with a sort of heavy feeling, like being off balance, and I didn't like the work I was producing. My gallery started getting anxious; I was feeling all this pressure, and nothing seemed to make me happy. I began to think that the money was really getting in the way of my life. I had to restore the balance.

One day I was leafing through this financial magazine (in a dentist's office, of course) and came across an article about giving money away systematically, and for some reason it felt as if it had been written just for me. I've always supported certain causes, fifty dollars here, fifty dollars there, but now I began to think since I had more I should give more. I began giving money away every month, just like the article said. Don't misunderstand—I wasn't reckless. I kept plenty and invested plenty. But I decided I could do more. The first cheque I wrote was for five hundred dollars; that felt scary, but I sent it. Not long after, I sold a painting for more money than I ever had before; then I sent a cheque for a thousand dollars. I really felt exhilarated about that, but more in control in a funny way. I know it sounds odd, but I really did begin to feel better about my work, and my work got better, too—other people could see it, so you don't have to take my word for it.

Last year for Christmas I opened investment accounts for my two nephews, which gave me this incredible feeling of power, and then I began to get it. It's true that money is power, but as with any kind of power, you have to use it in the right way. That's where the balance comes in, for me anyway. Keep too much, and you weigh down your side of the scale. Let go of some, and you will feel released.

Do you see the lesson here? Every charitable act enhances you, without diminishing what you have. What happened after Pamela's first big donation? She sold a painting for more than she ever had before, which meant that her gift came back to her. Then she made an even bigger donation of thanks, and her gift restored both her inner harmony and her financial harmony. She found the courage to be rich.

Whether it is harder or not, it is your duty to overcome your internal resistance and give as much as you can. My belief is that if you see your work in the world as an offering to God, and are, as the expression goes, richly rewarded, then it becomes your duty to give on behalf of those who cannot themselves currently give. Once you and your family have more money than you will ever need, then your offering of thanks must express gratitude for all that you have, and all that you can afford to give. You needn't be limited to 10 percent; for some of you it could be 30 percent or even more. If your true offering has thought behind it, has reverence for the world, and shows an appreciation for what you have, then you have chosen the right amount to give, and you also have joined in the worldwide flow of abundance. You have offered a gift, and you will be rewarded for that gift. Rich thoughts, rich words, rich actions, rich offerings. With those elements in place, you are living a rich life indeed.

THE COURAGE TO BE RICH

If you are a professional athlete, your achievements are apparent in your numbers—the number of goals you scored in today's game compared to yesterday's; how many minutes and seconds it took you to run your last mile; whether you were over or under par; and bottom line, what you are paid for your achievements. If you manage other people's money for a living, you measure your professional worth by what return you earned for your clients, and what those returns then netted you. If you remain in one job or profession year after year, you measure the money you earn, how fast your practice is growing, what you made this year compared to what you made last year and the year before. There are other achievements most of us can't quantify in numbers, of course—the teacher who helps an unruly student to excel, the doctor who spends extra time with every patient, a toll taker who has a kind word for each car that passes through his tollgate, the bus driver who makes every bus ride a pleasure for her passengers. Overall, though, if we let it happen, our self-worth and our net worth become bound inextricably together. This is what I make, therefore this is who I am.

I hope you come away from this book with a different message, which is that who you are, and not how much you have, is the most important thing. If you are respectful of yourself and your money; respectful, too, of what money means and how you spend it, and always mindful, when it comes to your money, of how the actions you take affect the people you love, then you will be rich.

I also hope you come away from this book knowing that what you make is far less important than what you do with what you make. Every fortune begins with a balance of zero. And great fortunes can be created from very little.

We all have seen stories of the custodian, the laundress, the couple who lived modestly down the hall, all of whom were in the end richer than anyone imagined, all of whom in the end left staggering amounts of money to charities they cared about, all of whom felt all along—despite their modest way of life—safe, rich, grateful . . . and proud of what they had. They had drawn upon their courage to be rich. They were rich. And rich in more than just a bottom-line way.

Life is a journey, and if you open yourself up to its possibilities, it can take you in directions you never imagined. A rich life doesn't necessarily take you there wrapped in cashmere, weighted with gold, or travelling first-class. You need not compete with anyone else. Your journey is your own.

SUZE'S STORY

The courage to be rich. I have it, but where did it come from? I think about my mother and my dad, and all that they tried to do—and failed and succeeded in doing—and that is a great part of it. Even though often they didn't have much hope, they had courage, and like most parents, they always did the best they could for my brothers and me. Like most parents, too, they sent us all kinds of mixed messages. And like most kids, my brothers and I ultimately had to find our way in this world. And we have.

I have written before about working for many years after college at the Buttercup Bakery, how comfortable I was there, how unimaginable a better life seemed. But then, a better life (or so I thought) presented itself, when I was offered the chance to work at Merrill Lynch and then at Prudential-Bache. What is harder to remember and write about, though, is how terrifying each of those moves felt to me. How scared I was to enter each new realm. I was afraid to be found out, as little Suze Orman, without a rich credential in this world. I have to tell you, I was always so much more afraid when I was seeking more than when I was settling for less.

From there, from Wall Street, to nearly being destroyed in trying to start my own financial firm, I was scared. It was so hard to learn to reach for more. Never mind the idea of writing books! If anything, entering the publishing world was more intimidating to me than Wall Street had been, because at least when I was working with money, I was working with numbers, and with numbers, I always felt at home. For the longest time, every expansive act I took made me feel not richer but smaller, poorer, afraid of what I might lose. So many times I felt like retreating, going back to who I had been—but I didn't. I kept going as if I were propelled by some force far greater than me.

For me, it was fortunate that throughout this journey, I was also pursuing my spiritual course—trying, like all of us, to earn money, always as much money as I could, but also trying to find meaning in the money, to make the money matter. There are those who will say that there is no emotional or spiritual quotient attached to money, that the point of money is only to make it, invest it, and spend it—but this view seemed empty to me, and it wasn't enough. I studied ancient scriptures; I attended classes, seminars, and retreats; and I began threading what I was learning into my work. Finally, I began to understand that in order for money to bring true riches, it cannot simply pass in and out of your hands but also must pass through your heart. Let the financial naysayers say what they will. I have met plenty of people with lots of money who could never be called anything other than poor, and I have met people with far less money who lead lives that could only be described as rich. I don't mean to suggest—not for a minute—that I don't think money is important, because it is very important. It is so important, in fact, that I believe that if you can get your financial house in order, then many, many other kinds of richness will follow you into that house.

As we've seen, getting your financial house in order means valuing people over money and valuing money over things. It means putting money in the right place in your heart, and in the right investments. It means having all that you love, and loving all that you have. It means turning toward your money, and turning your money, some of your money, toward righteous causes. But money alone, as important as it is, can never make you truly rich.

LAWS OF MONEY, LAWS OF LIFE

From my spiritual quest alone, I would never have learned how to deal with money, how to spend it, invest it, use it to infuse relationships with clear and righteous actions. In the same way, from my financial practice alone, I would never have learned how the laws of money and the laws of life can work together in such perfect harmony to create true abundance.

About twelve years ago, I attended a seminar about the Five Laws of Life, which seemed, I remember thinking, like a tidy way to be sure to get everything right—just five laws. But the lessons that emerged from the seminar were anything but easy. They were, in fact, lessons of true richness—richness beyond money, richness of the soul. It was here that I began to understand the ways in which your thoughts, words and actions create your destiny. I learned, really learned, what I still think of as the lesson of oneness: In order to live a rich life, in every realm, everything about who you are must be one, in alignment, and in pure harmony. It was a dazzling lesson to learn, because, to me, it explains why each and every one of us matters so much to the world. And it has been a profoundly challenging lesson to live ever since, because desiring wealth and choosing to be rich in every way possible takes immense courage, courage that, one way or another, we all have to draw upon every day.

In fact, I was deeply moved by this seminar, because up until then, I had thought that spiritual pursuits took place in private, removed from the larger world. Not so, I learned. Instead, our souls are on display every day. Rich or poor, as we make all our daily offerings, we leave a much bigger imprint on the world than we know.

These are the laws I learned and took to heart, and I ask you to consider doing so for yourself.

Rich or poor, your life will touch many other lives, and the way in which it touches them is your choice and will determine the legacy you leave to the world. Please accept these laws as an offering and make your legacy a rich one.

THE FIVE LAWS OF LIFE

1. *May every thought that you think be etched in fire in the sky for the whole world to see, for in fact it is.*
2. *May every word that you say be said as if everyone in the world could hear it, for in fact they can.*
3. *May every deed that you do recoil on top of your head, for in fact it will.*
4. *May every wish that you wish another be a wish that you wish for yourself, because in fact it is.*
5. *May everything you do be done as if God Himself is doing it, for in fact He is.*

THE REWARDS OF COURAGE

Our journey, remember, started with the act of forgiveness, an act that was the first step toward unifying thoughts, words and actions. Through forgiveness, I hoped you would find the clarity and strength to look ahead, with courage and hope. Only when this sequence is in harmony can we achieve what we dream for ourselves. Now I want to complete that sequence, for I believe the sum total of your actions makes up your character, and your character determines your destiny. Thoughts, words, actions, character, destiny—when they all are in concert, your life is free of confusion and uncertainty—moral, emotional, financial, or otherwise. When any two elements in the group are at odds, your life can be thrown off balance. Do you see why it was so important for me to begin this book with exercises to cleanse your thoughts? Because thoughts begin the journey that ultimately delivers you to your destiny.

I hope you will take the lessons in this book to heart. I hope you will remove the clutter that prevents more from coming into your life. I hope you will value people above all, and that you will come to value money itself over things. Please spend wisely, whatever it is you're buying, be it a car, a house, or any of life's necessities or luxuries. Always keep in mind tomorrow's dollars when calculating what you want today. We have learned, too, about funding your future—how to keep money safe and how to separate myths from realities. These are lessons about money, it's true, but they also are the lessons that will enable you to care for yourself and your loved ones, today, tomorrow, and perhaps even long after you are gone.

If you have taken these lessons to heart, you now know, too, how to embrace and truly value your money and how to give purely, to make offerings, by passing your money through your heart and hands out into the world, to make the world a better place. Last but not least, you have learned the laws of money and the laws of life, vital laws indeed. If you follow them faithfully, they will never let you or your money down.

Please take the courageous actions necessary in order to be rich, for the rewards of richness are so great, and the deprivations of poverty so crippling and so often needless. Think beyond today, into tomorrow; think beyond yourself, to the people you love. Think what you can create from what you have—the most you could possibly create—and create it. See the world clearly—from a material standpoint and from a spiritual standpoint. However much money you have right now, turn toward it today, for with courage, you can make it grow into enough, into more than enough. Seek abundance, and you will have abundance. With all my heart, and with all the courage I possess, this is the message I hope you will take into your heart, every day for the rest of your life.

May you always have the courage to think great thoughts and relish small treasures.

Suze Orman

VALUABLE RESOURCES

◆

Here are some excellent additional sources of information on some of the subjects covered in this book.

Banking Ombudsman (for all banking complaints)
All states:
PO Box 14240
Melbourne City Mail Centre
Melbourne 3001
Telephone: 1800 337 444

Credit Reference Association of Australia (for a copy of your credit report)
PO Box 964
North Sydney 2059
Telephone: 02 9464 6000

Level 40, 55 Collins Street
Melbourne 3000
Telephone: 03 9281 1676

Level 15, 348 Edward Street
Brisbane 4000
Telephone: 07 3853 6617

157 Grenfell Street
Adelaide 5000
Telephone: 08 8223 4309

Level 8, 16 St Georges Terrace
Perth 6000
Telephone: 08 9221 7783

New Zealand readers can contact the following credit bureau:

The Baynet
15 Hopetoun Street
Ponsonby
Auckland
Telephone: 09 356 5855

The Family Law Court (for counselling/mediation and information)
97–99 Goulburn Street
Sydney 2000
Telephone: 02 9217 7326

570 Bourke Street
Melbourne 3000
Telephone: 03 9604 2900

GPO Box 9991
Brisbane 4001
Telephone: 07 3248 2200

25 Grenfell Street
Adelaide 5000
Telephone: 08 8205 2666

150 Terrace Road
Perth 6000
Telephone: 09 224 8222

39–31 Davey Street
Hobart 7000
Telephone: 03 6232 1725

Cnr Mitchell & Herbert Streets
Darwin 0800
Telephone: 08 8981 1488

The Financial Planning Association of Australia (to find a financial planner)

Suite 404, 89 York Street
Sydney 2000
Telephone: 02 9299 8300

6/50 Queen Street
Melbourne 3000
Telephone: 03 9614 2289

Level 23, 66 Eagle Street
Brisbane 4000
Telephone: 07 3229 0455

28 Greenhill Road
Wayville 5034
Telephone: 08 8373 3936

11 Angwin Street
East Fremantle 6158
Telephone: 09 319 1941

Financial counsellors (for help with debt)

Credit Helpline
Telephone: 02 9951 5544 or 1800 808 488 (NSW & ACT)
Telephone: 03 9602 3800 or 1800 803 800 (VIC)

Financial Counselling Services (QLD)
Telephone: 07 3257 1957 (QLD)

Department of Family & Community Services
Telephone: 08 8226 7000 (SA)

Family & Children's Services
Telephone: 09 222 2555

Anglicare Financial Counselling Services
Telephone: 03 6223 4595 (TAS)

The Insurance & Superannuation Commission (independent advice on superannuation and insurance)
Telephone: 02 9395 7222 (NSW)
Telephone: 06 247 2299 (ACT)
Telephone: 03 9246 7500 (VIC)
Telephone: 07 3221 2533 (QLD)
Telephone: 08 8232 5130 (SA)
Telephone: 09 481 8266 (WA)

For advice on a range of investment products

Investment Funds Association of Australia
345 George Street
Sydney 2000
Telephone: 02 9262 3599

The Australian Stock Exchange (courses and information on brokers)
20 Bond Street
Sydney 2000
Telephone: 02 9227 0660

530 Collins Street
Melbourne 3000
Telephone: 03 9617 8611

Shop 3, Retail Plaza, Riverside Centre
Brisbane 4000
Telephone: 07 3835 4014

91 King William Street
Adelaide 5000
Telephone: 08 8216 5028

2 The Esplanade
Perth 6000
Telephone: 09 224 0044

86 Collins Street
Hobart 7000
Telephone: 03 6234 7333

Citizens Advice Bureaus (free legal advice)

Check with your local council or chamber magistrate at your local court.

State Government Trustees (Public Trustees for advice on wills, estates, financial planning, tax, trusts)

19 O'Connell Street
Sydney 2000
Telephone: 02 9252 0523

4 Mort Street
Canberra 2601
Telephone: 06 257 1222

168 Exhibition Street
Melbourne 3000
Telephone: 03 9667 6444 or 1800 133 095

444 Queen Street
Brisbane 4000
Telephone: 07 3213 9313

25 Franklin Street
Adelaide 5000
Telephone: 08 8226 9200

565 Hay Street
Perth 6000
Telephone: 09 222 6777

116 Murray Street
Hobart 7000
Telephone: 03 6233 7598

47 Nuckey Street
Darwin 0800
Telephone: 08 8992 7271

Social Security (for information on pensions, family allowance and
government benefits)
Telephone: 13 24 68

Australian Taxation Office (tax enquiries)
Telephone: 13 23 00

INDEX

◆

ABOUT THE AUTHOR

◆

Suze Orman is the author of the #1 *New York Times* bestseller *The 9 Steps to Financial Freedom* and the national bestseller *You've Earned It, Don't Lose It*. A Certified Financial Planner® professional, she began her career as an account executive at Merrill Lynch and went on to become a vice-president of investments at Prudential-Bache before founding her own firm in 1987. She has hosted two PBS specials, based on *The 9 Steps to Financial Freedom* and *The Courage to Be Rich;* writes a monthly column for *Self* magazine; and has appeared numerous times on *Oprah, Good Morning America,* CNN, CNNfn, and CNBC.

THE 9 STEPS TO FINANCIAL FREEDOM
Practical and spiritual steps so you can stop worrying
Suze Orman

The Australian Edition of this number 1 New York Times *bestseller.*

Are you in control of your money, or is your money in control of you? This revolutionary book, from popular *Oprah* guest, Suze Orman, shows us the steps that will let us break free of financial anxieties and take power over our money.

Orman believes it's important to not only have the practical means to right the financial wrongs in our lives but to also truly understand the relationship between our emotional life and our financial one. *The 9 Steps to Financial Freedom* helps us come to terms with our past as a way of coping with the present.

In this Australian paperback edition, readers can gain the benefits of Suze Orman's inspiring message within a familiar and locally relevant financial framework.

Bantam paperback
ISBN 1 86325 225 8